A SINK OF ATROCITY

A SINK OF ATROCITY

Crime in 19th-Century Dundee

Malcolm Archibald

BLACK & WHITE PUBLISHING

First published 2012
by Black & White Publishing Ltd
29 Ocean Drive, Edinburgh EH6 6JL

1 3 5 7 9 10 8 6 4 2   12 13 14 15
ISBN: 978 1 84502 420 8
Copyright © Malcolm Archibald 2012

A CIP catalogue record for this book is available from the British Library.

Typeset by Ellipsis Digital Ltd, Glasgow
Printed and bound by MPG Books Ltd, Bodmin, Cornwall

FOR CATHY

Acknowledgements

I would like to thank the following people for their help and guidance while I was researching and writing this manuscript: The staff of Local History Department, Central Library, Dundee; Iain Flett, Richard Cullen and Angela Lockie of Dundee City Archives; Rhona Rodgers, Ruth Neave and Christina Donald of Barrack Street Collection Unit, McManus Galleries, Dundee; Kristen Susienka of Black & White Publishing, for her patience and skill during the editing process and, most important of all, my wife Cathy.

Contents

'Dundee, the palace of Scotch blackguardism, unless perhaps Paisley be entitled to contest this honour with it.'

'Dundee, certainly now, and for many years past, the most blackguard place in Scotland.'

'Dundee, a sink of atrocity, which no moral flushing seems capable of cleansing. A Dundee criminal, especially if a lady, may be known, without any evidence of character, by the intensity of the crime, the audacious bar air, and the parting curses. What a set of she-devils were before us!'

Henry, Lord Cockburn, *Circuit Journeys*

Foreword
A Sink of Atrocity

When *Circuit Journeys* was first published in 1888, the reading public was able to see the thoughts and experiences of Henry, Lord Cockburn during the seventeen years he worked as a Circuit judge. In this impressively readable tome, Lord Cockburn both praised and condemned the people he met and the places to which he travelled. While some towns earned plaudits, Dundee was treated with nothing but condemnation. Cockburn's comments bear some repetition: 'Dundee, the palace of Scotch blackguardism,' he wrote, 'unless perhaps Paisley be entitled to contest this honour with it.' And again, 'Dundee, certainly now, and for many years past, the most blackguard place in Scotland.'

After a brief verbal tour of the Fife and Angus district, Cockburn returned to vilify Dundee a third time: 'Dundee a sink of atrocity, which no moral flushing seems capable of cleansing. A Dundee criminal, especially if a lady, may be known, without any evidence of character, by the intensity of the crime, the audacious bar air, and the parting curses. What a set of she-devils were before us!'

Lord Cockburn's statements influenced the writing of this book. If a judge, with all his experience of crime in its worst, most sordid, saddest and most wicked forms, thought so harshly about Dundee, the town must indeed have been a grim place. I decided to investigate further. It took only a brief glance at contemporary and near-contemporary accounts to realise that others also painted Dundee in negative colours, and sometimes they were disappointingly close to Cockburn's opinion. For instance, there was 'Philetus', writing in the *Dundee Magazine* in 1799, who stated that 'Vice, manufactures and population . . . kept a steady jog trot together'. By making this statement, Philetus seems to blame the rise in manufacturing concurrent with urban industrialisation for a growing crime rate; but Dundee had experienced the occasional bout of law-breaking before manufacturing dominated the town. For example, according to Christopher Whatley et al. in *The Life and Times of Dundee*, in 1720, John Brunton, deacon of the Weavers' Incorporation, led a mob to sack a merchants' house and loot food from a vessel in harbour. In the absence of a police force, the authorities sent a body of military from Perth to quell the troubles and one man died and others were arrested before peace was restored.

However, mob rule was rare, and was perhaps an indication of hunger-politics more than criminal intent. By the nineteenth century and the time of Henry Cockburn, Dundee was a rapidly-industrialising town, fast becoming a city, with all the vices and horrors that were attached. In its own way Dundee was a microcosm of the period, and as such is worth investigating.

When I first envisaged this book I had a notion of an academic work with every fact referenced and tables of statistics to guide the reader. But the more I researched the more I realised that, while such an approach might appeal to a limited number of intellectuals, it would more likely repel the majority of readers. It would also litter each page with little numbers that would make reading difficult. Accordingly, I altered the approach to make the contents more accessible. This book was not written to prove an argument but to paint a picture, to try and explain not why Dundee was what it was, but how it felt to be there in the nineteenth century.

Although this book is about crime in nineteenth-century Dundee, it is equally about the people: how they coped with their environment and how they acted and reacted to the trials and stresses of life. It is about the pickpockets and footpads, the husband-beaters and vitriol-throwers, the murderers and thieves, the rioters and rapists, the mill girls and seamen, merchants and prostitutes, fish sellers and masons; it is about the people who occupied the tenements and villas and whose often-raucous voices filled the streets. Some of the incidents are tragic, others are sordid, some show elements of chilling brutality, others a sense of social justice that is humbling in these more selfish times. Often one can feel sympathy with those forced into desperate acts, but sometimes there is a sensation of creeping horror that such people exist in the same sphere as the rest of us.

Researching this book was an interesting procedure in itself and involved many hours in the libraries and archives of Dundee and Edinburgh. Dundee is fortunate that the archives hold the Police Board Minutes, while the local press filled in many details that were missing elsewhere. It was sometimes frustrating that many perpetrators were mentioned only by their surname, but that seemed to be the style of the period. However, that anomaly was counterbalanced by the double naming of married women. In Scotland, women could keep their maiden names even after marriage, which is why they were frequently referred to as, for example, Mary Brown *or Smith*. For the sake of clarity, this book will refer to married women solely by their married name.

The book has a simple format: sixteen chapters dealing with various forms of crime or crime prevention. Some chapters deal with a type of crime or a historical period, others are more specific. What will become apparent is that while some crimes are very much fixed in the past, others are recognisable today. In Scotland, grave-robbing and infanticide are hopefully confined to history, but theft and drunken behaviour are probably as common in the twenty-first century as they were in the early nineteenth. It is perhaps encouraging to learn that crimes we consider as products of modern life were known 150 or 200 years ago; child abuse, assault and brawls are not creations of the media, but were part and parcel of life for our ancestors as much as for ourselves. The nature of people does not change despite advances in technology.

Throughout the book I have not attempted to either prove or disprove the words of Lord Cockburn. That I will leave to the reader, basing his or her answer on the evidence presented in the following pages.

There is only one piece of advice: Keep your doors and windows locked.

Malcolm Archibald
Dundee and Moray, 2012

Introduction
Nineteenth-Century Dundee

Trade was vital to Dundee: trade with the landward farmers who grew the produce that fed the population, coast-wise trade with the other towns and cities of the British Isles and overseas trade that imported raw produce which Dundee converted to sellable goods. At no time was the importance of trade more apparent than in the nineteenth century, when Dundee expanded from a small town into an industrial powerhouse that was the world capital of jute, a major linen manufacturer, the largest whaling port in Europe and a shipbuilding centre of note. However, the ordinary Dundonians paid the price for prominence with poor housing and poverty wages. Not surprisingly, such conditions helped create a criminal under-class. Given the hell's kitchen in which so many lived, it is more surprising that most people remained honest.

Perhaps it was their environment that made the Dundonians such a unique people. While industrialisation and the associated factor of over-crowding scarred their city, the people evolved a toleration that is hard to match. Beneath faces often aged by poverty and deprivation, the vast majority of the population exudes a comfortable warmth that extends a welcome to visitors and incomers alike. It may have been Dundee's nine-teenth-century ordeal by industrial fire that created this character, and if so, then something good was hammered from the horrendously long working hours, the starvation poverty and the constant battle to survive.

For those unfortunate enough never to have visited, Dundee sits on the north bank of the Firth of Tay, sheltered from the worst of the weather by the Sidlaw Hills and from the grind of the North Sea by eight miles of river. At the beginning of the nineteenth century Dundee had a population of around 30,000, and she was centred on just a handful of principal thoroughfares. Nearest to the coast was the Shore, with the docks, dockyards and fish market, from where the rapidly deteriorating Fish Street slanted down towards the docks. Slightly to the north and east, past a maze of closes and buildings bisected by the broad new Castle Street was the Seagate. This long, narrow street ran past a score of timber yards and whale yards that emitted a noxious stench when they boiled blubber into oil. Continuous with Seagate and curving eastward to Peep o' Day and the rural hamlets of Lilybank and Craigie was The Croft, not yet darkened by industry to its Victorian name of Blackscroft.

City Churches

© Author's Collection

North of and parallel to the Shore was the High Street, the centre of religion, administration and justice. Here were the City Churches, the Mercat Cross from where official proclamations were announced and the William Adam Town House. This iconic building was arguably the most important single structure in the town, housing the council officials, the archives and the jail in one impressive building. Nearly closing the east of the High Street was the Trades Hall, meeting place of the town's businessmen. Beyond that stretched the Murraygate, at first narrow, congested between overbearing buildings, and then broadening out as it poked a long finger toward the Cowgate and the meandering Dens Road. Slicing northward from the junction of Murraygate and Cowgate was the Wellgate, leading to the steep slope of Bonnethill, later to be known as Hilltown as it gradually industrialised and the land between there and Dens filled with tenements, mills and factories. A few miles to the east lay the fishing village of Broughty from where many of Dundee's seamen came. Not yet part of the town, the countryside between Broughty and Dundee was pleasantly rural, speckled with farms and the houses of gentlemen.

The High Street split just west of the Town House. The northern branch eased through the bustling, congested and lively Overgate, heading toward the ancient gateway of West Port. Here the road split again, one branch heading north-west along the evocatively named Witchknowe to merge with the road to Coupar Angus and the not-yet-significant village of Lochee. The other branch was named the Hawkhill and included the densely and largely unregulated industrial suburbs of the Scouringburn. The working people who lived there shared their world with the reeking smoke and clattering machinery of the mills and factories that dominated their lives.

The southern Nethergate Road slunk from the High Street to the right of the City Churches and onward to the prosperous Perth Road and the open space of Magdalen Green, home of cricketers and swimmers. Here in Dundee's first suburb substantial stone-built villas smiled over tended gardens, or were sheltered behind the security of isolating surrounding walls.

To the north of the High Street was the Howff, once the grounds of the Grey Friars, then a combination of a meeting place for the town's Incorporated Trades and a burial ground, but by the early nineteenth century it was purely a graveyard, enclosed by high walls and holding the remains of the great, the good and everybody else whose time on Earth had passed. Beyond that, spreading in flat green dampness, was the open ground of the Ward and the Meadows, used for public recreation and bleaching linen. From there Barrack Street and Constitution Brae pointed the way to the military barracks around the ancient Dudhope Castle.

Dundee was not large; an active man could stroll across it in half an hour, but it had considerable civic pride. The *Dundee Directory* for 1818 states it was a 'well-built town, consisting of several streets', while the High Street was a 'spacious square 360 feet long by 100 feet broad'. In 1847 George McGillivray painted a fine illustration of this High Street, which can be viewed in Dundee's McManus Gallery. Top-hatted gentlemen and wide-skirted ladies converse in convivial knots while the tight architectural group around the Trades Hall and the bulk of the City Churches speaks of the combination of a continuity of commerce and Christianity that will maintain the status quo and ensure future prosperity. Perhaps it is fitting that the Town House is not included in the picture, for that might tell a different story.

With its frontage of Ionic pilasters and bustling shops, the 1776 Trades Hall was a meeting place for businessmen and trade, but the Town House was the administrative heart of Dundee. Unique in Britain for having two facades, one facing the Tay, the other the High Street, the Town House was a splendid building, created by William Adam in 1734 and would have graced any street in Europe. In a lecture in 2010, Charles McKean, then Professor of Architectural History at Dundee University, described the Town House of 1776 as 'the finest new public building north of London'. Beneath the 140-foot-high spire and behind the piazzas were the Guild Hall and the town clerk's office, the town records and the Court House, and rooms in which the Dundee Banking Company attended to its financial affairs. It was perhaps ironic, yet typical of the nature of Dundee, that the upper storey of this most impressive piece of architecture was the town's prison, so the blackguards and ne'er-do-wells, the thieves and drunkards and swindlers rested their predatory persons only a few feet above one of the largest stores of money in Dundee.

The 1818 *Directory* also lauds both the Old Church, with its 156-foot-high tower, and the nearly-as-lofty spire of St Andrews Church. Naturally for a town bred to the sea, the Sailor's Hall was also mentioned, and the infirmary, lunatic asylum, the schools and colleges. The 'neatness and elegance' of the most recent streets is pointed out, as well as the good supply of 'excellent water conveyed in leaden pipes'. It would not be for many years that the danger of such pipes was known, and it was not until relatively late in the century that Dundee truly had an adequate supply of clean water.

On either fringe of Dundee were pockets of luxury where the wealthy merchants built their houses and lived apart from the common mass of humanity. In the west, the area around Magdalen Green and Perth Road saw a gradual build-up of fine houses, either ornate terraces or individual mansions. However, the preferred relocation area for Dundee's elite would be to the east, with the jute barons of the 1860s building mansions in West Ferry and Broughty Ferry, so it earned the sobriquet of the 'richest square-mile in the world'. Other parts of the city were not so fortunate.

As a seaport, it would be expected that Dundee had good connections by water, and most Dundonians were familiar with the regular packet boats to Perth and the ferries to Fife. Travel to Edinburgh was more likely to be by sea than by road, although by the 1820s there was a network of stagecoaches. Merchants Hotel in Castle Street saw the Royal Mail coach arrive from Edinburgh at seven every morning, having crossed the Forth at Queensferry and rattled through Perth with its guard clearing the way with a post horn and the horses lathered with sweat and dust. From Dundee it continued up the coast by Arbroath to Aberdeen, and returned with the northern mail to Merchants at about half past four in the evening.

There was also a coach for Forfar too, the *Thane of Fife*, that arrived at Morran's Hotel in the High Street at nine, and the *Coupar Angus Caravan* that filled the road at the same time. A Caravan was a slower and less luxurious vehicle, with bench seating and more space for luggage. With the *Saxe-Coburg*, the *Commercial* and the *Fife Royal Union* also searching for business and touting for travellers, Dundee was well connected with the rest of the country.

In 1800, Dundee was very much a linen town, with ships bringing raw flax from the Baltic and exporting the finished material. Although linen remained extremely important throughout the century, from mid-century on there was a gradual shift to jute and the number of mills and factories multiplied, bringing their own problems. As early as the 1830s there was concern about the volumes of smoke pumped over and through the town from the tall factory chimneys, but while some voiced concern about the possible effect on people's health, others said that more smoke meant more employment, which could only benefit the town.

The nineteenth century was a time of change and movement like no other. Scotland altered from a country whose inhabitants were largely based in rural areas to one in which the majority of the population lived in urban centres. As a growing population was unable to find full employment in the countryside, they moved to the towns, a continual shuffle of people that was seldom met by adequate house building. The result was an ever-worsening congestion in a finite number of houses, with inevitable tension. Many of these new Dundonians originated from Ireland, bringing with them a strong religious attachment that was not always present in Scotland. The Irish influence altered the character of Dundee, and the clash between Scots and Irish, Orange and Green, added to the confusion of rapid urban expansion.

Between 1788 and 1801 Dundee's population rose from just over 19,000 to 26,000. In the next twenty years it rose by nearly fifty per cent to 34,000 and in the next twenty to over 59,000. The depressed decade of the hungry forties saw up to 20,000 more souls arrive, a nearly twenty-five per cent increase in a mere ten years. It was no wonder that many of the people cramming into the already overcrowded town turned to crime. For some it might well have been a lifestyle choice, for others there was simply no other option.

Yet while the city expanded and altered, its main reason for being remained constant: it was a town of trade. In 1818 there were 150 vessels registered in Dundee, from the sixteen-ton coaster *Elizabeth* to the 364-ton *Tay* that braved the Arctic seas in search of whale. As the century progressed, steam gradually ousted sail and the larger and more numerous vessels necessitated constant improvement and enlargement of Dundee's docks. More shipbuilding yards brought skilled and relatively well-paid jobs as Dundee looked beyond Europe to an increasingly global market.

As in every major trading port, where there were docks there were prostitutes and pubs. Dundee had its share of both. Public houses from unlicensed shebeens to extremely ornate drinking palaces were scattered thickly around the town. There were also a number of streets and alleys with a reputation for houses of ill repute or brothels. The narrow Couttie's Wynd that cut like the slash of a seaman's knife from Nethergate to Yeaman's Shore was notorious for brothels and low lodging houses, while the Broad Close in the Overgate was another area best avoided by those of more refined susceptibilities, but such streets were part of the price Dundee had to pay for its international trade.

Finishing the transport trilogy was the railway, which came to Dundee in the early 1830s, altering the geography of the town as it rattled north-ward toward the new village of Newtyle and the fertile fields of Strath-more. Much more disruptive than the steam ship, in many ways the railway was the epitome of the century just as much as was industrialisation. By bringing inexpensive transport to the people it shrank the country, but the sidings and embankments were a divisive influence, and the gangs of labourers, the railway navvies, who built the initial lines, could bring mayhem in their wake. Dundee was fortunate to avoid that particular form of crime, but criminals certainly did use Dundee's railways and one of the most mysterious of Dundee's robberies took place on a steam train.

Industrialisation brought many changes. It brought factories and pollution, fixed and long working hours and streets of bleak basic tenements, but it also supplied regular work so that when the Industrial Revolution matured, the people of Dundee no longer had the great periods of dearth that marred their rural ancestors. With factory-based employment backed by the Christian charities of the mid- and latter-century, and with the parish workhouse, the dreadful Union, as a last resort, it is unlikely that people actually starved to death by the 1880s and 1890s. That, however, was not the case earlier in the century.

In the depression years of the 1820s, and especially in the terrible hungry 1840s, death by starvation was not unknown even in the most densely populated areas of Dundee. For example, there was the case of Ann Wilson, a single woman who lived in Jessman's Court, Seagate. One evening in February 1829, she begged for a potato to eat, and spent the entire night at her spinning wheel, desperate to earn some money. In the morning a neighbour found her dead with her work unfinished and no food in the house. There was a similar case in the middle of January 1844 when a widow named Mrs Cameron was found dead in her garret. Mrs Cameron had lived in Argyll Close in the Overgate, but ended her life lying on the pile of rags that was the only furniture in her house. She had died of starvation, still holding her seven-year-old son in her arms.

For many people, even late in the century, poverty and hunger were dark shadows waiting. The middle-aged would remember the pangs of childhood; the elderly would recall the daily struggle to survive, so for them the rattling din of a mill would signify the sound of wages, however poor. Yet although the nineteenth century lacked the famines that had created meal riots in the 1770s, the alternative also had dangers. Scarcely a week passed when there was not a death or injury at work.

Accidents could happen in a hundred different ways. Seamen could fall from a ship in Dundee harbour nearly as easily as they could in a

Baltic squall or in the blinding ice of the Arctic; carriers and coachmen risked death on winter roads, quarrymen worked with gunpowder and terrible weights, but the workplaces in the city were equally deadly. Sometimes accidents resulted in horrific injuries, such as the case in April 1836 when an unnamed boy lost his arm in a carding machine at Balfour and Meldrum's mill in Chapelshade. He survived to be taken to hospital, but others were not so fortunate. The following year an eight-year-old boy named James Templeman was also victim of a carding machine into which he fell backward. He sustained appalling injuries, so it was probably merciful that he died before he reached the infirmary. Another man who died was Archibald Menzies. In 1844 he was working at the Dron distillery when he fell into boiling copper. He was hauled out but died of his burns.

Sometimes people were so terribly injured they might have wished they were dead, such as the fourteen-year-old Robert Thoms who worked at Midmills Bleachfield on the Dichty Burn. He got himself trapped between two of the great wheels and his left leg was literally rolled together to form a single mass of bone, muscle and sinew, while according to the *Dundee Advertiser,* 'the integuments of the lower part of the belly and fork were torn off.' The surgeons at the infirmary immediately amputated the mess that had been his leg, but could do little about his other injuries. On 19th June 1828 another unfortunate fell into a tub of not-quite-boiling lees at Taylor's Soapworks. He dragged himself out and lingered for two agonising days before he died.

Even home life had its dangers. With houses heated by open fires and children often unsupervised while their parents were at work, death by burning was common. To give one example of many, on 27th December 1826 a three-year-old girl living in the Long Wynd died when her dress caught fire. The ballooning clothes worn by women were terribly susceptible to catching fire, and every so often some unfortunate creature would run screaming into the street enveloped in flames.

Augmenting the dreadful poverty and frequent accidents was the constant worry of childbirth and disease. Childbirth was a major killer of women well into the century, but unless there was something unusual in the circumstances, it hardly merited a comment. In July 1824 there was a double tragedy when two women died in childbirth the same day. The incident was worse because both women were married to whaling seamen. In common with every other urban centre, Dundee had areas where disease was rarely absent, and such horrors as smallpox, typhus and cholera made periodical ravages. The cholera year of 1832 alone claimed 511 lives in the town, but it was the slow dribble of childhood deaths that would suck joy from people's lives. Infant mortality was as bad in Dundee as anywhere else, as a single visit to the Howff graveyard can prove. It is sobering to read the names and ages on many of the gravestones, and one can only bless the medical pioneers who have alleviated much of that monstrosity.

A final, and sad, cause of death was suicide. Every week seemed to bring another instance of man or woman who terminated their own life by hanging, drowning, jumping or wrist slashing. Each death was a family tragedy and a failure by the community to recognise that one of their own was in trouble. Suicide seems to have been prolific in the nineteenth century, and Dundee was no exception.

Yet the Dundonians struggled on. Seamen mutinied against inefficient ship masters, workers fought for something approaching a liveable wage and working hours that would give them some life with their families, and charities, usually Christian, combated the worst effects of poverty. Sometimes, perhaps more often than was recorded, quick anger banded people together to combat crime. The sudden cry of 'Murder!' or 'Stop, thief!' invariably invoked a response in old Dundee as people co-operated in chasing a housebreaker, wife beater or pickpocket.

If there was often a deep sense of justice in the hard-used Dundonians, there was also a fierce independence that resented any authority considered overbearing. The old nightwatchmen – the Charlies – and the early police force were often given a rough time by the people they set out to protect. Sometimes a whole street would rise against the peacekeepers, and on a Saturday night when the drink flowed free the police seem to have been regarded as legitimate targets by many of the less respectable inhabitants of the burgh.

To live in nineteenth-century Dundee would be to live in a constant barrage of noise and smells. The noise would be from the wheels of carts and coaches across granite cobbles, the clump of horses' hooves, the shouting of street traders trying to sell their wares and the pleas of a dozen different types of beggars. In the background, and dominating the narrow streets, was the hum and clatter of machinery from the scores of mills and factories. The smells were, if anything, more offensive. Hundreds of horses meant the roads would be covered in horse dung. Houses with no interior plumbing led to cesspits for household waste. These household middens were meant to be emptied every night, but reality did not always match the theory. And there was the smell of rotten fruit and vegetables and at times the sickening stench of boiling whale blubber. In common with every urban centre, Dundee employed scavengers, men whose job it was to remove the 'nuisances' (as the piles of human excreta were known), but their numbers were small and the city constantly growing. Over everything, sometimes choking, sometimes drifting, was the all-pervading smell of smoke from scores of factory chimneys and hundreds of household fires. Edinburgh may be known as Auld Reekie, but smoke dominated Dundee as well. To live in industrial Dundee was to wade through smoke, avoid assorted unpleasantness and grow used to the varieties of smells that assailed the nostrils and noise that battered the ears.

So that was Dundee in the opening decades of the nineteenth century: a hard-working, hard-living town rapidly changing into an industrial city. It was a town at the heart of an international trading network. It was a place of startling contrasts, of sickening deprivation close to some of the most luxurious trade-created mansions in Britain, a place of cramped tenement living and of mobs that could attack the police at the skiff of a broken bottle, a place of rattling mills and men often numbed by unemployment. Perhaps it was this terrible contrast that created the criminal element, for Dundee was also home to just about every kind of crime known to the nineteenth-century man and woman. Murder and petty theft, smuggling and Resurrection, child stripping and thimble rigging, rape and prostitution, housebreaking and hen stealing, riot and child exposure – Dundee knew them all.

As the century rolled on, some of the types of crimes became less familiar, while others were as well known to the Bobbies of the late 1890s as they had been to the Charlies of the 1820s. It has often been said that people do not change, only circumstances and technology. That is certainly true of Dundee's nineteenth-century crime, and the blackguards and footpads of Peter Wallace's gang in the 1820s would have fit easily into the garrotters of the 1860s or even the teenage thugs of the present age.

This book does not pretend to cover the entire story of Dundee's nineteenth-century crime. It has been selective, leaving out far more than was included, but it aims to give a flavour of life in Dundee at a time when Scotland was in the forefront of the world of industry and trade. It shows Dundee through a period of major change, when shipping advanced from sail power to steam, when the iron juggernaut of the railway cleaved through the centre of town and life moved at an ever faster pace. It brings the reader to the claustrophobic closes and unhygienic tenements of the city and eases through the smoke-swirled streets. Was Dundee such a sink of atrocity? Enter the gas-lit confusion of the nineteenth century and make a judgement, but be aware: the pitiless eyes of the criminals are watching.

1
The Body Snatchers: 'Bury Them Alive!'

Body on the Coach

On 9th of February 1825 the *Commercial Traveller* coach rumbled on its usual route through the small towns of Fife. Crammed together, with their feet shuffling in the straw, the passengers would normally have stared at the dismal winter weather outside or spoken to the people within, but not this time. Instead they sat in some discomfort, very aware of the man in their midst. He was young, well-mannered and respectably dressed, but they were still wary of him; he had boarded the coach in Dundee and had behaved perfectly politely, but they were highly suspicious of his luggage.

Rather than the usual selection of bundles and bags, the young man carried a single but extremely large box, which aroused great curiosity in the rocking coach. Naturally, if not exactly politely, the other passengers had asked him what it contained, but the man had been evasive with his replies. By the time the coach stopped at Kinghorn for the ferry across the Forth, the other passengers were restless on their leather seats. Without a word, the young man left the coach, hefted the huge box on his back and fled, but by then the curiosity of the passengers was too strong.

Bundling out of the coach, they followed. When the young man tried to run, the weight of the box slowed him down and the other passengers caught him, held him secure and wrenched open the huge box. They peered inside, with some recoiling in horror and others nodding as their suspicions were confirmed. The dead eyes of an old woman stared sightlessly up at them. There was only one reason for anyone to carry a dead body across the country in the second decade of the nineteenth century, and the passengers looked at their captive with mixed horror and disgust: he must be a Resurrectionist.

At the beginning of the nineteenth century Edinburgh was one of the leading medical centres of the world. The University's medical school was famous for teaching and innovation, but human bodies were essential to teach anatomy and the legal supply had just about dried up. In an era when religion was still important, people believed that the dead should be left undefiled so when God called them on Judgement Day they were whole. That notion, however, only applied to God-fearing folk; those who broke God's word were unimportant, so there was some leeway for doctors of dissection. The law stated that babies who died before they were christened and orphans who died before they signed articles for an apprenticeship could be dissected, although the parents of the former probably raised some objections. In other parts of Europe deceased prostitutes could be legally dissected, and the Terror in France produced a crop of fresh corpses. Sometimes the dead were shipped from Europe and Ireland to Britain for dissection. Nevertheless, throughout the eighteenth century and well into the nineteenth the most common corpses in anatomy labs had been those of hanged criminals.

Such a situation was fine and dandy as long as there was a healthy crop of condemned men, but the swinging old days of full gallows were past. By the 1820s there were few crimes for which hanging was prescribed, and unless Scotland was flooded with murderers and rapists, the noose would wait in vain for its victim and the anatomy table for its cadaver.

To rectify this situation, medical students and strong-stomached entrepreneurs became Resurrectionists, scouring the graveyards of the countryside, watching for funerals so they could unearth the grave, remove the recently interred body and carry it to an anatomist. Stealing a body was reprehensible, but carried only a fine. Stealing the clothes in which the body was clad was worse, for clothing was valuable, so the Resurrection men would strip the corpse and run with a naked body. The most unscrupulous would even murder to obtain fresh meat: Burke and Hare were not the first in this trade. That dubious honour goes to a pair of women, Helen Torrence and Jean Waldie, who murdered a young boy as early as 1751 and were duly hanged for their pains. However, the rewards for body snatching, with or without the accompanying murder, were good. A prime body could fetch as much as £10, which was a small fortune at a time when a working man was lucky to earn £1 a week.

The town authorities took what precautions they could to deter the Resurrectionists. Many graveyards had a watchtower in which men stood watch over their silent charges, shivering as cold moonlight cast long shadows on the ranked memorials of the town. Others had a mort house or dead house in which the dead were securely placed until they decayed to a condition unlikely to interest even the most avid of anatomists. Even after burial there were mort safes, heavy cages that could be hired to protect the coffin, but for those without funds, the best defence was to stand guard night after long eerie night, so dim lanterns often lit Dundee's graveyards as the bereaved huddled over the graves of their departed. The young man who had carried the box on the Fife *Commercial Traveller* had obviously succeeded in circumventing any defences, but until he was questioned, nobody knew who he was or whose grave he had desecrated.

Dragged back to Cupar, the county town of Fife, the Resurrectionist was closely interrogated until he admitted everything. He was a medical student and he had dug up the body from the burial yard of Dundee. There were two graveyards in Dundee: Logie on the Lochee Road, and the Howff beside Barrack Street and the Meadows. When the student finally confessed he had dug up a grave in the Howff, word was sent to the Dundee Procurator Fiscal, who sent men to search the fresh graves.

Sure enough, an elderly lady had been buried on the previous Friday but now the coffin was empty. It is impossible to gauge the feelings of the relatives upon discovering the theft of their bereaved, but some travelled south on the Fife ferry. The Magistrates at Kinghorn greeted them in person and when they confirmed the identity of the body, the old lady was reburied in the graveyard in Kinghorn. Rather than a lonely, sad affair, the funeral was well attended, not only by the relatives but by local people who showed their support and sympathy for the bereaved.

Defending the Dead

Although it was unusual for a Resurrectionist to be caught actually carrying the body, the people of Dundee had taken precautions to protect their dead. There were two doughty men standing guard over the burial ground at Logie, and for night after dark night they waited with nothing happening, and then in early May 1824 the body snatchers struck. Rather than sneak in to quietly dig up a grave, they jumped the wall of the graveyard and attacked the watchmen. There was a desperate struggle around the tombstones in the dim of the summer night, but the watchmen held their ground and chased the Resurrection men away. There was little time to celebrate their victory, however, for only the following night the body snatchers returned, but once more the guard fought them off, and Logie rested secure, at least for a while.

There were other, more ingenious methods of ensuring the peace of the deceased. Throughout the nineteenth century the death rate among children was shockingly high. A visitor to any old graveyard only has to read the inscriptions on any random selection of gravestones to realise that many were erected for children from a few minutes to a few years old. It was natural that the parents wanted their children to rest in peace, undisturbed by the Resurrectionists, and in July 1823 one Dundee father went further than most. When his child's coffin was lowered into the grave, the mourners noticed an array of lines and cables criss-crossing the lid. The father explained that the cables were connected to an explosive device, so if any grave robber attempted to steal the body, they would be blown to pieces.

Perhaps there was a bomb in the coffin, or perhaps the bereaved father had merely tacked on cables in the hope of bluffing the body snatchers. Either way, the sexton was fearful as he looked down on the tiny coffin at the foot of the newly dug grave. Scratching nervously as the pile of earth that lay on top of the grass, he dropped the first shovelful, panicked and jumped back, with many of the mourners immediately joining him. He could hardly be blamed: if the coffin was rigged to explode if a Resurrection man grabbed it, what result might a spadeful of earth bring?

Although the anatomists were probably more interested in dissecting

© Author's Collection

The Howff

adults' bodies, children were certainly not immune from Resurrectionists' predatory claws. In October 1824 a child's body was stolen from the burial ground at the Howff, and the magistrates of Dundee offered a reward of twenty guineas for its recovery or information about the thieves. Twenty guineas was about twice the going rate for a fresh body, but still, there was no follow-up notice of a capture so it seems these particular body snatchers escaped. The theft of a child must have been particularly distressing for the parents, and there were a few incidents in the town that reveal just how high feelings ran and how fearful people were of these ghouls who prowled the graveyards.

The first scare came in April 1826 when George Law, a shoemaker in Baltic Street, a short street between the Wellgate and the Meadows, investigated a thump at the door. Finding his nine-year-old son on the doorstep in a state of near paralysis, he carried the boy inside and rushed for a doctor, who took a brief look and gave his opinion that the boy was merely drunk. However, Law and his wife were not so convinced and when their son was still insensible the next morning they called a second and more sympathetic doctor. The boy told a strange tale: two well-dressed men had forced him to drink something from a bottle, and then tried to drag him to the Meadows. He had objected, saying he was going home, but the two men had accompanied him all the way, only running when George Law heard his son collapse against the door.

As the people of Dundee digested this disturbing event, they heard of a similar attempt to drug and kidnap a young girl named Orchiston near the Water Wynd, again at Baltic Street. Again there were two well-dressed men, and again they forceed the child to drink from a square bottle, with similar results. Already shaken with the actions of the Resurrection men, the good citizens of Dundee reached a predictable conclusion: the two men were obviously body snatchers intent on murdering the children and selling them to the anatomists. Even as the fear and anger surged around Dundee, the truth seeped through. The first doctor had been correct. Young Law had drunk himself into a stupor and made up a colourful story to avoid his parents' wrath; young Orchiston had probably heard the tale and jumped on the Resurrectionist bandwagon.

However, there was no doubting the truth of the events of a dark night in March 1825. At that time the Howff was surrounded by a high stone wall, pierced with two tall doors. Between the night and the high walls, the interior was dark, with the serried ranks of the gravestones dimly seen in the moonless night. There were two men on watch in the Howff, guarding the grave of a recently buried woman. With their swinging lanterns casting bouncing shadows on the ground and emphasising the darkness beyond, the watch distinctly heard the creak of one of the doors. It was between eleven and twelve on Saturday night, no time for anybody to have lawful business in the Howff. The watchmen moved forward. When they heard the muffled whispers of men through the rustling of the trees, one raised his lantern and shouted a challenge.

'Who's there?'

The whispering ended, but muted threats hissed through the dark, followed by a pregnant silence. The watchmen returned to their posts at the grave, glancing into the sinister dark, wondering who was out there, how many there were, and if they had been scared away. The answer came about half an hour later, when there was a whistle from one edge of the Howff, with an instant reply from the other. Then came calls in what might have been a code but was certainly in words that the watchmen found incomprehensible. Then silence again, and the gravestones, unconcerned, stood in the stern darkness.

That night passed slowly, but the watchmen had no more alarms. They returned to their post the next night, no doubt a little more apprehensive, but also more prepared. As well as their lanterns they carried pistols and were ready to defend their position. Even so, the first part of the night passed peacefully, but about half an hour after midnight the watchmen saw movement among the gravestones and the yellow glow of a lantern.

'Who's there?' the watchmen called again and added that they were armed and would shoot anybody who came near the grave they guarded.

There was no reply, but the scuffling continued so both watchmen fired, one after the other, the orange muzzle flare bursting the dark and the roar of the shot tearing apart the silence of the night. The result was immediate: the hollow thump of running feet and the creak of a door as the body snatchers made a quick retreat. Once again the watchmen had guarded their charge well. They picked up a spade and sack the intruders left behind as sure proof of their intentions, but listened with some concern to the threats that were shouted from the other side of the boundary wall. However, the watchmen could be satisfied; the remainder of that night passed peacefully.

The watchmen were back the next night, but so were the Resurrectionists. It was shortly after ten o'clock, dark and crisply cold, when the watchmen turned up for duty. As they stepped into the night, one immediately gave a cry and vanished foot-first into a gaping hole where the grave should be. The body snatchers had come early and had already dug half-way down to the coffin. As the watchman struggled to escape from the grave, two shadowy figures emerged from the night, but rather than threats, the men offered bribes, saying if the watchmen looked the other way they would be rewarded.

True to his salt, the watchman refused, which was a brave thing to do when he was up to his knees in a freshly dug grave. The nearest body snatcher reacted instantly, swinging his spade at the second watchman. The blow missed; the watchman drew his pistol, moved forward to take hasty aim but stumbled over a grave and swore as the priming of the firing pan fell out. He cursed again as he reloaded, but by then the Resurrectionists were retreating through the ranked gravestones. The watchman fired anyway, the shot going nowhere as the intruders scurried over the wall and vanished. Chasing them through the dark graveyard, the watchman tripped over something, looked down and realised it was a sack containing a freshly dug-up body. The glazed eyes of elderly Jean Anderson stared sightlessly up at him.

Naturally, with Dundee already on edge with the threat to their deceased, the sound of gunshots and shouting brought crowds, all asking questions, all looking for scapegoats. Two visitors from Edinburgh, probably entirely innocent of any attempt to unearth a Dundonian corpse, became targets for the fear and anger of the mob. As the crowd turned angry, the visitors pleaded for police protection. After a night in the cold cells of the Town House they may have wished they had chanced the mob, but they managed to persuade the police they were not grave robbers.

Early on Tuesday morning, a huge crowd of women, sprinkled with a few dozen men, squeezed into the Howff. There was no reason for being there, no Resurrectionists to chase and nothing to do but ask each other what was happening, voice their anger and search for somebody, anybody, on whom to fix the blame. Around seven in the morning Begg the gravedigger appeared with his wife, and the frightened mob turned their anger on them. Surging forward, they threw both into an open grave and crowded around, chanting, 'Bury them alive, bury them alive!' Despite the threats, the Beggs scrambled clear and fled, ducking and dodging as the mob pelted them with stones and turf. Reaching their home, they cowered there until noon when Begg was summoned to fill up an open grave.

Strangely, the crowd were quiet while he worked, but once the coffin was covered and the turf levelled, they again began their attacks, hurling abuse and missiles at the unfortunate gravedigger. Once again Begg had to run home and the crowd remained where it was, packing the burial ground and overflowing outside the gates. It was late afternoon before the Dundee magistrates ordered the Howff cleared, but the people were reluctant to go. They protested but eventually obeyed, amidst much grumbling and muttered threats against any Resurrectionist they should happen to catch.

With many of the crowd still watching suspiciously from outside the walls and the slight eminence to the south, Jean Anderson was returned to her rightful place under the turf. The authorities questioned Mr Begg, the watchmen and Mrs Duncan, a nearby resident who claimed to have seen some men acting suspiciously among the graves. However, nothing was learned that helped catch the body snatchers.

Not surprisingly, feelings in Dundee remained high. Immediately after the weekend skirmishes, the Town Council recruited two watchmen to mount a nightly guard over the burial ground and ordered one of the town officers to help whenever he could, but the Howff was large, the nights were dark and the Resurrectionists were cunning and could be violent. More security was needed. Somebody proposed knocking down the tall surrounding walls and replacing them with a low parapet topped by iron railings so passers-by could see into the graveyard and grave robbers could not hide in dark shadows. However, the tall walls remained in place and people continued to fear for the peace of their departed. Equally abortive was a suggestion to build a house at the entrance and install a guard with a pack of mastiffs.

As the ideas rolled in, the paranoia continued. When one of the town scavengers died in the infirmary, many of his friends and family came down from the Highlands for the funeral. There was no trouble until Dr William Dick ordered the coffin carried to the burial ground, but then the Highlanders steadfastly refused to move. They obstructed everything and everybody, turning what should have been a dignified procession to the graveside into something of a riot. As usual in Dundee, a crowd gathered to watch the fun and soon the rumour spread: the Highlanders believed somebody had stolen the scavenger's body and sold it to an anatomist. When the protests grew unbearable even Dr Dick agreed to check. The coffin was placed on the ground, the lid unscrewed and the Highlanders crowded round to see the dead body of the scavenger. Once they were satisfied, the procession continued and the coffin was decently interred. It was a minor story, but one that reveals the impact Resurrectionists had on Dundee.

As the grave-robbing spree continued and people began to get ever more nervous, the burgesses of Dundee debated how to protect their dead. They met in the Howff in March 1826 but news of the meeting had leaked and over 300 people crowded into the graveyard. Inevitably there was chaos, until a brave spokesman took the initiative and shouted out what the meeting was about. Only when the surplus population had drifted away was there any progress. The burgesses who remained crammed into the watch house and decided to put a more secure guard on the burial ground. Spurred by fear, they drew up a document of thirteen articles.

The burgess' document stated they would form a body of 'voluntary police ... for preventing the violation of the graves by those unfeeling wretches who bear the ignominious title of Resurrectionists'. The anger in this statement is so obvious it nearly crawls out of the page and shouts down the centuries. Adding that 'to prevent crime is more pleasant than to punish it', the document sets out a plan to have watchers to 'record anything unusual'. One man would be the 'captain of the guard' in charge of five others. They would watch the burial ground from the first day of November until the first of March and from sunset until six in the morning. There would be subscriptions into a general fund that would pay for fire, lights and weapons, but the guards must provide their own refreshments. The plan was well considered. Six armed men with the backing of the town and, it turned out, the approval of the magistrates. When a call for volunteers went out, there were 2,000 subscribers; the people of Dundee had a strong desire to look after their dead. Six were immediately chosen to man the watch that same Thursday night.

Perhaps it was because of the guard, or perhaps the previous gunfight at the burial ground had sent out a strong message, but there were few scares at the Howff after that date. While Cupar and Montrose had their grave robbers, and Edinburgh suffered the horrific depredations of Burke and Hare, Dundee was virtually secure from the Resurrectionists. There was only one more incident of note.

In February 1827 the grave robbers tried again. A party of three or four entered the Howff from the south side, where the wall was lowest and the entrance easiest. One man slipped inside and eased himself into the midst of the gravestones, but the watchmen were alert and moved toward him, with their lanterns casting yellow pools of light among the gravestones. The grave robber ran, clutched a rope his companions had thrown down the wall for him, but the watch were faster. One of the watchman lunged forward and thrust his makeshift weapon, a bayonet tied to the end of a pole, hard into the intruder's buttocks. With a yell of 'Murder!' the man dropped on the far side of the wall and in spite of a hot pursuit by the watchmen, neither he nor his companions were seen again.

Although that was the last known attempt by the Resurrection men at the burial ground in Dundee, there was a final flurry of excitement in February 1829, just after the scares of Burke and Hare in Edinburgh. The Captain of the burying ground found one of the graves uncovered and suspected the watchmen themselves were digging up the dead. Calling the watchmen into the watch house, he locked the door and ran for the police, who escorted the watchers to the police office in St Clement's Lane. When the police discovered that the relatives of the deceased had uncovered the grave, the watchmen were released.

The watchmen of Dundee remained in the graveyards for a few more years, but after the murders of Burke and Hare in Edinburgh the law was changed, making it easier for anatomists to legally get their hands on corpses; the need for that grisly trade had ended. The Anatomy Act of 1832 'provided for executors and other people legally in charge of dead bodies to give them to licensed surgeons and teachers of anatomy unless the deceased had expressed conscientious objection to being dissected'. With that Act, there was no longer a market for dead bodies and peace descended on the Howff. There was plenty other crime still in Dundee.

2
Nautical Crime

For much of the early nineteenth century, linen was Dundee's staple industry. There was an extensive trade with the Baltic and Russia for flax, while sailcloth and other linen articles were exported to half a dozen destinations. With a thriving trade with the Mediterranean and northern Europe added to the mix, it is not surprising that there were thousands of seamen based in Dundee and as many again visiting from other ports. It was nearly inevitable that many of these men spent time and money in Dundee's pubs and some called in at the lodging houses that doubled as brothels. It was also inevitable that some should end up on the wrong side of the law.

Most of the crimes were petty – simple theft or drunken misbehaviour. For example there was the smartly-dressed seaman James Johnstone who was fined five shillings for simply 'lurking' in the passage of a house in the Seagate in November 1824, or the three apprentices who in October 1825 stole a warp and ropes from a Perth smack because a seaman on the vessel said it was all right, or the seaman from the Aberdeen schooner *Dee* who was fined half a guinea for using abusive language to people in the Perth Road in November 1826. None of these crimes would shake the foundations of the city, but when similar incidents took place day after day, night after night, they would be an irritation to the citizens.

Thefts, Riots and Pistols in the Night

Ships moored in harbour were tempting targets for the petty thieves and juvenile vagabonds of the port. One example out of many was the case in January 1826, when two boys were caught robbing the cabin of the whaling ship *Estridge*. They had four days on bread and water to ponder their actions. Just over a year later four young sailors, together with a woman named Susan Frazer, plundered the brig *Scotia*. While two of the seamen were handed thirty days each, Frazer, a known thief and troublemaker, got sixty days in jail. By 1839 the penalties had become even

© Courtesy of Dundee Art Galleries and Museums

The Docks

stiffer as a man named James Stalker was given a full year in jail for thieving articles from the whaling vessel *Fairy*.

On other occasions stranger mariners, those who did not belong to Dundee, caused the trouble. In August 1823 an English seaman had participated fully in the hospitality of Dundee's taverns and was weaving his way about the docks. Drunken seamen were easy prey and a bunch of hooligans attacked the stray Englishman as he searched for his ship. By the time the sailor escaped he had been considerably roughed up and was looking for revenge. Finding a pistol on his ship, he returned to the shore, but rather than hunt for the men who attacked him, he fired at random, shooting at everything and anybody from the bottom of the Seagate all the way to the High Street. The watchmen eventually hustled him to the lock-up house for the night. Luckily the Englishman's aim was no better than his judgement, for he injured nobody in his shooting spree.

In June 1825 a trio of stranger mariners appeared in Dundee's Police Court for causing a riot in Jamieson's pub in the High Street. The sequence of events is probably familiar to most Dundee policemen and publicans today. The three men were drinking quite happily in Jamieson's most of the afternoon, but they took a glass too many and began to sing. Either they were too raucous or the song was too bawdy, for Jamieson asked them to quieten down. Instead they drank some more, so Jamieson sent for help. The arrival of the police signalled a general melee and when one seaman, James Brown, kicked down a partition wall within the pub, Sergeant Thomas Hardy arrested him. It took four police to carry Brown to the police office, where he was held overnight with his two companions, John Wilson and John Wyllie.

A Fishing Dispute

Not only deep watermen but also fishermen could cause trouble. The fishermen of Broughty were famed as pilots and smugglers but could also be as aggressive as any other Scottish seamen. On the first Saturday of

November 1849, two rival fisher crews argued in the Dundee fish market. When the police moved in to calm them, both crews moved away with dirty looks and threats, but they knew the situation was unresolved. At four o'clock that afternoon the first crew, Watson Bell, Lawrence 'Dick' Gall and George Bell, hauled up their sail and left the harbour, with the second crew of John Lorimer, Thomas Knight and George McCoull following in their oar-powered yawl a few moments later.

The sailing boat arrived at the Hare Craigs first and waited for the yawl. As the oar-powered boat tried to pass, the sailing boat ran alongside and the crew boarded. Watson and George Bell simultaneously attacked McCoull while Lawrence Gall shouted encouragement, but within minutes everybody was involved. The fight lasted for about ten minutes with injuries on both sides, but the eventual victors were the harbour police, who fined George Bell a pound with the option of twenty days in jail, while Watson Bell and Lawrence Gall were fined 10/- or ten days.

The Exciseman's Awa' wi' the Wine

Not surprisingly, smuggling was not uncommon in nineteenth-century Dundee. Usually it was small-scale stuff, such as the brandy, tea and tobacco the Customs and Excise officers seized from the vessel *Thistle* when she arrived from Gothenburg in November 1826, or the tobacco and spirits seized from an unnamed sailor who had just arrived from America in July 1824. On other occasions the amounts seized were much more impressive. For example, in 1821 the vessel *New Delight* of London put into the Tay to shelter from one of the savage North Sea squalls that blew up out of nothing. When *New Delight* anchored off Broughty, Customs officers boarded her. Her Master said she was bound for Montrose to load potatoes, but something about her made the Customs men suspicious and they searched her, without success.

Still sure that something was wrong, but not sure what, the Customs men brought a pilot to steer *New Delight* off the Lights of Tay, those lights that marked the dangerous sandbanks. They searched her again, and again they found nothing. Only when they were reluctantly about to allow her to sail did one of the officers notice the quarterdeck was fairly high, but the accommodation below had little headroom. It was the work of a few moments to find a hidden compartment between the two, and the Customs men delighted over their discovery of nearly six tons of contraband tobacco. The crew were bundled into Dundee's Town House jail.

However, even Customs officers could be tempted. On Friday 29th October 1841 *Vestal* of Bo'ness waited off Tayport to enter the Tay with a cargo of Oporto wine. Her master, Captain Meikle, signalled all day for a pilot to guide them to Dundee, but without success. Eventually he tried without a pilot, but the entrance to the Tay is notoriously tricky. *Vestal* was driven onto the Gaa Sands, a sandbank at the tip of Buddon Ness just north of Dundee and around a third of the cargo was lost. Rather than whisky galore, it was wine galore in the Firth of Tay as the people of Broughty and Tayport and the places all around descended on this bonanza. For days there were scenes of drunkenness around *Vestal*, with even the Customs officers joining in. Apparently, though, the officials from Dundee did not become involved in the spree.

Seamen and Ladies of the Night

While most seamen ashore in Dundee headed toward the public houses, a considerable number ended up in the disreputable lodging houses, many of which doubled as brothels and were often dens of thieves. In the early years of the century, the narrow gulley of Couttie's Wynd was one of the most notorious areas for these establishments. One of the public houses on this street was owned by James Davidson. He was commonly known as Humphie, and his establishment as Humphie's House. At the end of October 1825 the master of a visiting ship was ill-judged enough to enter Humphie's House and whatever happened there he also met the ubiquitous Susan Frazer, notorious as a prostitute and thief. When he realised he had somehow lost all his money he complained to the police and both Frazer and Davidson were arrested. While Davidson was set free, Frazer admitted to picking the captain's pocket and was sent on to a higher court and eventually sentenced with a long spell in the jail.

Couttie's Wynd was too dark a street to attract many respectable people and for much of the century it remained a place of prostitution and drunkenness. In September 1861 Frederick Leverdowitz, Master of the barque *Lavinia* of Libau, visited one of the houses and came out minus a gold watch and chain and £90 in cash, which was a huge sum at the time. The police arrested three suspects: Catherine Grant, Catherine Hughes and her husband John Hughes. Catherine Grant, officially a millworker, was sent to jail for sixty days while the husband and wife team were given longer sentences.

There were other areas of Dundee with nearly as interesting a reputation, including Fish Street, square in the heart of the old Maritime Quarter. At one time Fish Street had been the home of some of Dundee's elite, but by the beginning of the nineteenth century it was a place of mildly dangerous pubs. At the beginning of September 1824 three English seamen were at large in Fish Street when a trio of local ladies took them in hand. With promises of great favours they helped the seamen into one of the low houses and departed with the Englishmen's money. The ladies were never found.

Mutiny

Sometimes disputes at sea could be continued on land. The 1830s had been a bad time for the whaling industry with large numbers of ships sunk by the ice and others trapped over the winter. One of the latter was the Dundee vessel *Advice*, which lost most of her crew to scurvy. So in the summer of 1842 when Captain John Buttars of the whaling ship *Fairy* gave orders that they head deeper into the ice, it is not surprising the crew were worried. When they thought the ship was short of supplies they refused to go any further.

On a ship there are only two options when faced with the master's orders: duty and mutiny. Anything the master orders the hands to do is their duty; anything they refuse is mutiny. Accusing the crew of mutiny, the master returned them to Dundee and dumped them on shore with no wages and no access to the possessions they had on board. The situation was bad enough for the local men, but for the seamen from Shetland, the majority of the crew, it was desperate. On the evening of 6th August, the thirty-two Shetlanders arrived at the police office and requested a bed for the night. Rising manfully to the occasion, the Dundee police gave each man access to a cell and a free penny roll. Next day Peter Twatt, one of the Shetlanders, went to court to argue for his pay. In such a seafaring town it is not surprising that the crowd cheered when the Justices, Alexander Balfour and David Milne, found in favour of Twatt. The victory was only the first as the Shetland men all gained their wages.

The Dundee Scuttlers

After mutiny, perhaps one of the worst crimes at sea was scuttling, sailing a vessel to sea and deliberately sinking her for the sake of insurance money. Dundee was not immune, with cases at either end of the century. In 1816, a man by the name of James Murray, alias James Menzies of Lochee, embezzled the cargo of *Friends* of Glasgow, which was then scuttled off Jutland for insurance.

The 1893 case was far more complicated, with a group of shipbrokers and ship masters alleged to have sunk a number of vessels. The vessels were *De Cappo*, *Gretgelina*, *Tryst*, *Barrogill Castle* and *William and Martha* of Wick. The death of any ship is sad, but a deliberate sinking purely for profit must be the worst ending for any vessel. The supposed facts of each sinking are stark.

On 24th August 1891, the tug *Earl of Windsor* was towing the lighter *De Cappo* from Aberdeen to the River Tyne. Commanded by Captain Andrew Baillie, *De Cappo* had a cargo of stones, and as they passed

Girdleness, the weather turned foul. *De Cappo* began to leak and although the crew took to the pumps, the water level inside the lighter gained steadily. When Baillie told the master of *Earl of Windsor* the lighter was sinking, they decided to head for Montrose but as they changed course the bow was under water and the crew chose to abandon. *De Cappo* foundered within half an hour.

Gretgelina was a Grangemouth-registered vessel of thirty-five tons commanded by fifty-five-year-old Captain Joseph Severn, who worked for David Mustard Hobbs of 30 Dock Street, Dundee. On 22nd December 1891, sailing from Grangemouth to Invergordon, she sprung a leak off the Redhead, by Montrose. As the water within *Gretgelina* rose, the crew took to the boats, and within quarter of an hour *Gretgelina* had sunk. They were then fifteen miles off Bodden, south of Montrose, and rumours soon circulated that Severn had either forced out the bow plates of *Gretgelina* or bored holes in her to make her sink. Adding to the speculation was the fact that *Gretgelina* was insured for the fairly large sum of £925, spread over three different companies.

William and Martha was carrying a cargo of potatoes and paving stones from Castlehill in Caithness to West Hartlepool. She sunk in March 1892, just a short time after leaving harbour. Her owner was once again Hobbs, who insured the ship, together with her freight, cargo, captain's effects, disbursements and outfit stores. He also insured a small fishing boat the ship was meant to have on board, but before the vessel left Castlehill Harbour, three small holes were bored in her hull, then carefully disguised. When they were at sea, the holes were re-opened and the vessel sank.

Not content with merely claiming insurance for *William and Martha*, Hobbs also presented a false bill of lading for £28, claiming there had been 120 bags of potatoes on board the vessel, rather than the twenty-five bags that were actually there. As if that was not enough, in June Hobbs also claimed for a gold watch worth £8, a £3 clock and a collection of other nautical equipment that in total amounted to £70. In July he also produced a false receipt and bill of lading for £75, for the fishing yawl that was said to have been on board. This claim was made to Thomas Crosby of Sunderland. Finally, he told Thomas Crosby that he had paid £385 for the vessel rather than the £195 he had parted with. In total, Hobbs claimed £1043 in insurance for this vessel and received £518.

There was also a lighter named *Tryst* that sank in October 1891. Again the scuttling was an insurance fraud. *Tryst* was underwritten by Lloyds and insured by the Maritime Insurance Company. The charge was that Hobbs insured the freight, cargo, salvage plant and commission on the sale of the cargo. As a lighter, *Tryst* was to be towed from Thurso in Caithness to Montrose, but Hobbs was accused of having the ship's illustrious master, Joseph Severn, bore holes below her watermark so she sank some three miles off Clythness in Caithness. The tug *Granite City* of Aberdeen was towing her from Thurso to Montrose when she hit a heavy sea. The crew moved to test the pumps and were shocked to find the hold was partially filled with water. Leaping to the pumps, they tried to keep her afloat, but when it became obvious they could not, they signalled to the tug, which took all three of them off a few moments before she sank.

The final vessel was the schooner *Barrogill Castle*. Hobbs was again the owner and he was accused of ordering Severn to set fire to her in November 1892 so he could claim her insurance of £600 from the West of Scotland Fire Office. *Barrogill Castle* had been berthed in Inverkeithing as she was unfit to sail. Hobbs brought a shipwright from Dundee to inspect her to see if she could be taken to the Tay, but before that happened she was burned at her moorings.

In July 1893 Hobbs and Severn appeared before Sheriff Campbell Smith. Both pleaded not guilty although Hobbs was said to be very pale; their second appearance was before Lord Kyllachy at the High Court of Justiciary in Edinburgh on 8th August. Both admitted to some of the charges. With 117 witnesses against them and an indictment nine pages long, things looked bleak for the defenders, but although Hobbs was clearly upset when he appeared at the bar, Severn appeared virtually unaffected. They pleaded guilty to scuttling two vessels, *William and Martha* and *Gretgelina*.

The defence argued for Hobbs' previously good character, showing certificates of character given by previous employers and the Reverend Robert Duncan of Montrose. Hobbs also said his father was a sea captain and he had come under the influence of older men who later turned Queen's Evidence. Severn's council pleaded he was only an accessory to the crime, that at fifty-five he was quite an old man and there had never been any danger to life. Even so, the judge was not convinced. Lord Kyllachy gave Hobbs seven years' penal servitude and Severn, as Hobbs' instrument and a man of less intelligence and education, five years' penal servitude.

But that was not the end of the case. A fortnight later twenty-nine-year-old machinery merchant William Stewart of Royal Park Terrace in Edinburgh was arrested for his involvement in the scuttling of *Tryst*. His arrest was followed in October by the arrest of a seaman named William Ellington of Aberdeen, who had been *Tryst*'s master. The police had been searching for him, but he had been at sea until lately. Hobbs had sold *Tryst* to Stewart. Buying the engine and boiler of a grounded vessel named SS *Speedwell*, Stewart loaded them onto *Tryst*, insured her for a whopping £2390 through the Maritime Insurance Company Limited and got Ellington to bore holes in her so she sank. When the case came to court in January 1894, Hobbs was again accused of being involved in the scuttling of *Tryst* and the trial was set for 13th February. He came as a witness and gave the following story:

In April 1892 he and Stewart discussed buying the engine and boiler of a wrecked vessel called *Speedwell*, then lying in the Thurso River. After buying the engine for £200, Hobbs suggested that Stewart have a hull built into which they could put it. Hobbs and Stewart met again at the Tay Bridge Station in Dundee and Stewart bought *Tryst* for £120. Hobbs had paid just £25 for the lighter. A tug was to tow the boiler to Leith and Hobbs insured it for about £900, on Stewart's instructions. By that time Hobbs and Stewart had agreed not to build a hull but to lose the boiler and claim insurance. After loading *Tryst* with stones to ensure a fast sinking, Ellington bored holes in her bottom. Hobbs agreed he knew about the scuttling beforehand, but he claimed he was not involved and got no benefit. As in his previous trial he broke down in tears under cross-examination. In this case Stewart and Ellington were found not guilty. Hobbs was obviously out of his depth dealing with crime, but at least there were no deaths.

How to Steal a Whale

Nineteenth-century seamen often lived lives different from those men on land. They used a different vocabulary, experienced half the ports of the world and had unique customs and superstitions. It stands to reason that when seamen turned to crime, they could be just as unique. People steal anything, but sensible thieves prefer an item that is small, portable and easy to conceal. Probably the least likely object to be stolen would be eighty feet long, weigh upwards of fifty tons and have to be messily butchered and publicly processed to make it sellable, particularly if the initial theft was carried out in full view of the legal owners and about fifty other witnesses. Nevertheless, that is exactly what happened when George Thoms of Dundee saw an item he deeply desired.

It was 23rd August 1829, deep in the Davis Strait, that treacherous stretch of iced water that separates the western coast of Greenland from the eastern seaboard of Canada. The whaling vessel *Traveller's* master, George Simpson from Peterhead, sighted a whale and was in hard pursuit, with a couple of other vessels, *Princess of Wales* from Aberdeen and a Dundee vessel called *Thomas*, close by, but everybody was there for the same end.

Traveller sent out her boats and the oarsmen pulled toward the whale, with the boatsteerer ensuring the boat was out of range of the flukes of the whale's tail. Alexander Buchan stood up in the bows, aimed and threw the harpoon. The barbs stuck in deep and the crew released a mighty shout of triumph. 'A Fall!' they cried. 'A Fall!'

Alex Buchan heaved his foreganger over the boat and took the line a turn around the billet head, securing the whale to the boat. He hoisted a jack, a distinctive flag that announced he had harpooned a whale and the animal was now *Traveller's* lawful property. They were the 'fast boat', the boat held fast to a whale. All they had to do now was kill the animal and they were guaranteed oil money to supplement their wages.

As was expected, the whale fled, pulling the boat behind it. The whaleboat held a number of lines but one by one they were used up, so although the whale and boat were still attached, the whaling seamen were in danger of losing their capture. Providentially, a boat from *Princess of Wales* thrust in one of her own harpoons, known in the trade as a 'friendly harpoon' to help tire the whale. However, the whale was still full of fight and struggled, dragging lines and boats behind it, until the lines of *Princess of Wales* were also finished. The whale remained alive, panting on the surface of the sea. Exhausted but triumphant, Alexander Buchan's crew crept closer, readying their lances for the killing blow, but before they could strike, a boat from *Thomas* raced past and Alexander Kilgour, a Dundee harpooner, thrust his harpoon deep into the whale.

Giving a jerk that unbalanced one of the men in *Traveller's* boat, the whale raced away, hauling *Thomas's* boat behind it. It is easy to imagine the scene, with the waves heaving around, possibly dappled with icebergs and speckled with the Arctic birds that knew a kill meant free food. Eventually, and inevitably, the whale tired and lay on the surface, sobbing its exhaustion as the whaleboats circled around like the predators they were. A seaman from *Traveller* thrust in another harpoon. The whale barely stirred and the killing lances came out, thrusting for the lungs, the heart and the brain. The hunters of *Traveller*, the Peterhead Greenlandmen, congratulated themselves on a job well done.

But the Dundee men had other ideas. Ignoring the imprecations and complaints from *Traveller's* boat, *Thomas's* men surged forward to claim the whale as their own. Tying lines to the whale's tail, they prepared to tow it back to their ship but the Peterhead men objected. Harsh words were exchanged, and no doubt so too were threats, but there were more men from *Thomas* than from *Traveller* and weight of numbers told who'd be the victors. The whale was towed to *Thomas*. It was blatant theft, carried out in the full light of the north in view of a dozen men from Peterhead – or so *Traveller's* crew claimed. The men from Dundee had another version of events.

Alexander Kilgour did not deny that Buchan had thrust the first harpoon. On the contrary, he mentioned that he saw *Traveller's* harpoon sticking out of the whale. However, he also said that there was no line attaching the whale to the boat; it was a 'loose whale' and therefore fair game. The whale was free to whosoever could harpoon it next.

At the time, the men from *Traveller* could do nothing but protest. They were outnumbered and far from any law save that of tradition and that imposed by a master on his ship. Captain George Simpson of *Traveller* complained to Captain Thoms of *Thomas*, but to no avail. When Captain Simpson brought his complaint to the Dundee Union Whale Fishing Company who owned *Thomas*, the trustees of the company backed their captain's actions. Eventually, the owners of *Traveller* took their case to law, and the High Court in Edinburgh had the unusual experience of deciding who owned a captured whale.

The case was heard in Edinburgh on 8th March 1830, with traffic rattling past and the formal, learned judges a world away from the savagery of the Arctic seas. By that time, of course, the whale no longer existed in body. The whole idea of whale hunting was to secure the blubber and the whale-bone or baleen. The blubber would be melted down to oil, which was used for lighting, heating and, increasingly, for softening textiles. The baleen was cut up and used for a hundred different household purposes, from hairbrushes to netting to stays for women's fashion. So the case was now over the value of the whale, and both parties agreed that £600 was about the correct figure.

After the advocates listened to the evidence they realised the whole case hinged on one fact: Was the whale 'fast' or 'loose'? If it was 'fast', or attached, to Alexander Kilgour's boat by a line, then *Traveller* had the right to compensation, but if it was what the whaling men termed a 'loose fish', a whale with no lines, then the Dundee boats had every right to harpoon and claim it for themselves. The judge made the problem as clear as he could:

A 'fast fish' which is entangled by any means, such as the entanglement by the line round it or the like, to the boat of the first striker … any harpoon struck by another person into the fish while so entangled is said to be a 'friendly harpoon' and that the fish belongs to the first striker … on the other hand, the instant a fish … gets free … it becomes a 'loose fish' and belongs to the person who next succeeds in making it fast.

With this advice as a background, the legal experts listened to the evidence, with Greenlandmen from opposing vessels giving vastly different versions of the events, each of which proved conclusively that their vessel owned the whale, until Henry Cockburn, later to become Lord Cockburn, gave his exasperated opinion: 'I would confess that in all my experience,'

Whale Alongside Whaling Ship

he said, 'I never saw any class of men on whose evidence I had less reliance than on the depositions of Sailors. At all times, under all circumstances, they are ever ready to depone that their own ship was indisputably in the right.'

Despite the tangled evidence, the court gave its judgement. It was decided the evidence from *Traveller*'s crew was more reliable than that of the crew of *Thomas*. In essence, the judge said *Thomas* had stolen the whale and he ordered the Dundee Union Whale Fishing Company to pay £600 to the owners of *Traveller*.

In this incident, only Dundee's pride and the Whale Fishing Company's bank balance were injured but there were other occasions when whaling voyages created more tragic results.

Every year whaling ships sailed to brave the ice and vicious storms of the Arctic. They were hunting for whales, seals and anything else they could bring back to make money for the ship owners and shareholders. Whaling was not an easy job. It was hard, dirty, often bloody and frequently dangerous. Many Dundee ships ended their careers crushed by the ice of the Davis Strait. Every voyage could end in injury or death for the Greenlandmen, so it was no wonder that the families crowded to the dockside when the ships sailed, and the farewells were always emotional as wives said goodbye to the men they would not see for many months.

By the same token, the homecoming was joyful as the Greenlandmen erupted into the bars of Dock Street and the Overgate. The men picked up their wages from the whaling company offices in Whale Lane or Seagate, and alone, in groups or with their wives, they relaxed after the tensions of the voyage. In most cases the whaling men were good husbands and fathers, for the museums and archives of Dundee contain many documents showing wages being paid to their wives, or photographs where husband and wife stand united. However, there was always an exception to the rule.

The *Terra Nova* Murderer

Sometimes an area of a city will attract a bad element, and for a period of time will suffer from a notoriety that is unfair to the majority of the inhabitants. The Whitechapel area of London was such an area during the murders of Jack the Ripper and the Grassmarket of Edinburgh when Burke and Hare went on their rampage in the 1820s. Dundee did not quite have such a district, but in the late 1880s and early 1890s the streets around Dudhope Crescent became known for casual acts of violence. Dudhope Crescent no longer exists; a dual carriageway has obliterated the entire area, but in the later years of the nineteenth century it was the scene of possibly the only Dundee murder by a whaling man.

Richard Leggat was a Greenlandman on board the famous *Terra Nova*, the last whaling ship built in Dundee, but when he returned from the Davis Strait in 1896 he was not a happy man. At thirty years old he was an experienced seaman; he knew the Arctic seas well, and was used to bringing back a fat pay packet after his exploits in the north. The wage system for whaling men was fairly complex: There was a low basic pay augmented by oil money, striking money, fast money and bone money. Oil money was based on the amount of blubber the ship brought home, paid in proportion to the rank of the seaman. Bone money depended on the weight of baleen, or whalebone, brought back, while striking money was paid to the harpooner who actually fixed his harpoon into the whale, and fast money to men who were in the boat, or boats, that got 'fast' to a whale. In a good year, the whaling man could at least double his basic wage; in a poor year he would get only the basic, which was perhaps the equivalent of a minimum wage – a poor return for months of stress and effort.

The season of 1896 was not good for *Terra Nova* or Richard Leggat. The ship captured around 5000 seals but only one whale, so the wages were as low as the spirits of the men. Not that Leggat was a stranger to hard times; in 1888, while he was sailing on *Nova Zembla*, he took ill with what the doctors called 'inflammation of the lungs and dropsy' and had to leave the ship at Holsteinborg in Greenland. Although a Danish ship brought him back to Scotland, his wages would be drastically cut, for a seaman's wages stopped the moment he left his ship. Perhaps that was one reason for the constant arguing that marked Leggat's marriage.

At that period many Dundee whaling ships worked out of St John's in Newfoundland, with the hands spending time and money in the local taverns. However, amongst a breed of men renowned for their heavy drinking, Leggat was noted for his quiet sobriety. In appearance he was thin-featured, almost gaunt, with a straight, prominent nose and a red, drooping moustache. As a line manager he had a position of some responsibility, rowing out in the small whaleboat from which the whale was harpooned and ensuring the line connecting the harpoon to the boat did not kink around the leg or head of any of the seamen. Their lives depended on his skill and concentration.

In her mid-twenties, Elizabeth had been married to Leggat for three years. She worked as a weaver in Mid Wynd Works at the Hawkhill, and that autumn moved from her home at Lawrence Street to a two-roomed attic in a John Street tenement, four floors above the flickering gas of a streetlamp. There was also a fourteen-month-old daughter to care for. John Street was a short street between Dudhope Crescent and Dudhope Crescent Road. Because Leggat's wages were poor that season, Elizabeth had to work longer hours at the mill to make ends meet. 'What will become of us? There's only my wages to keep my man and myself and the bairn,' she said once, and that single remark reveals so much about the constant work of ordinary people in Victorian Dundee. Neither Richard nor Elizabeth were great conversationalists, so save for the occasional brief greeting, their neighbours did not know much about them, but they did hear their frequent arguments and knew that all was not well in the Leggat household.

It is obvious that such a marriage was subject to stress: A man away for months at a time and a family dependent on wages that could fluctuate wildly from season to season. There was one other factor that was probably hidden from the outside world: Richard Leggat was racked with jealousy.

There is no knowing how Elizabeth Leggat acted when her husband was at sea, but when he was home she seemed hardly to have a life. Leggat controlled everything she did, and beat her if she did not obey. On one occasion she told her sister, Jessie Crichton, that Leggat had beaten her so badly she could barely walk. At times he had threatened to murder her, but nobody believed he would. The neighbours knew the marriage was not perfect – the internal walls of a Dundee tenement were too thin for secrecy – but there were many quarrelling couples in the city and few thought twice about it. Marriage, like life, was never easy in an industrial city and people preferred to close their ears, mind their own business and hope other people minded theirs.

Late on the morning of 7th December the couple fell out, and their raised voices echoed around the close. Mrs Kendall, in the house immediately below, had heard such things before, but at one in the afternoon there was something that momentarily startled her. It was a sound, she thought, 'like the breaking of a bed', but save for a brief, semi-humorous comment to a friend, 'Is that somebody being killed?', she pushed the incident to the back of her mind.

When Mrs Kendall heard somebody running down the common staircase she peeped outside her door and saw Leggat hurrying past. On a lower floor, Mrs Smith greeted Leggat with a cheery 'Hello,' but met with no response as he rushed outside into the dark winter street. Presumably both women gave a metaphorical shrug of their shoulders and returned to their homes. The police arrived a couple of hours later.

Until then only Richard Leggat knew what had happened. During the long months he was at sea, he was intensely aware that his young, attractive wife was alone. Leggat was a quiet man who did not join in the revelries of his comrades, and perhaps this solitariness enhanced his jealousy until it became an obsession. By the time he returned from the Arctic he was convinced that Elizabeth had been cheating on him, and he gave her dog's abuse. Combined with the lack of money, Leggat's suspicions must have unhinged his mind. Up in the ice, the Greenlandmen would hunt anything, from birds to polar bears to whales, so perhaps that is why Leggat owned a large, central fire revolver. He produced it as Elizabeth stood in front of him, taking a pinch of snuff. He shot five times, hitting her twice, with one shot going into her thigh and another straight through her heart.

There does not seem to have been any build-up to the murder, no more arguments than usual, but the neighbours beneath did hear loud noises. Afterwards Leggat placed the revolver on the dresser in the kitchen and left the house. His daughter lay in her bed, half naked and apparently undisturbed by the violence and the death of her mother.

Running down the stairs, Leggat walked straight to the harbour, climbed onto the West Protection Wall and jumped into the Tidal Basin in an attempt to commit suicide, but his instincts for life were stronger than either guilt or grief and he remained afloat. Some time before three in the afternoon he swam back ashore, walked to the Central Police Station in Bell Street and gave himself up. At first the police did not believe him. It was not common for a soaking wet man to arrive and confess to a murder, but they searched him, found a handful of revolver cartridges, and decided to act.

The arrival of Deputy Chief Constable Carmichael and Inspector Davidson with a gaggle of uniformed police alerted half the neighbourhood that something was amiss. People emerged from their homes and bustled to John Street, some hoping for scandal, others perhaps genuinely shocked. Searching the house, the police found the corpse of Elizabeth Leggat and her still unaware daughter. The police doctor, Charles Templeman, announced that Mrs Leggat was dead and her body was quickly taken to the Constitution Road Mortuary.

Leggat was as quiet and unassuming in custody as he had been on board a ship, but when he appeared at the Police Court he denied murder, claiming he remembered nothing until he came to his senses in the Tay.

As he waited for his trial, his daughter was taken to the Children's Shelter in Constitution Road. Possibly because of his plea of temporary insanity, Leggat was found guilty of manslaughter and sentenced to fifteen years' penal servitude.

Murder, however, was uncommon among Dundee seamen. Assault, drunkenness and theft were much more likely. In one case in February 1824 three sailors arrived at an Overgate lodging house. They paid for a night's board but when the owner slipped out for a few moments, one of the seamen began to search through all the drawers. The owner returned before anything was stolen but the man ran too quickly to be caught. The police found him later and dragged him to the police office, where he was strip-searched. Only then did they realise that he was actually a woman. When dealing with Dundee mariners, anything was possible!

3

Crimes of Passion

Burning Passion

At first sight, there seemed nothing out of the ordinary about Mary Sullivan. In common with many thousands of other Dundee women, she was over forty years old and worked in a textile mill. Although she was sometimes known as Mary Killen and lived in fair harmony with a man of that name, the two had never been married. Nevertheless they had acted as man and wife for years, so when Killen left her for another millworker named Margaret Page, it is not surprising that Sullivan was a little upset.

In such a case it would be expected for Sullivan to confront her man and tell him exactly what she thought of him. She might also have tried to win him back or challenged her rival for his affections, but instead she took more direct and more drastic action. Gathering a bundle of waste paper and a piece of a discarded willow basket, Mary Sullivan soaked them in paraffin. Sometime after dark on the night of Wednesday 29th July, she placed her bundle against the door of Page's house in Lilybank Road, scratched a Lucifer match and set it alight. Within a few minutes the flames had spread to the door, burning through the wood and spiralling blue smoke inside the house. Fortunately for the occupants, and probably for Mary Sullivan, the flames spread only as far as the surrounding wood-work and nobody was hurt.

Sullivan never denied the act and within days she was in the Police Court, charged with wilful fire-raising. Bailie Doig thought a higher court would be more appropriate for such a serious accusation and in mid-September Sullivan appeared before Lord Craighall at the Circuit Court. Once again she pleaded guilty, so there was no need for a trial. Lord Craighall listened to the reasons for Sullivan's actions and pointed out that the fire might have spread from Page's house to others around, so putting others in great danger. He reminded her that the law considered fire-raising as a serious crime and sentenced her to twelve months' imprisonment. He also said that Sullivan had 'done it under the influence of passion'. That same passion was evident in some of the worst crimes in nineteenth-century Dundee.

Lock Me Up

However they are depicted on the television, murders are sordid affairs with nothing of romance or excitement about them. There is usually a lot of sympathy for the victim and occasionally a twinge for the perpetrator, but there was one case in Dundee where the murderer was viewed with pity by just about everybody. Even stranger, this was a domestic murder, where a husband killed his wife, but the murder of Margaret Balfour was unusual right from the start.

On the morning of 22nd December 1825 David Balfour, a seaman, and Thomas Houston, who worked for the Dundee & Perth Shipping Company, walked into Mr Dalgairny's spirit shop at the Shore. After he had knocked back half a gill of whisky, Balfour told Houston he was determined to end things; he said he would put his wife away because he could not take any more, and he did not care if he hanged for it. With that the men parted and Balfour headed to the Fleshmarket. He may have intended to buy meat, but instead he borrowed a knife from one of the butchers, 'to kill a lamb'. When the butcher asked him where the lamb was, Balfour told him it was in the Murraygate.

With the knife in his jacket, Balfour walked to his father-in-law's house in the Murraygate. According to his own account, his wife, Margaret, was standing alone beside the kitchen fireside.

'Margaret,' Balfour said, 'will you give me the shirt?'

'Yes, yes you blackguard,' Margaret replied. 'Do you want anything else?' As she fetched a shirt from another room, she asked again, 'Do you want anything else, you blackguard?'

'Oh Margaret,' Balfour said. 'Margaret . . .'

Grabbing him by the shoulders, Margaret tried to push him out of the door, but Balfour drew the knife from within his jacket and stabbed her, there and then. Even as Margaret crumpled to the ground, Balfour left the house, but rather than try to escape from justice, he ran straight toward it. He walked the few dozen yards from his father-in-law's house to the Town House, knocked politely at the door and when Charles Watson, the turnkey, answered, Balfour confessed he should be locked up; he had murdered his wife.

Even faced with such a confession, Charles Watson did not welcome Balfour into jail with open arms. Instead he said that the jailer was not there, but if Balfour could wait outside? Balfour did, kicking his heels around the Pillars and walking away the last hour of freedom he would ever know. Eventually John Watson the jailer appeared and ushered David Balfour safely into a cell.

That same morning Balfour wrote a confession that told his whole sad, sordid story. Like so many before him, Balfour had gone to sea as a young boy, and after four years, the Royal Navy pressed him. It was then 1801, the French Revolutionary War was at its height and Britain was struggling for her existence against a continent in arms. A few years later and still in the Navy, Balfour met Margaret. She was a Dundee girl, and her father worked in the Dundee Sugar House. She was very attractive, and he was a fit, virile young seaman. It is possible that Margaret was pregnant when they married in July 1805, and Balfour was very much in love, despite his more worldly-wise shipmates warning against her. Knowing women from a score of ports, they would recognise her type immediately.

However, Balfour was as brash and confident as any other seventeen-year-old boy and set up home with his new wife in the Seagate, no distance at all from the harbour of Dundee. Perhaps it was because of her that he deserted the Navy, but there is ambiguity over that period of his life. He certainly served in the Navy until 1813 when he was discharged with a pension, which for some unknown reason he claimed under the name of Mitchell. During that period Margaret picked up half his pay, as was customary with nearly every seaman's wife – the Custom Records in Dundee are littered with such instances.

By that time the Balfours were considered an old married couple by nineteenth-century standards, but in David Balfour's case, at least, the love survived. He seems to have been a decent, good-natured, hard-working man who did his best for his wife despite growing doubts about her fidelity. It was this good nature, combined with the wayward streak in Margaret, which was to begin the slide to murder. Perhaps David remembered the warnings of his shipmates before they married, but if so he tried to ignore them and remain faithful as they produced three children. Unfortunately only one boy survived.

Notwithstanding his troubles at home, it was not hard for a seaman in Dundee to find a berth, and once Balfour was back at sea Margaret took in a lodger, Alexander Hogg, to help with the bills.

Then Margaret's brother, Robert Clark, needed money. He asked his father and Balfour to act as security, and in time the repayment was due. But as neither Robert nor his father had the wherewithal, Balfour became liable for the full amount. He did not have the money, but Margaret Balfour asked the lodger to help, and the difficulty eased. Nevertheless, there was a cloud to the silver lining, and Margaret and Hogg became more than friends.

With Balfour at sea much of the time, the relationship between Hogg and Margaret had taken root and Balfour found himself a stranger in his own house. He suggested that Margaret and he leave Dundee together, but when Margaret's mother applied pressure for her to stay, Balfour moved out alone. For the next three years he lived in Aberdeen, where Margaret occasionally visited him, while Hogg moved in with Margaret's parents. Eventually David and Margaret moved to Greenock together, with their surviving son and Margaret's brother.

In Greenock the Balfours rented a house from a local inn-keeper, Torquil Macleod, who was a widower with a small boy. Margaret soon transferred her infidelity from Hogg to Macleod, and Balfour had renewed cause for jealousy. When he came home early from a voyage from Belfast, he found his house empty and it took little deduction to guess where Margaret was. Balfour waited outside Macleod's house until two in the morning when he saw Margaret emerge. Naturally he confronted her, heard her admission of guilt and promptly forgave her, but it was obvious they could not stay in Greenock.

The game of musical chairs began again. Margaret crossed the country to Dundee and moved in with her recently widowed father. She took Macleod's son with her, and Macleod followed like a hungry dog with Balfour close behind, determined to keep his wife.

Once again Balfour had to intervene to salvage his marriage. He chased Macleod back to Greenock and ordered him to take his son with him. Macleod left, his retreat possibly sweetened by his consolation prize, for he had transferred his affections from Margaret to her younger sister, a girl of sixteen. Satisfied he had regained his wife, Balfour returned to sea.

In late 1825 Balfour was shipwrecked off the west coast of England. Such occurrences were part and parcel of a seaman's life, and he returned to Dundee as a passenger on a packet ship. When he arrived home his wife refused to let him in, saying, 'You have got Macleod's boy away, but it will cost you dear.' She spoke the truth, and Balfour had only his own thoughts and the wet December streets for company. He returned home at night and despite opposition from his wife's brothers, stayed until morning, but Margaret was anything but friendly and her brothers gave

Balfour unpleasant advice to leave Dundee. When he tried to win Margaret back the next day she swore at him and said 'she loved Torquil Macleod's finger better than his whole body'.

At least that statement, unless shouted in thoughtless anger, would have removed any lingering ambiguity about where Margaret's affections lay, but the sentiment would sink deep and fester. Balfour and Margaret argued again that evening and Margaret stormed into the bedroom, dragged a chest of drawers across the door and kept Balfour out. He asked her to pass him out a clean shirt but Margaret refused. All night Balfour remained in the kitchen, fully dressed and probably fuming.

Sometime during the night Margaret must have removed the barricade, for at the back of seven the next morning Balfour came to her bed and tried once more to patch the relationship.

'Oh Margaret, why will ye no' mak' peace atween us?'

But Margaret was having nothing of it. 'Be gone, you vagabond,' she said. 'I'll have nothing to do with you, and some misty morning you will find me away from Dundee. As for you, I will have you fixed before twelve o'clock this day.'

It was then that Balfour left the house, to return with the knife and murder his wife.

On 20th April 1826 Balfour was tried at Perth. On the advice of his advocates he pleaded not guilty and Alexander Macneil, speaking for him, argued he had suffered mental derangement brought about by jealousy. The judge, Lord Pitmilly, had little sympathy. After advising the jury against feelings of compassion for the prisoner, he said, 'Jealousy, revenge, anger from insult or other provocation and every other passion to which human nature is subject, are aberrations of the mind, but not such as to justify the commission of so heinous a crime as that with which the panel is charged.'

The jury was out for an hour, but when they announced that Balfour was guilty, they also asked for mercy. Once again the judge disagreed and sentenced Balfour to be hanged on the afternoon of 2nd June.

Balfour remained composed between the sentence and his death. He read the Bible, spoke of death as a happy event and seemed not to let a petition for mercy affect his equanimity. Even after all the provocation he had endured he spoke of 'his dear little wife, his poor little woman, whom he loved as he loved himself'.

It was a short walk from the condemned cell through the Guild Hall of the Town House to the gibbet that had been erected outside the window. Probably the calmest person in Dundee, Balfour stepped outside, sang a hymn and spoke to the estimated 18,000-strong crowd. He was hanged at ten to three and less than an hour later his body was taken into the Guild Hall preparatory to be sent to Edinburgh for dissection.

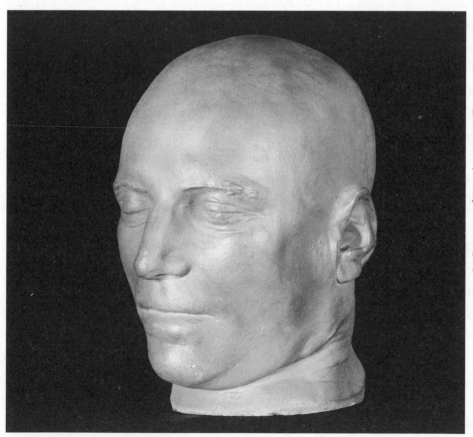

© Courtesy of Dundee Art Galleries and Museums

Death Mask of David Balfour

There was still one final act, however. After Balfour's execution a cast was made of his head, for at that time the supposed science of phrenology, when so-called experts attempted to explain the character of a person by the shape of his or her head, was popular. The idea was to examine Balfour's head and see if there was a typical criminal or even murderer's head. The cast still exists, sitting on a shelf within the Barrack Street storage facilities of Dundee's McManus Museum.

A Face Full of Vitriol

Of course not all crimes of passion resulted in murder, and sometimes it was the male partner who was the victim. As Lord Cockburn pointed out, Dundee women could be passionate in their actions, so a Dundee woman scorned was best avoided.

At midday on 28th December 1864 Princes Street was busy. Carriages and carts clattered over the cobbles, merchants marched purposefully from their places of business, chimney sweeps carried their long brushes, shop keepers watched out of crowded windows, hoping for trade in the post-Christmas lull, blacksmiths and boilermakers, carpenters and cowfeeders, mechanics and millworkers, the myriad workers of Dundee all hustled along, lost in their own lives.

Young David Nicoll probably should have been at work. Not yet a teenager, he was growing out of boyhood and enjoying the bustle of the expanding city. It was a boom time for Dundee, with the docks packed with ships, the mills and factories buzzing nonstop and jobs for anybody who wanted one, but David was more interested in the drama that played itself out only a few yards from where he stood.

The woman was a looker, a respectable millworker standing with a handkerchief in her hand. She was at the bottom of Crescent Street, just where it met Princes Street, and had been there for some time, obviously waiting for somebody. Eventually she saw a man and shouted over to him. The man replied, but David did not hear what was said through the growl of traffic. He watched the woman hurry over to the man and they spoke together for some time, but it seemed the man was less enthusiastic about continuing their conversation than the woman was. As David watched, the woman produced a small tin canister and threw the liquid contents in the man's face, before turning and running away. The man collapsed to the ground, screaming and clutching his face.

Although David Nicoll did not know it, he had just witnessed a jilted lover's classic act of revenge.

It had all started in July 1862, about a month after James Killeen had left Ireland to seek work in Dundee. He had an aunt in Todburn Lane, and while visiting her he had got to know a young woman named Elizabeth Hay, a quiet, decent millworker. Unmarried and in her mid-twenties, Elizabeth lived in Horsewater Wynd while Killeen stayed in his own house in Princes Street. As a cooper he was a skilled man and made a respectable wage, although he would certainly never be rich. The two got on so well that Elizabeth believed Killeen was courting her for marriage, although in his own words he believed 'it would not answer'.

After more than two years with Elizabeth, Killeen met and married another woman. It is not difficult to imagine how Elizabeth felt about that, in an age when women married fairly young. Her own words, spoken at her trial, 'This injured my feelings very much,' were probably a great understatement. She would undoubtedly be devastated.

There are two versions of what happened next: James Killeen's and Elizabeth Hay's. According to Elizabeth, Killeen and his wife began to spend more than they earned, and he was desperate for money. He came to her door, apologised for the way he had treated her and asked her for a loan of some money. She loaned him £2.

Killeen had a radically different story. He claimed that he had been married for just over a year when Elizabeth came into his King Street shop. At first Killeen believed she had come to buy one of the tubs he made, but instead she showed him a portrait and asked if he knew who owned it. He did not know and handed it back, and she pressed two shillings and eleven pence halfpenny, (about fifteen pence) onto him. Killeen tried to hand it back, saying he had enough money, but Elizabeth was insistent. At the beginning of September she met him again, handed over £1 16/- and suggested that he leave his wife, go down to Newcastle and find work there. When he was settled she would come and join him. Naturally, Killeen refused. He refuted any suggestion that he had ever asked for money from Elizabeth.

During Elizabeth's trial for assault, Killeen's legal representative, Mr Campbell, asked him if he had ever asked Elizabeth to forgive him. When Killeen said no, Elizabeth had become agitated, saying, 'Didn't you now? Didn't you?'

Killeen did sail to Newcastle, but after a few weeks he returned to Dundee. According to Killeen's account he was barely back when Elizabeth visited him in his aunt's house. They drank together, but before he could repay the loan Elizabeth left the house.

Once again, Elizabeth's version does not agree. She claimed that Killeen was 'doing well' in Newcastle and when she heard he was back she called on him to ask for her loan back. She said she had loaned him a full £2 – a lot of money for a millworker in the 1860s – but he refused, instead starting an ugly rumour that she was 'trying to seduce him from his wife'.

Once again Elizabeth was emotionally injured. Killeen had hurt her when he had strung her along with hopes of marriage and then rejected her in favour of another woman, and now he had hurt her again when he spread cruel and, according to her, false tales about her. In Elizabeth's words the rumours 'affected' her 'very much'. Not surprisingly she became ill. One of her friends, Isabella Darling, advised her to take a solution of vitriol (sulphuric acid) for her health. Darling said that a few drops of vitriol in a glass of water helped settle her own stomach and Elizabeth tried the same solution.

There was more disputing about the meeting between Elizabeth and Killeen on Tuesday 28th December. Both agreed that they met in Princes Street at twelve o'clock, but the accounts of what happened next differ widely. Elizabeth said that she just happened to have her vitriol with her when she met Killeen that day and 'he spoke cruelly to me' and gave her a slight push. By the time of her trial she thought the push might have been accidental, but, 'I took the bottle and threw some drops of the liquid over him,' she said.

Killeen said Elizabeth had called over to him, but he told her he wanted 'nothing to do with her as I was a married man'. At that point Elizabeth put her hands beneath the handkerchief she was carrying and threw a red liquid over his face and his clothes.

'Take that!' Elizabeth said, and ran away along Princes Street.

The vitriol landed on Killeen's face, mouth and neck. He said he felt a 'burning sensation' so painful he would 'as soon have had a pistol bullet through my head'. With the corrosive vitriol burning his eyes and inside his mouth, he yelled for the police and chased after Elizabeth. He caught her outside James Milne's grocer shop, and they both went inside to try and ease the pain.

As soon as Milne learned what had happened he cut away the damaged part of Killeen's clothes and dabbed olive oil on his burned face. 'She must have been an awful woman that would do the like of that,' he said, but Elizabeth denied everything and blamed Killeen for throwing the vitriol. Milne did mention that her dress was also damaged. Elizabeth also advised that Killeen put water on his burns.

When they were in the shop somebody handed the near-empty canister of vitriol to David Ogilvy, a police lamplighter. He kept it as evidence, followed Elizabeth into Milne's and held her until she could be properly arrested, but once again Elizabeth denied that she had thrown vitriol into Killeen's face.

After Milne's first aid, Killeen sought more professional medical help, but the pain continued to gnaw at his face. He was in bed for over a month, for the first two weeks of which he was unable to eat. Even during Elizabeth's trial at the Perth Circuit Court in April, his eye and cheek still bore the marks of the burns, and Lord Cowan, the presiding judge, said that some of the injuries could be permanent.

The jury listened to all the evidence, and although they thought it obvious that Elizabeth Hay had thrown the vitriol, there was also a measure of sympathy for her. Perhaps they thought that Killeen had reneged on a previous agreement, stated or unstated, by marrying another woman after having courted her for so long; and possibly they believed at least part of her story. Whatever their reasoning, they found her guilty of assault, but under common law. Lord Cowan gave his final comments on his jury's decision: 'The crime of which you have been convicted is divested of much of its aggravated character. There are certainly circumstances connected with the crime that weigh with the court.' In other words, he said that Elizabeth had certainly thrown the vitriol, but the jury thought she had some justification or excuse for her actions. Lord Cowan sentenced her to eighteen months' imprisonment.

Vitriol-throwing seems very Victorian, but sometimes a crime of passion was so horrible that it still manages to chill the blood. The actual assault in the next case only lasted for seconds, but still raises a curl of disgust.

Knifed in the Groin

'Jessie Dand!'

The young voice, laced with pain and fear, would have echoed up the close that late night of 7th May 1867. 'Jessie Dand!'

The girl staggered up the stone stairs, her skirt sodden with blood and leaving a red trail behind her. She stopped at one of the doors. She was pretty but she was crying hard; realising her exertion had caused the blood to flow faster from her wound. She felt her petticoats soaked and heavy against her belly and legs.

'Jessie Dand!'

The door opened at last and she nearly fell in, throwing herself on the bed that stood only a foot or so inside the room. Jessie Dand knew Elizabeth Laing, who lived below her in the same close. She knelt at the girl's side and asked what had happened.

'See what the villain has done,' Elizabeth said. 'He's stabbed me!'

By the light of the low gas, Jessie looked at the girl's hands pressing against the lower part of her belly. They were also cut and bleeding. She asked, 'Who? Fred?'

Before Elizabeth told her story, Jessie sent her husband for a doctor. It was obvious that the girl was in increasing pain and losing a lot of blood.

Jessie already knew much of what had happened, but she listened to Elizabeth's version of what she knew was not all a one-sided story. Elizabeth lived with her father at 24 Dudhope Crescent, right at the corner of the street and with an entrance that penetrated the building from the front to the court and Number 25 at the back. Her attacker was Frederick Robertson, a mechanic from Princes Street in Dundee and she had known him for quite some time. In fact, the two had been sweethearts, a courting couple, and some people had thought they were destined to be married. Frederick had believed that, but Elizabeth had other ideas. In her own words, she 'did not care if he stayed away or came'.

It was about August 1865 when the then eighteen-year-old Elizabeth who worked at Fergusson's steam loom first met Frederick Robertson. Frederick was a mechanic at Baxter's Foundry in Dens Works and the two got along very well. They met each other about two or three times a week, and Frederick planned marriage, but Elizabeth was not sure. As the weeks and months passed she began to see flaws in Frederick's character. It was not drink. Although he took a drink now and then, he was not a habitual drunkard, but he could be a very excitable man. All the same, she met him frequently and wrote to him when they were not together, so Frederick could have no doubt about their mutual attraction.

Elizabeth's father, Thomas Laing, had a great influence over her and shared her mixed opinion of Frederick. More than once he asked young Frederick to leave his house, but despite these setbacks, Frederick continued to court Elizabeth and believed she shared his intentions. Nevertheless, when he asked her to marry her, she turned him down – more than once. Some people thought it strange that Elizabeth should continue to walk out with a man she had no intention of marrying. It appeared that she was just stringing him along, offering him false hope while she toyed with him and possibly searched for somebody she considered more suitable.

Matters began to come to a head on Monday 6th May 1867. Elizabeth spent the afternoon with her sister and two young men, but when the men took the train to Arbroath she returned home, arriving there about nine in the evening. Not long afterward, Frederick came to the door. He had been drinking but was far from drunk and he said it was not right that she spend time with another man. Trying to calm him down, Elizabeth said she had spent the afternoon with her sister, but when Frederick became agitated Thomas Laing ordered him out of the house.

Frederick left, but returned later. Not surprisingly, Laing did not allow him back inside. There was a nasty moment when Elizabeth believed Frederick would hit her, but perhaps because Laing was there, Frederick left again. Next day, Frederick sent Elizabeth a note asking to meet him in nearby Parker Street. Although it was obvious she had no intention of marrying him, she still agreed. After asking her if she would forgive him, he suggested they meet again, but Elizabeth refused, saying her parents were against the relationship continuing. This time Elizabeth made her position clear and said she wanted nothing more to do with him. When he pressed, she said that no, she would not meet him again that night.

'If you come tonight it will be the last night I will seek to see you,' Frederick promised, but Elizabeth was adamant.

As she walked away, Frederick shouted out, 'Will you not come?'

Elizabeth replied simply, 'No.'

Frederick followed her down Parker Street, insisting, asking if she would declare to God that she would come. After so many refusals, now Elizabeth promised that she would, but as she later declared, she had no intention of keeping her word but only wanted rid of him. After work she walked home and remained behind her own front door, but about half past nine Frederick asked Jessie to arrange a meeting. This time he wanted to see Elizabeth at the foot of the Lochee Road. Instead Elizabeth walked upstairs to Jessie's house.

Perhaps she suspected that Frederick was already there; she certainly mentioned he was pleased to see her. They remained in Jessie's house for about ten minutes, perhaps longer, and left together, with Jessie thinking they appeared quite happy, as she said later at Frederick's trial, 'with no coldness on Elizabeth's part'. They spent some time at Mrs McMath's which was, according to Elizabeth, a respectable public house at 13 Dudhope Crescent. They were not alone there, for they met a woman named Margaret Macrae at the foot of the stair.

Having had supper and a glass of beer, the three of them left together. After Frederick and Elizabeth escorted Margaret home to West Port, things got a little fraught. Frederick wanted to go back by Brown Street, a route made forbidding by tall mills on either side. Elizabeth was not keen to enter such a dark and, with no houses, lonely place. They seem to have got over that disagreement, for they were still together when they reached Dudhope Crescent, and Frederick continued to ask Elizabeth to marry him. And still she said no.

Once again Elizabeth seems to have been playing with Frederick's emotions, for after spending the evening with him, she said she would not see him again. Perhaps she enjoyed the power she obviously had over the man, or maybe she really was naive enough to believe she could handle him.

'If you do not take me,' Frederick said ominously, 'you will not get another, for this is the last night I will see you.'

Elizabeth thought Frederick was 'quite cool' as he said these words.

As he finished speaking, Frederick ducked and produced a knife. In nearly the same instant he shoved his hand under her skirt, under her petticoat and thrust the knife into her groin, slashing upward toward her belly. Frederick did not normally carry a knife. As a non-smoker he did not use one to cut tobacco and there was no other reason for a man in his position to be armed. He could only have brought it to use on Elizabeth.

Doubling up in agony and shock, Elizabeth grabbed for the knife and attempted to wrest it free. Frederick pulled the blade out of her grasp, cutting her hand. Still holding the knife, he shoved at her, perhaps trying to knock her down and then fled out of the back court, shouting he was going to drown himself. With the blood pouring from the savage slash in her groin, Elizabeth screamed to Jessie Dand for help.

As Elizabeth writhed in pain, Jessie held the edges of the wound together for the full hour it took until Doctor Pirie arrived. The wound was about nine inches long and an inch deep at the bottom where the knife had initially penetrated, but shallower further up. Frederick had obviously thrust the knife into her left groin and slashed upward. For some distance it ran parallel with, and dangerously close to, her private parts. After his examination, Doctor Pirie carefully stitched Elizabeth together.

After Elizabeth spent a night in Jessie's house, her father carried her home, promising to have Frederick arrested. There was a touch of naivety in Elizabeth's reply that there was no need as he was 'away to drown himself'. There was no real need for Laing to tell the police what had happened, for the trail of blood from the spot where Elizabeth was stabbed to Jessie's door spoke for itself. It was the end of May before the doctor considered Elizabeth was no longer in danger. She lay in bed for weeks as the wound slowly healed and her parents fretted.

When the case came to the Circuit Court Frederick tried to deny the stabbing, but Jessie, Margaret MacRae and a woman named Elizabeth Miller had all seen them together. Miller had heard Elizabeth cry for Jessie Dand and saw Frederick run into the court at the back. As these facts were incontestable, the defence concentrated on Elizabeth's previous treatment of Frederick. He was known to be a man of intense passions and his brother, James Robertson, explained why. 'He burst a blood vessel about four years ago,' James said, 'and has not been so strong since. He is easily excited. If he gets into an argument he gets very excited. The least quantity of drink affects him.'

The defence tried to blame Elizabeth for her cruelty to a man with such a temperament. They brought up her earlier behaviour when she raised and dashed his hopes and kept him dangling like a puppet on a string, but nothing they said altered the horror of the stabbing. Margaret

MacRae and Jessie both mentioned that Frederick and Elizabeth were 'sweethearting' but neither was sure whether or not they intended to marry. Elizabeth's father claimed he 'did not understand they were to be married ... I would have advised her against him – he would have been a bad husband'.

During the trial Sergeant Dow said he had arrested Frederick for assault in July 1866. He was not quite the slighted and bewildered innocent the defence claimed.

Strangely, at least some of the people of Dundee sympathised with Frederick and booed Elizabeth when she appeared outside the court. The judge, Lord Deas, had none of it. When the jury, after an absence of just eleven minutes, found him guilty of the attack, Lord Deas sentenced Frederick to twenty years' penal servitude, which sounds a savage punishment for a crime committed in a fit of passion.

But was it so savage? There is no doubt that Elizabeth had an unpleasant side to her nature and her treatment of a genuine suitor was unkind, but as Frederick did not normally carry a knife he must have had some intention of stabbing this girl when he arranged the meeting, and the manner of the stabbing was undoubtedly brutal. Elizabeth was scarred for life and might well have been killed, while Frederick had a history of violence. Was the attack something that occurred in a fit of passion, or was it a planned revenge for a year of frustrated hopes? Only Frederick Robertson knew all the facts. As he left the courtroom to begin his two decades in jail, he looked pale and calm. He glanced toward Elizabeth, but she appeared as unconcerned about his sentence as she had been about his feelings when she had pretended to court him.

These cases show only a few examples of the passion that was never far from the surface in Dundee, where men and women held strong feelings for one another. Those feelings were often displayed in marriages that endured periods of unemployment and depression, but when they were roused by injustice – particularly in personal relationships – they could be perverted into acts of extreme violence.

4
A Decade with Patrick Mackay

Films, books and folklore have maintained the fame of many nineteenth-century lawmen. The names of Pinkerton and Wyatt Earp are well known; in the 1860s Edinburgh had detective James McLevy, while the fictional Sherlock Holmes spawned a huge genre of stories based on brainpower and detection. Dundee, however, also had a man who stood out against the underworld and although he has now disappeared from public memory, his name can still be found in the records of faded court cases and in many newspaper columns. His name was Patrick Mackay.

Before the 1824 Dundee Police Act introduced professional policemen to the streets of Dundee, the streets were guarded by night watchmen, the much-derided 'Charlies' who were often recruited from the aging ranks of paid-off soldiers. These men were backed by the elected constables and the far more professional servants of the courts. There were two levels of the latter: Sheriff Officers and Messengers-at-Arms. While Sheriff Officers had local responsibility and could pursue warrants within the burgh of Dundee, Messengers-at-Arms were officers of the Court of Session, with the responsibility of serving legal documents and enforcing court orders across the entire country. Patrick Mackay was one of the latter. He had a commission as a sheriff officer, but with his wider remit, was also able to pursue and arrest criminals all across Scotland.

The position is ancient; officially Mackay was an Officer of the King, but since at least 1510 the Lord Lyon King of Arms has been their ultimate controller, and he had a fixed scale of fees set by an Act of Sedurant passed by the Court of Session, Scotland's supreme Civil Court. Patrick Mackay, then, was a powerful official, and as an energetic man, he was arguably a dangerous enemy of Dundee's criminal population.

Born in August 1772 to Patrick Mackay and his wife Isabel Meek, Mackay was a native of Dundee and spent his life working for the peace of the burgh. He married comparatively late, on 21st November 1818 when, according to the Old Parish Register, he chose Anne Scott of Auchterhouse as his wife. Their marriage was not to last, though, and Anne died not three years later. Her gravestone in the Howff is still as moving as it must have been to Mackay when he set it up. 'Erected by Patrick Mackay, Messenger at Arms Dundee,' it says, 'and dedicated to the memory of Anne Scott, his spouse, who died the 29th May 1821.'

© Author's Collection

Anne Scott's Gravestone

After the loss of his wife, Patrick Mackay seems to have redoubled his efforts to quieten the turbulent underworld of Dundee. He lived in Methodist Close in the Overgate, the heart of Dundee, and was also active in the commercial world, holding shares in the shipping that was the lifeblood of Dundee. However it was his crime-fighting skills that made him well known and probably well-hated by the seething Dundee underworld. Despite his position, his pay was not always remitted promptly. For instance, there is an entry in the Collectors Book in Dundee Archives for 19th July 1831 when he still had not been paid the £2 16/6 that was due to him for apprehending two smugglers, David Dick junior and James Paterson senior, in 1823.

Mackay's work was surprisingly varied. For instance, in April 1823 he was called to control a prize fight in the west end of Dundee. The combatants were to be a heckler and a baker, and thousands of people gathered in expectation of blood and gore and bravery. Patrick Mackay brought three peace officers with him to control the unruly thousands, but when only one of the fighters turned up the throng dissipated reasonably quietly and his services were not required.

Thiefy Doig and the Wallace Gang

A few months later, in August of 1823, Mackay swooped down on one of Dundee's most notorious characters, a man named Doig, but who was better known by the name of 'Thiefy'. Doig was a well-known petty thief, in and out of trouble, and when Mackay searched him he found a collection of false keys in his pockets. Thiefy Doig was hustled to jail, where he belonged. In October Mackay was busy again. There had been a robbery at the house of Colonel Chalmers, one of Dundee's elite, and the forces of authority were under pressure to catch the burglars. One man named James Ferguson was caught and thrown into Dundee's jail, but when he turned King's Evidence and named his accomplices, the others were hunted down.

Three of the thieves were speedily caught and lodged in various jails, but one must have had a loose tongue, for two women, Mrs Cook and Mrs Wallace, were implicated for receiving the stolen property. Cook was quickly captured, but Wallace fled to Edinburgh. Patrick Mackay caught the packet boat and traced her. When he reached her and declared her under arrest, Wallace had a petticoat, some shifts and a shawl that belonged to Mrs Chalmers, so Mackay escorted her back to Dundee. The whole operation had been neat and effective; it proved how efficient Dundee's crime detection service could be, but it did little for crime prevention.

Only two days after Wallace had been deposited in jail, Mackay caught two other women named Robertson and Mary Thomson strolling the streets. Both had been outlawed for creating counterfeit coins, so Mackay quietly locked them up.

He had barely settled their paperwork when there was further trouble as five of Dundee's most notorious criminals escaped from the Town House jail. During this incident, Mackay was in Forfar, but a rider notified him what had happened and he began to hunt for the absconders. Eventually, he found them, but more on this particular story later.

A Trip to Leith

Save for the constant but necessary routine paperwork of his office and recapturing and incarcerating the banished Thiefy Doig, Mackay seems to have enjoyed a fairly quiet period over the next few months, but in June 1824 he was off on his travels again. A female pickpocket had charmed her way into the company of two visiting farmers, smiled sweetly, patted them fondly and relieved them of their pocket books and all their money.

When one of the farmers ran to the authorities for help, Patrick Mackay asked around his informants. Contacts on the fringe of the Dundee underworld were a vital component of the King's Messenger's armoury; Mackay discovered the pickpocket and her friend had boarded *Quentin*

Durward, one of the steam packet boats that sailed between Dundee and Leith. Catching the next boat, Mackay apprehended both women and kept them secure in the police office in Edinburgh, from where they were brought back to Dundee and jailed.

Not all Mackay's arrests involved a hectic dash across Scotland, however. Most were routine, such as the incident on Thursday 8th September 1824 when he again picked up previously-incarcerated David Scott, who had returned to Dundee despite a sentence of banishment. Two weeks later he arrested another well-known criminal, Rose Bruce, for exactly the same reason.

In October 1824 Mackay reached the peak of his professional career. Dundee was in a fervour about creating a new uniformed police force and debating who should be the first superintendent. It was not surprising that Patrick Mackay's name should be mentioned and for a while it seemed that Dundee's most energetic peace officer would be given the position of head of Dundee's police. However, he was not selected for the post as he was already in a position of responsibility. Apparently he was too good at his present job to be spared. It would have been fascinating to see the impact an experienced and dedicated officer could have had on Dundee, but that was not to be.

A Busy Period

The second half of 1825 was destined to be one of the busiest periods in Mackay's career. On 2nd June he arrested David George, who was charged with attempted rape on the Coupar Angus Road. During the same week, Thomas Abbott, an ex-watchman turned weaver, was accused of stealing twenty spindles of yarn from the bleach field of Turnbull and Company. Abbott defended himself vigorously, claiming that the mill foreman had sold him the yarn, but while Mackay had not arrested Abbott, he did capture William Stewart, who bought the yarn. On 23rd June Mackay was again busy when he hunted four men, John Robertson, David

Lamb, John Smith and George Thomson who had assaulted David Simpson of Wester Gourday near Longforgan Market. Leaving Dundee and travelling west, Mackay scooped three of them up, and completed the task by capturing the fourth, John Robertson, at Kingoodie.

Despite this constant run of success and his name being linked to the police superintendent's job, Mackay found himself in trouble. Only a few days after Mackay arrested Robertson, John Home, the superintendent of police, accused him of employing Jeffrey Goddart, a serving police officer, as his assistant. While Goddart promptly resigned, Mackay argued that Goddart had only worked for him in his spare time, and never when he should have been on duty. Home pulled strings and found Goddart a job as town officer in Cupar, but the situation had revealed a tension between the new, raw police force and the established body of peace officers.

Despite this newly created division, Mackay had another success in July 1825, when he arrested Mrs Malcolm of Bucklemaker Wynd and Mrs Anderson of Nethergate for stealing and resetting yarn. In a textile town, such thefts were perhaps not unexpected.

Beaten by Blackguards

On 11th November of that year, 1825, Mackay himself was involved in a violent situation. Together with his assistant and solicitor David Ramsay Forrest, and the Sheriff Clerk Depute, James Jones, he visited Mr Myles at the inn at Mile House, Lochee, to witness a disposition being signed by a duo of solicitors, James Lees and Ramsay Forrest. However, when there was a barrage of noise from an upstairs room, the landlord, Mr Souter, sent his maid to ask Mackay to remove 'four blackguards' who refused to leave. As soon as Mackay entered the room, three or four men attacked both him and Mrs Souter, who was also present.

Of the men in the upstairs room, three Lochee weavers, Robert McGavin, Andrew Taylor and John Gray, were the most aggressive. When McGavin knocked Mrs Souter aside, Mackay shouted, 'Be still, that won't do,' and tried to intervene but had to block McGavin's attack on him. Moving from defence to offence, Mackay grabbed hold of McGavin's jacket, pushed him to the ground and knelt on him.

Hearing the commotion upstairs, Ramsay Forrest grabbed a pair of fireside tongs and rushed to help. He arrived in time to see Andrew Taylor attack Mackay, delivering a swift punch to the face and thumping him on the head and back until he released McGavin. Forrest, who seems to have been a handy man to have around, smashed the tongs into Taylor's shoulder. Enraged, Taylor closed with him and they fought, with Forrest receiving brutal cuts on the face and one of his knees.

At this stage Mackay was on the ground, and a man described as wearing a 'sailor's suit' was attacking him with a sharp object that, according to James Lees, 'peeled' the skin from his fingers. Mackay struggled free and escaped downstairs, bleeding heavily, as Taylor, having finished with Ramsay Forrest, turned his attention to Jones, the Sheriff Clerk Depute.

As quickly as it had erupted, the disturbance was over. The weavers poured down the stairs and into the street, leaving Mackay's party to lick their wounds. Mackay was probably the most badly hurt, with three bleeding gashes on his head and another on his hand. James Lees had a bone-deep cut on his forehead; the solicitor David Ramsay also had a cut on his forehead and another on the top of his head, while Mrs Souter was understandably upset by the turmoil in her house. However, the excitement was not yet complete. Almost as soon as they were outside, McGavin and his band returned, hammering at the outside door with great stones as the people inside debated what was best to do.

Despite Mackay's advice not to let them in, Robert Souter opened the door. Strangely, when the weavers returned the atmosphere had altered completely. After spending about quarter of an hour trying to kick pieces out of Mackay and his colleagues, now they said they wanted to come to some sort of agreement. Lees turned them down, but according to Mrs

Souter, all the men were 'good billies' – good friends – and Mackay paid for half a mutchkin of whisky. It is an interesting scenario, but one that is difficult to believe, given that Mackay's wounds seeped blood for some hours.

When the case came to court in April 1826, the defence lawyer attempted to lay the blame on Mackay, but the jury disagreed, and Lord Pitmully awarded Taylor nine months in prison, with Gray and McGavin receiving six months each.

After the excitements of 1825, the following year was comparatively quiet for Mackay, but there were still moments of drama. Around the time he gave evidence about his own assault, Mackay escorted the wife-murderer David Balfour to Perth for the Circuit Court. While others due to stand trial travelled by the steam packet, Mackay took Balfour in a chaise, passing crowds of people who had come to watch him go. In this case, the crowd were full of sympathy, for they knew Balfour had been sorely tested before he killed his wife.

That year Mackay also arrested Mrs Swan, an elderly midwife charged with assisting with an abortion, and he had an interesting episode in the Nethergate. The police had been watching John Robertson, whose house was notorious for the disreputable crowd that gathered there, but they did not have enough proof to arrest him. Then in early December of 1826 there was a robbery in Auchtermuchty in Fife and a man named Robert Anderson was arrested and placed in the jail in Cupar. Anderson mentioned Robertson's name to Inglis, the local jailer, who in turn came to Dundee and approached Mackay.

Mackay and Inglis searched Robertson's house very thoroughly, with Robertson watching, knowing that previous searches by the police had found nothing. This time, however, Mackay was on the job. He found a secret cupboard, full of watches, silk handkerchiefs and other portable valuables. When he saw his hoard was discovered, Robertson made a quick dash to climb out the window, but he was stopped, and along with his wife, Elizabeth, and a certain David Walker, was escorted to Dundee jail. The material Mackay and Inglis found was later identified as having been stolen in Auchtermuchty and St Andrews.

Swimming with Convicts

Strangely, it was again the closing months of 1827 that saw Mackay break out of the normal routine of his job. As Messenger-at-Arms he was responsible for ensuring that convicted prisoners were taken to whatever jail they had been consigned to. On 4th October 1827 Mackay and two of his assistants were escorting three men onto the smack *Glasgow* to be taken to English hulks prior to being sent to Australia. All six had to board a small boat that would take them to the smack, and as the convicts were handcuffed together, they had to step on the gunwale of the boat simultaneously. The sudden weight capsized the boat, sending all six into the water of the wet dock. It was nearly an execution rather than transportation. Fastened together, the convicts could not escape, but fortunately one of Mackay's assistants was an excellent swimmer and dived under the water to unlock the handcuffs. Sodden wet but alive, the convicts were dragged on board the smack and Mackay had another small adventure to add to his list.

The Final Arrest

In 1828 there were a number of minor incidents. In May Mackay sent one of his assistants to arrest Alexander Gordon, an Auchterhouse smuggler. Gordon was a daring man who had been arrested and held in Forfar Gaol, preparatory to standing trial at the High Court. Rather than face the judge, he escaped and remained free until Mackay's man put on the handcuffs. Three weeks later Mackay picked up four men accused of assaulting a seaman walking along the Perth Road. It was a fortnight before he learned that two of the men were actually trying to save the seaman from the others, and the case collapsed when the victim returned to sea.

After that frustrating experience, Mackay's next arrest must have given him more satisfaction, when he brought in John Dean, a millwright from Feus of Carnoustie, accused of forging an £18 bill. At that period Dundee was notorious for supposed lodging houses, a name that was a cover for brothels, and it was often these places that were notorious hideouts for thieves. In September 1828 Mackay made a tiny dent in the proliferation when he travelled to Perth to arrest a young prostitute named Easson, who had robbed one of her customers that March. In July the following year he made a significant arrest when he captured a man named Low who had assaulted and attempted to rape a farmer's wife. In 1830 he arrested Billy Cook in Ogilvie's Close, Fish Street. Cook was a noted forger and Mackay scooped up over £52 in forged silver money, but frustratingly the sheriff freed Cook because there was no proof he had actually made the coins or used them as currency.

That was Mackay's last major arrest. He died of consumption on 9th August 1833, aged just forty, and the criminal fraternity of Dundee would have breathed their relief if they did not have other worries. The professional beat bobby, with his top hat, rattle and truncheon, was now patrolling the streets, and if the police had a lot to learn about crime prevention, they were growing better every year.

5
The Watchmen

Charlies on Watch

In 1824 the first Dundee Police Force came into existence. In the opinion of some, it was not a moment too soon, as the watchmen, or 'Charlies', seemed swamped by an increasing tide of crime. Armed with a long staff or baton, the watchmen carried a lantern to help them through the dim streets of Dundee. They had specific beats, and if they were in need of help they could either bang the butt end of their staff on the cobbles or 'spring their rattle'. This rattle was a large wooden affair, which when 'sprung' or rotated created a distinctive noise that would bring all other watchmen within earshot. However, as their wages came from subscribers and not the town, and those subscribers were the property owners of the area they patrolled, they were responsible only for their own specific beat and nowhere else.

The Charlies were natural targets for the unruly or drunken who infested the mostly-unlit streets, and by 1821 assaults were common, as in the case on the night of Saturday 6th January when four men attacked two watchmen in the Murraygate. Despite being outnumbered, the watchmen gained the upper hand and chased their attackers up the Wellgate, where a second scuffle began. This time the attackers won, with one man cracking a watchman over the head with his own baton. However, three of the attackers were later arrested, with housebreaking and robbery added to the charge for good measure.

On Saturday 16th February 1821 a gang roamed the Nethergate, first attacking an innocent servant and then assaulting the watchmen, who nevertheless managed to arrest three of them. Despite the odds against them, their efforts were pointless. Two of the men were freed due to a lack of evidence and the remaining man only fined a guinea. Yet the much derided watchmen did have the occasional success.

On Tuesday 19th of February a watchman was at home in the West Port when the door was forced open and a well-known thief named Francis Christal burst in, demanding money. Showing his official staff, the watchman announced who he was and arrested Christal instead, but even when caught red-handed the thief was only given two days in jail and released on his word of honour to leave Dundee.

Charlies in Disgrace

Perhaps this lack of support, and the ludicrously meagre sentences awarded to the criminals they did catch, caused some frustration among the watchmen. In October 1821 a number of them caused their own riot in the street.

The trouble began when a couple of half-drunken carters accused a watchman of sleeping at his post and demanded he do his job and shout out the hours. Whether the watchman had been sleeping or not, he over-reacted by grabbing hold of one of the carters and springing his rattle to summon support. More watchmen arrived but rather than calming the situation they beat up the carter. The carter's shouts brought a crowd, who the watchmen decided to arrest. Within a few moments a struggling mob filled the street. Some of the watchmen's lanterns were smashed, a handful of people arrested and then rescued by their comrades, but when the dust cleared the watchmen got the blame. Two lost their positions and the town authorities decided a captain should be appointed to keep them under control.

Charlies at Work

It was becoming obvious that the growing industrial centre of Dundee needed a more efficient body of lawmen, but in the meantime, the Charlies did their best. In early June 1823 when a gang of five men roamed the streets attacking everybody, the local watchman sprang his rattle to summon aid. Once a number of watchmen gathered they pursued the gang and arrested four of them. The fifth escaped. A month later two members of another raucous gang attacked a couple of young gentlemen who were unfortunate enough to cross their path. The local watchman arrived just as the kicks and punches began to rain down and the attackers ran away. Nevertheless, crime in Dundee continued to rise.

© Courtesy of Dundee Art Galleries and Museums

The Vault

One period in August 1823 gives an example of the typical crimes in Dundee. One Friday night a group of thieves tore the padlock from a spirit cellar in the Vault, but ran away when somebody shouted a challenge. On the same night, and possibly by the same people, there was an equally abortive attempt on a spirit cellar in the Horse Wynd, while a more successful thief eased into a Barrack Street shoemaker's with a false key. It might have been the same person who tried to rob another shoemaker in the Overgate, but once again a passer-by scared him off. During the week there was a break-in in Hilltown, where a girl, lying sick in her bed, could only watch as the thief casually sorted through her possessions to see what was worth stealing. On Monday a High Street house was robbed, while three masons beat up two men in Lilybank. Two of them tried the same thing on a lone gentleman walking in the Murraygate, but they found they had a tiger by the tail as he fought back, knocking both down.

A pickpocket found easy prey in the crowd waiting for the Perth packet boat on Tuesday, and at nine that same evening three men jumped a lone woman walking past Logie on her way to Lochee. They grabbed her basket and a respectable twenty-five shillings. After a surprisingly quiet Wednesday, a thief roamed the Craigie Estate on Thursday, picked the lock of a bothie and a chest inside and stole the overseer's clothes. The following Monday brought more trouble to Craigie as two horsemen carrying smuggled whisky met a customs officer head-on. There must have been a few seconds of hesitation, but when the local farm workers backed the officer, the smugglers dismounted and escaped in a wheat field.

The following week was not much better, with pickpockets rife in Dundee. They infested the first fair on the Monday, and that night a male and female team picked the pocket of a visiting countryman. When the victim noticed and protested, the Dundee crowd gathered in support and chased the thieves into a house, grabbed the watch from the woman and dragged the pickpockets to the Town House jail. In a touch of typical Dundee irony, while the pickpockets were safely tucked away, an opportunist thief stripped their Blackness Road house of anything valuable.

That robbery was only one of a clutch. On Saturday night thieves took the bedclothes from a house in Overgate while a gardener's house in Perth Road was also robbed. Later in the week the watchmen stopped a man who was carrying an armful of clothes through the Scouringburn. Although he claimed to have found them on the Seabraes, the watchmen arrested him anyway, while Patrick Mackay arrested the notorious Thiefy Doig and found a number of false keys in his pockets. False keys were quite common in Dundee, and in another incident, a thief used them to rob a warehouse and heckle house (an area in a spinning mill where flax was teased and combed out) in the West Port. He took a quantity of hemp and yarn.

There was a new type of pickpocket at the Fish Market on Saturday 12th September 1823, when a man had his pocket literally cut out and his pocketbook stolen, while in a High Street close a man was attacked and robbed of 7d and a piece of beef, all the money he had in the world and his Sunday dinner. On the second Sunday in September 1823 there was a riot in Couttie's Wynd and the watchmen moved in and arrested four people.

So the merry-go-round continued: petty theft and petty robbery, footpads and pickpockets with the occasional riot. The Charlies tried their best, but when they were absent, the Dundee public fought crime without them. For example, at the beginning of May 1824 four gentlemen ran riot in Monifieth until the locals rose in justified wrath, chased them into a house in Broughty Ferry and remained outside as the gentlemen cowered behind locked doors. That same month a con woman and her daughter took up position at the Dens Bridge, buying eggs and butter from the countrywomen with counterfeit money. When the countrywomen realised they were being duped they took swift revenge with their fists. The con woman had to grab her daughter and run.

The first week of July 1824 was also busy. It started with a footpad attacking a mason and grabbing his week's wages and his coat, and continued when two men assaulted a woman near Trade's Hall. In the latter incident a passing gentleman chased the muggers before the watchmen arrived. There was also an ugly riot in Chapelshade. This last was fairly serious, with a couple of young men badly injured and a gang of thugs rampaging down Dudhope Wynd. The watchmen kept well out of the way.

There are a couple of obvious trends in this catalogue of crime from the 1820s. The first was that the watchmen were struggling to cope, and the second was that the ordinary Dundee people were neither overawed nor frightened by criminals. When the opportunity arose, they did their bit to help. However, they were unhappy at the performance of the official guardians of the law.

Early in December 1823 thieves placed a ladder against the wall of the New Inn Entry in the High Street, scampered up it, drew up the window sash of the writing offices of John Ogilvy and Son, smashed one of the shutters and snaked in. The fact that they robbed the offices of a few pounds and about twelve shillings' worth of stationery was less important than the fact that the whole affair took place only a few yards from the beat of the local watchmen.

Charlies Under Pressure

Some Dundonians believed there were four watchmen in the High Street, and their image was of a group of idlers who lounged in the piazza, the covered area in front of the Town House, gossiping and taking snuff for the bulk of their watch, pausing only to shout out the hour as the clock struck and then return to their seat on the Town House stairs, safe and snug behind their lantern. In reality there were only two watchmen for the entire High Street. From ten at night until six in the morning, one man would patrol from the offices of the Dundee Bank at Castle Street to the English Chapel at Nethergate, a beat that took half an hour. The second man worked the north side of the street and the luckenbooths. Neither beat included the New Inn Entry, so the watchmen could only have interfered with the robbery by neglecting their duty, to the detriment of the subscribers who paid their wages. It is significant that no robberies took place in the shops and offices these men patrolled. However, that same week, a gentleman was wending his uneven way homeward when he saw a watchman sleeping beneath his lighted lantern. Removing the lamp, the gentleman used it to find his way home but discarded it in the street so as the watchman could later find it.

As 1823 slid into 1824, the situation in Dundee did not improve. Crime continued to dominate the night-time streets. The first week in February saw a thief rob a house in the Lower Chapelshade despite the entire family being home; a footpad badly beat a pedestrian in Lochee Road; and a man assault a woman in the Overgate and then, for reasons known only to himself, jump into a well. A compassionate Dundonian crowd rescued him. Even worse was the pack of men who set their dogs on a lone woman walking at the back of the Law. She escaped but her clothes were ripped to shreds. The second week saw a girl robbed in the Cowgate and a number of attempted break-ins. On Saturday night in the Murraygate thieves bent aside a metal security bar across a shop window, tore open the wooden shutters and got inside. After rifling the place they left through the front door. As so often happened in Dundee, though, a passer-by chased them, but they escaped in the labyrinth of closes and lanes behind the Murraygate. It was little consolation to the shop owner when some of his property was later found concealed in a Wester Craigie haystack.

The same night in the Chapelshade a dog chased away a robber from a fleshers' shop, while in Castle Street a hopeful thief climbed up a lamp-post to the second-floor window of Mr Aitken's warehouse. He managed to smash the window, but when the shutters held, he was heard to say, 'Damn it – it won't do,' and retreated in defeat. In Barrack Street, a thief used a crowbar to break into Scott the watchmaker's. When the brand new steamboat *George the Fourth* was on fire at the West Protection Wall, the thief wandered down to watch the fun, but in the confusion he dropped his booty, which was recovered from the sticky mud of the dock. On the Monday night a man dressed as a seaman robbed Keiller's the confectioner's, but the watchmen did succeed in rounding up seven young men who were causing trouble in the streets.

There were more personal assaults, too: footpads robbed a man in the Murraygate; a man attacked a woman at Peep o' Day; and in the Kirk Wynd a gang of thieves stole a watch from a man. When the victim recognised one of the thieves, the watch was discarded.

Too Dangerous to Interfere

Sometimes the watchman was in the right place at the right time, but he still did not help. Such a situation arose at the end of May 1824, when a watchman in the Meadows saw a group of men surround a lone woman and knock her down. Rather than going to her aid, the watchman merely watched, as he was afraid he might be the next victim. A month later a gang attacked a helpless drunk in the Wellgate. Again the watchman thought it too dangerous to interfere, but instead loosed his dog, which scared off the attackers. Nevertheless, the security of the innocent in Dundee could not depend on a dog; every year it was becoming increasingly obvious that the current system of watchmen required a drastic overhaul.

Given the propensity of the people of nineteenth-century Dundee to take care of their own affairs, it is hardly surprising that they should take measures to protect themselves and their possessions. While some were rumoured to carry weapons, in February 1824 the people in the Murraygate banded together to hire four watchmen exclusively for their own property. The *Advertiser* of 4th March 1824 claimed that the previous week had seen 'assault, shop breaking and petty theft . . . in every quarter of the town'. The same newspaper said there was not enough room to print all the crimes, and added that some shops had employed night watchmen.

The Dundee Police Act

On 24th June 1824 a Police Act for Dundee received the Royal Assent. The Act covered lighting, cleansing, paving and crime prevention, including the establishment of a new jail. It was a holistic approach to the organisation of the town and included extended boundaries, westward as far as the Blackness Toll, northward to Clepington and eastward to Mayfield. The River Tay was a natural boundary to the south.

Within these enlarged boundaries, the new Dundee police force began their task of reducing crime. They retained the system of watchmen, but added a day patrol and a night patrol. A Police Court was also established, sitting at ten o'clock every morning. The judges were all men of authority and presumably of common sense, if perhaps lacking in legal knowledge. They were the Provost and the magistrates, the Dean of Guild, the sheriff and his substitute. These men dealt quickly with the petty offenders, imprisoning for up to sixty days or fining up to a £5 limit, but any serious offences were passed to a higher court, with the worst offenders being held in Dundee's jail until the next Circuit Court.

The Police Act did not remedy all Dundee's ills, however. There were not enough police, not enough watchmen and the areas on the fringes or just outwith the boundaries were badly lit and without the benefit of a law officer. But it was a start, and the newly-formed police force prepared to walk their beats and make the streets safer for the respectable citizens of Dundee.

6

The Unsolved and the Strange

The Great Railway Robbery

Mr Andrew Cunningham of Carlogie House was an eminently respectable man. As the factor of the Right Honourable the Earl of Dalhousie, Lord Lieutenant of the County, he was responsible for ensuring the Earl's estates ran smoothly and the rents were collected on time. It was a responsible job with many benefits, including first-class travel on the railways. Yet at the end of 1866 Andrew Cunningham was at the centre of perhaps the biggest mystery to hit nineteenth-century Dundee and one which was discussed the length and breadth of the British Isles.

Towards the end of December 1866, Cunningham collected £1862 in rents from the Panmure Estate. He rolled the money, mainly in £100 notes, into a single bundle, tied it securely and placed it in a travelling bag. On the morning of Thursday 27th he slung the bag over his shoulder, left Carlogie House and took a coach to the railway station at Carnoustie. He stepped into a first-class carriage. It was just after half-past eleven and he intended to place the money safely in a Dundee bank.

There were two gentlemen already seated in the carriage and they asked him, quite politely, if he would mind if they smoked. He said he did not mind and they filled their pipes and began to smoke. The next thing Mr Cunningham knew, the guard at Dundee was shaking him awake, the gentlemen had gone, his travelling bag had been moved and all his money was missing.

The police created a picture of the theft. The two gentlemen were seen boarding the train at Arbroath, and at Broughty Ferry a lady tried to enter Cunningham's carriage. She found the door locked and called the guard but when she saw Cunningham sleeping heavily on the seat with his legs sprawled across the floor and the place reeking with smoke she decided to find another carriage. There was no sign of the other gentlemen. The next stop was West Ferry Station, and an entire party entered the carriage. There was the merchant Peter Stewart and his lady, together with Charles Smith of Bartley Lodge, Broughty Ferry and his female companion, and they had to step across the recumbent form of Cunningham to reach their seats. They noticed that he was sleeping very deeply and after failing to wake him at Dundee they asked a guard to run for a doctor. Nevertheless, they did manage to wake Cunningham before the doctor arrived, and thought his face was slightly distorted and his eyes fiery and slightly protruding.

The Arbroath to Dundee section of the Caledonian Railway ran straight beside the coast, with no diversions. The stations were only a few miles apart, and there were only a few minutes between each. The two gentlemen must have somehow rendered Cunningham unconscious, robbed him of the money he was carrying and changed carriages, unseen, all in the short eight miles of line between Carnoustie and Broughty Ferry.

Once he was awake and as recovered as it was possible to be, considering he had just been drugged and robbed of a great deal of his employer's money, Cunningham caught a cab and travelled with Mr Smith and a guard to the office of Shiell and Small, the Earl of Dalhousie's agents in Dundee. Cunningham informed the police, and the Procurator Fiscal was soon involved. By this period the police were adept at using the telegraph and they contacted their colleagues in Edinburgh, Glasgow, Perth and some of the larger English towns. Banks, both in Dundee and elsewhere, were warned to be aware of strange customers with £100 notes; the numbers and banking companies were known and circulated and the police began their investigations.

They interrogated the guard at Barry, one and three-quarter miles down the line from Carnoustie, but he had not seen anybody leave the train – but then again, he had been busy packing game into the luggage-van for a few minutes, so somebody could have slipped past him, or changed compartments. The guard at Monifieth, three miles and eight minutes further on, was more helpful, for he was certain nobody had left. After that it was two and a half miles and five minutes to Broughty, where Cunningham had been awakened.

The police inquiries continued. They unearthed a witness, a friend of Cunningham's who had seen his head at the carriage window at Barry, but the carriage door was locked and Cunningham did not appear to notice him. It seemed entirely possible that at that early stage, just three rattling minutes from Carnoustie, the gentlemen thieves had knocked him out and stolen the money. Other people spoke of a pair of 'suspicious-looking men' who travelled from Broughty Ferry to Arbroath on the Wednesday, the day before the robbery, and it was supposed that these were the same men who were in the carriage with Mr Cunningham on the Thursday. Various people in Arbroath remembered the two strangers who had visited the Alhambra Music Hall on Wednesday and bought tobacco in Keptie Street. These strangers had also asked the time of the Dundee train. One of the men had carried a meerschaum pipe and they were the last passengers to board the train at Arbroath. It was also interesting that nobody had bought a first-class ticket from Arbroath, so possibly the two men were second-class passengers who sneaked into a first-class carriage.

There were many theories about the robbery, but most seemed to agree that the gentlemen had used some form of drug to knock Cunningham out. However, the people who entered the carriage afterward smelled only ordinary tobacco smoke. It was considered possible, if unlikely, that the fumes of tobacco had been enough. It was more likely, people speculated, that a drug such as opium was used, with the apparently weak smell hidden behind the stronger scent of tobacco. Rumours and speculations abounded: Cunningham had thought the smoke smelled strange; Cunningham had been knocked out with chloroform; Cunningham had been knocked out with opium; Cunningham had merely fallen into a deep sleep and the two so-called gentlemen had taken the opportunity to rob him. A letter published in *The Scotsman* pointed out that chloroform left a distinctive aroma, while administering it needed the co-operation of the victim. Somebody else said it would be impossible to knock somebody out by smoking opium without the smoker also being affected and yet a third person said that Indian hemp would most likely have been the drug used.

With humanity's amazing gift of hindsight, some people in Arbroath began to remember they had thought the gentlemen a bit suspicious even before they boarded the train, so between them and the guard and Cunningham himself, a description of the supposed robbers was created. They were somewhere between twenty-five and thirty-five and one had a black moustache.

The robbery gave rise to some interesting conversations and letters to the press. While some thought that smoking should be banned on trains, or at least only permitted in selected areas, others took the opportunity to complain about the filthy state of the first-class carriages, which, they said, showed the quality of people who travelled first-class in that degenerate age. Somebody else pointed out that, despite having a population of around 100,000, Dundee had only four detectives who spent most of their time in court or trawling through pawnshops for stolen property, and they had little time for detecting. Another letter spoke of the danger of travelling so fast – up to sixty miles an hour (or a little faster than the speed of a racehorse at full speed) – and with the passenger knowing he may 'be dashed to pieces in any second'. The same anonymous letter-writer gave his opinion that the first-class carriages on the Dundee and Arbroath Railway were 'private dens for insult, robbery and murder . . . without a possibility of detection'.

Cunningham collapsed several times during the day following the robbery and within a short time the Great Railway Robbery became a major talking point. Apart from Cunningham himself, nobody had seen his two fellow passengers, not even the station masters at Monifieth or Barry. If the men had changed carriages, other travellers would have noticed them. Nor did they leave the train at Broughty Ferry, where two boys, a woman and a man disembarked. Instead the thieves seemed to have vanished, along with Cunningham's money.

As he recovered from the effects of the presumed drug, Cunningham remembered little things that might have been significant. He said he sat nearest the door, facing the engine and immediately when the train started, one of the gentlemen stood up to look out of the window. Cunningham believed that the man locked the door then. There was a certain factory on the route that he had no recollection of passing, so he thought he was unconscious very soon after he boarded the train.

The Great Railway Robbery was never solved. It gives rise to a host of questions: If the two travellers had planned the robbery, how did they know which carriage Cunningham would pick, for they were on the carriage first? How did they manage to knock out Cunningham in such a short time, and to where did they disappear? And how did such a man come to be robbed by two gentlemen in a first-class carriage on a busy line with stops every few moments, and no witnesses? These are questions to which there has never been satisfactory answers.

Either the perpetrators were experts in their profession, or very lucky that Cunningham walked right into their predatory hands.

The Ghost of Baltic Street

Sometimes there were strange happenings that must have left the police confused, but which had aspects that showed the underlying feeling of fairness in Dundee. At the beginning of 1826 there were rumours there was a tall white ghost in Baltic Street. There had been a few reports, including one from the local watchman, who perhaps should have known better than to repeat such things. Not surprisingly, given the period, people were becoming a little nervous, although the more sceptical tended to scoff at such sightings. And then on the first Monday of February, a woman dressed as a man strutted drunkenly up the High Street. The police watched her, and when she tried to barge into a pub, they arrested her.

There was a scuffle when the police tried to put their prisoner in a woman's cell, but they succeeded, and in the Police Court next morning she was identified as one Elizabeth MacDonald from Aberdeen, who had only been out of jail for a few days. Still in her male attire, she was sentenced to four days for disorderly conduct, but by this time the rumour had spread that she was the ghost. A crowd waited for her appearance, but must have been disappointed to see only a rather scruffy woman dressed in a man's cast-off clothing.

Rumours of the ghost continued, however, spreading from person to person and no doubt being inflated with every pint of beer. On the following Monday there was a disturbance in Broad Close. An Irishman had struck his wife in the street and a number of witnesses had rushed to defend her. Within a few moments the Irishman was at the centre of a yelling mob, which stripped him of his coat, shoes and trousers and was inflicting its own brand of justice when the police rescued him. As they carried him away, the mob followed, chanting, 'The ghost! The ghost!'

Probably glad to be safe in police custody, the Irishman admitted the assault when he came before the court, but when the judges saw the tattered state of what remained of his clothes, they took pity and only fined him five shillings.

The mystery of the ghost remained unsolved.

Galloping Gentlemen and Naked People

Another strange event occurred at two on a late December morning in 1827 when a mounted gentleman cantered down the steep slope of Hill-

Aerial view of Dundee

town, carrying a double-barrelled gun. He reached the Wellgate, thrust in his spurs and, despite the roars of sundry watchmen, galloped madly along the Murraygate, passed the Exchange Coffee room and entered the Seagate. When the watchmen continued to shout the mysterious horseman brandished his gun and threatened to shoot them. One brave watchman named Abbot chased after him but the horseman fired at him, thankfully missing. Still riding eastward, the horseman fired the second barrel of his gun at the gas lamps, shattering two of them, and rode on into the dark. He was never identified and there was never a reason given for his actions.

Just as mysterious at the time was the naked man who appeared in St Peter's Church at the beginning of December 1842. Mr McCheyne was reading the Bible to the congregation when a voice came floating from outside the church: 'This is the last day and I must be in the church!'

Given the intense nature of religion at this time, with the Kirk in disarray and the Disruption looming, it is not surprising that there was instant turmoil among the congregation. Some rose from their pews, others clung to their wives or husbands, and the situation worsened when a naked man appeared, walking slowly down the gallery stairs. As some women fainted where they sat, men rushed to make the intruder decent.

In May 1861 it was a drunken woman who decided to strip herself. She was a stranger to Carnoustie who seemed to have a grudge against other women as she forced herself into every school class room she could, divesting herself of her clothes one by one. Swearing and cursing at the women she met, she did not seem to disturb the school pupils, who tried to calm her down by dousing her with cold water until the police could arrest her. Once again, there was no explanation for her actions.

'The Fenians are Come!'

Sometimes incidents in Dundee shifted from the bizarre to the completely crazy. In 1866 Britain was in turmoil over the Fenian Movement. Many Irish blamed the British government for the famine that created so much devastation in their country during the 1840s. They took the bitterness with them in the crowded emigrant ships that crossed the Atlantic and imparted it on their children born in the New World. By 1866 the legacy of half-truths and memory erupted into violence as a small army of US-based Fenians launched an attack on Canada while others created trouble in the British mainland.

Dundee was not immune. In October a rash of posters disfigured the town, and a £500 reward was offered to anybody who helped arrest the people planning to cause trouble in Dundee. Ordinary citizens watched each other with suspicion, people were wary of anyone with an Irish accent and strangers were in danger of being shunned. It was in the midst of this tense atmosphere that a body of 'brave' Scottish soldiers fled before a bunch of children throwing stones.

Having completed their evening's drill in the Barrack Park, a platoon of Volunteers marched along Dudhope Street near the barracks. They made a splendid show with their rifles on their shoulders, the fixed bayonets glinting in the gas light and the uniforms smart. It was only ten years since the close of the Crimean War, seven years since the Mutiny in Bengal had been crushed, and six since the British Army had marched through Peking. But these were Volunteers, not the regular red-coated army; they lacked the iron discipline. Somewhere in Dudhope Street, they began to argue and their raised voices carried far in the autumn evening. As usual in Dundee there was a gaggle of children nearby and in the dim light they saw the bayonets, heard the raucous voices and drew their own conclusion.

'The Fenians!'

Rather than run before this supposed invasion of Dundee, the boys launched an attack. Lifting stones and anything else they could find, they charged forward and unleashed a torrent on the surprised Volunteers. When the soldiers realised what was happening they retaliated in kind and volleys of stones flew back and forward along the street. More boys arrived until there were about fifty of them hurling stones at the Volunteers, but after half an hour, military might prevailed and the boys were forced back onto Constitution Road. Desperate to defend their town, the youths rallied and again shouted, 'The Fenians are come!'

This time the call upset the Volunteers, who realised that any police intervention would mean a spell in the cells. Picking up their rifles, they turned their backs and ran, to the jeers and cat calls of the victorious boys who were certain they had defeated a Fenian attack on the city. The irony of the situation became apparent when news filtered out that the Fenians had never intended an attack on Dundee; the poster was a spin to raise a crowd at the Alhambra Music Hall.

Ding Dong Bell, Naked in the Well

Perhaps even stranger was the event at the beginning of December 1828 when a young woman from the Scouringburn area of the town took her pitcher to the well to draw water. As she leaned over the parapet a voice boomed from the water below: 'Dinnae let doon your pitcher on my heid!'

Not surprisingly, the woman screamed and ran off. She returned with some friends, who looked cautiously over the parapet and saw a naked man at the bottom, supporting himself by clinging to the stones. After a lot of effort they succeeded in hauling him to safety. When he stood there, goose-pimpled with the cold, dripping wet and with the skin of his back and shoulders scraped raw, he claimed he had dropped his water pitcher and had taken off his clothes to retrieve it but could not climb back out. Perhaps he was speaking the truth, but it must have been a little unsettling for a woman to find a naked man shouting at her from the bottom of a well. But in nineteenth-century Dundee, anything could happen.

7

Gangs of Young Thugs

Harbour Thieves

Despite some starting work at an early age, despite the growing influence of the state that saw universal schooling, despite the genuine work of charities, there were always gangs of children and youths infesting the Dundee streets. They can be seen in most urban Victorian photographs, either standing in menacing groups or as blurred images passing by. To the citizens of Dundee there was nothing blurred about their presence, and they often faced theft, intimidation and sometimes assault by these groups of youths.

Although there were professional thieves in Dundee, most thefts were crimes of opportunity as people living on the borders of society saw a chance to enrich themselves at the expense of others. One place where gangs of potential thieves were commonly found was the Dundee docks, for there were usually ships being unloaded. Any goods left unattended on the quay were an obvious temptation for a hungry thief. One such instance occurred in April 1845 when the brig *Commodore Napier* was in the graving dock to be re-coppered.

When the old copper had been stripped off the brig it was packed

© Courtesy of Dundee Art Galleries and Museums

Youths at Couttie's Wynd

away into casks, which in this case were carelessly left on the quay – a fact that was soon ascertained by a nine-strong gang of young teenagers. Rather than just diving in, the gang organised themselves into small groups, with some posted as look-outs for the harbour police and others stealing as much copper as they could carry. In all the gang took away about twelve pounds of copper, some of which they sold to a rag merchant and some to a brass founder.

The youths still had around six pounds weight left when the harbour officials William Gordon and Thomas Rennie found them at the rear of a foundry in Trades Lane. As was usual in such cases, the gang scattered in different directions but Gordon and Rennie caught one unfortunate boy. Possibly due to a combination of threats and promises, or perhaps because the names were well known, the officers discovered six other culprits and dragged them to the Police Court. Mr Thoms, the Dean of Guild, was the judge and awarded sentences from ten to thirty days each. However, he also made a pointed comment that the people who bought the obviously stolen goods were equally guilty if apparently respectable.

Although juveniles were often the perpetrators, sometimes the victims were also young, as in the case of Daniel Dakers.

Robbery by Intimidation

In July 1874 Daniel Dakers began work with the grocery firm of Lindsay and Low, of Hilltown. He was twelve years old, fairly intelligent and as a messenger boy he ran around town with orders for various customers. Daniel settled into his new job quite quickly, but after a few weeks a youth named Charles Crammond approached him. Crammond was older, taller and stronger than Daniel, and also worked for Lindsay and Low. When Crammond demanded money, Daniel refused, but when Crammond threatened violence, Daniel became frightened and handed some over. Realising he was onto a good thing, Crammond gathered some friends and about three weeks later they cornered Daniel, again demanding money.

After that Daniel's life became a misery as a variety of youths regularly threatened him. The most prominent was William Watson, but he was backed by James McConvel and Charles Hackney, from Hospital Wynd, and the millworker George Boag. Outnumbered, outmuscled and frightened, one Saturday in September, Daniel took ten shillings from the till and handed it over to Crammond. Maybe he thought that was the end of the matter, but it was only the beginning. Within the month, Daniel had handed over another three pounds, and when he walked home on the Saturday evening, the gang followed him. Next day Watson grabbed him and demanded more money, and when Daniel said he had none, Watson said he had better find some, or else. Daniel took another two shillings out of the till. A few days later Watson again appeared, demanding yet more, but this time Daniel said he could not get any more.

No doubt hoping that was the end of the matter, Daniel continued with his work, but Watson was hunting for him. Ambushing the delivery boy in Caldrum Street, Watson held him down and rifled his pockets. The same thing happened later, with a group including Watson, James McConvel and a few others robbing Daniel of everything he had, and still looking for more. The intimidation continued, with Daniel being hounded and threatened, so he robbed the till and tried to pay off his tormentors, but always with the same result. By the closing months of the year nearly every day one or more members of the gang would wait for Daniel, demanding money.

It was a case of paying the Danegeld but never getting rid of the Dane, but the money had to come from somewhere and Daniel's employers were in business to make money, not to pay off bullies. In the first week of January 1875 the shop manager, Charles Henderson, performed a stock-taking, which means he physically checked every item of stock the shop contained. The firm was successful, taking in about eighty pounds on a Saturday alone, and Henderson hoped to continue to make profit. Unfortunately he found the stock was about £30 short. Every shop suffers from shortfalls through mistakes and shoplifting, but £30 was a sizeable amount to lose. Stocktaking was scheduled for every three months, so in early April Henderson checked again, hoping to find things more level, but instead the stock was £80 short.

It was obvious that the store could not continue with that level of loss, and equally obvious was the fact that something more than petty pilfering was going on, so Henderson called the police. When Inspector Lamb arrived, Daniel was probably relieved to tell him about the intimidation. But once again, Watson met him and asked for money. This time Daniel said he had none, but could get some later. At eight o'clock the gang ambushed Daniel in Church Street, Watson, Charlie Hughes, Charles Hackney, George Boag and James McConvel, five violent young men, all demanding that he give them money, and Daniel said no. It was Charles Hackney who punched him, bloodying his nose.

'I suppose you want us to be caught,' Watson said, as Daniel made his painful way back to the shop.

That night Daniel was in Glamis Street and the gang was hovering, but this time Detective Ross was present and they backed off, with Boag saying, 'There's something up.'

On Saturday 24th April 1875 Daniel was again sent on a message to Church Street, but this time he was monitored. Inspector Lamb and Detective Ross took up residence in a house opposite the shop, and prepared to watch everything that happened. As expected, Watson and his cronies followed Daniel all the way back to the shop. Inspector Lamb asked Henderson to send Daniel back out, and he watched as Watson and his friends immediately surrounded him.

Daniel returned within fifteen minutes, but Henderson sent him out again, this time with a basket and half a crown with which to buy a necktie. The gang was waiting when Daniel walked to Blair's Land in Alexander Street. As usual they crowded round, demanding money. When Daniel said he only had the manager's half-crown they backed off. Not long after, Watson harried Daniel again with McConvel and the others a few paces away, watching menacingly, probing for money, threatening violence, but Daniel said he had no more to give.

'You surely have some,' Watson said.

'No, I dinnae,' Daniel replied.

'Well then,' said Watson. 'This will be your last night.'

The threat was obvious. 'I'm going another message to Blair's Land,' Daniel said, 'and I'll try to get you some money then.'

Watson spoke over his shoulder, telling him friends that Daniel still had no money.

'What? Nothing yet?' somebody commented, and they watched as Daniel returned to the shop. They were still there when Daniel came out for the next message, but this time Inspector Lamb and Detective Ross hid in the close to which he was sent. Once again Watson and McConvel demanded money and again told Daniel it would be 'his last night in the shop,' when he said he had none.

By that time Inspector Lamb thought he had gathered enough evidence to secure a conviction and he rounded up Watson and his minions. The relief for Daniel must have been tremendous. The case came to the Dundee Circuit Court at the beginning of September. Watson and McConvel, Charles Hackney and George Boag were charged, but Hackney and Boag had ran before they could be arrested and were immediately outlawed. Watson and McConvel gave the customary plea of not guilty. Perhaps they thought Daniel would be too scared to speak against them, and maybe they were right, but there was a string of witnesses to back up his story.

Alexander Welsh, a millworker from Mains Street, had seen Watson's boys with Daniel on numerous occasions and named one specific event when Watson had stolen two shillings from Daniel's pocket. John Fyffe, another millworker from Mortimer Street, said he saw McConvel demanding money with threats. On that occasion Daniel refused. The Hilltown policeman, Constable Beveridge, had not seen Watson's boys rob Daniel, but he had often seen them surrounding him.

Inspector Lamb said that when he was taken to the police office, Watson and McConvel denied ever seeing Daniel. The police continued to gather evidence. James Down, a sheriff criminal officer, told the court that Watson had been convicted at the Dundee Circuit Court in 1872. But Daniel lost some of the sympathy of the court when he admitted keeping some of the stolen money for himself, and he added that McConvel had never physically assaulted him.

Whatever they thought of Daniel, the jury had no doubt at all of the guilt of the accused. It took them only a few moments to find both Watson and McConvel guilty. The judge, Lord Deas, reminded Watson that he was given eighteen months last time and sent him for seven years' penal servitude, with McConvel getting five. As he was led below, McConvel gave the customary farewell to a friend in the public gallery:

'See and watch yourself, Davie. Cheer up!'

Watson's goodbye was more sinister as he faced Daniel. 'Wait till I come back and you'll catch it!'

But that would be seven years in the future, and seven years in penal servitude could do a lot to what was still a very young man.

Murder at the Fair

Throughout Scotland, fairs were often an excuse for drunken debauchery and riots. The fairs at Dundee were no exception, with that at Stobbs having an evil reputation second to none. Stobbs, or Stobs, Fair was held on the Stobsmuir to the north-east of the town and was one of the most popular, possibly because it took place at the height of summer. The first Stobbs Fair was held on 23rd June 1679 on the Moor of Craigie, and it became known as a place best avoided by the faint hearted because of the riots, thefts and general mayhem. The Fair was a mixture of entertainment and functionality, where people from the town and country gathered to view the sideshows, but also a feeing fair where men advertised themselves as available for a new position and where cattle, sheep, horses and other produce of the farms were on the market. Holding a predominantly agricultural show so close to a town with such a strong urban identity as Dundee was a sure recipe for trouble, and clashes between Dundonians and the 'country jocks' were frequent. With so few days free from labour in a year that held only a handful of official holidays, fair days were an excuse to let the hair down and forget the cares and restrictions of virtually incessant labour. Petty theft and drunken fights were expected and usually the day ended in violence, but occasionally there was worse.

In 1809, with the Napoleonic War at its height, a party of the 25th Foot visited Stobbs Fair to recruit, but instead got itself involved in a fully-fledged brawl with the local rowdies and a group of gunners from the Royal Artillery. It was a case of swords and bayonets against cudgels and stones, with casualties on both sides and one man killed.

The Fair of 1823 was equally violent, with a great deal of theft and pickpocketing, the usual assortment of fights and assaults and the twelve constables on duty hard-pressed to keep even a minimum of order. However, four of them did manage to arrest one offender, but such events only strengthened Dundee's demand for a standing, professional police force.

July 1824 had already proved a violent month even before the Fair, with a riot in Chapelshade that nearly killed two men as a drunken mob rampaged along Dudhope Wynd, shouting challenges to any who dared interfere and scorning the feeble forces of the law. It was not a good omen a few days before the notorious Stobbs Fair.

Nevertheless, the morning of the Fair was quieter than normal despite lounging bands of what were termed 'vagrant Irish'. Yet save for the usual petty thieving, for which the Irish were blamed, there was no trouble worth reporting. As always, there were wheels-of-fortune tents and other ways of relieving hard-working people of their money by gambling, fair or foul, but nothing unusual occurred. Nevertheless, as the day drew on and the drinking increased, the Fair grew rowdier, disagreements degenerated to disputes and disputes escalated into fights. The magistrates of Dundee had sent a number of porters, a form of reserve police force, to try and keep the peace but there were more youthful gangs than normal and they used the porters as targets for stones, pelting them at every opportunity, leaving some badly hurt and unable to interfere when more serious trouble broke out. The evening was always the most dangerous time, possibly because the people from Dundee would explode from the mills and factories to descend on the drinking booths and other places of seedy entertainment.

At this time there was quite a sizeable quarry at Duntrune, and a group of nine masons walked from the quarry to the Fair to be paid. Such a practice was normal, and when their employer, Mr Scott of Hawkhill, paid their dues, two of the masons escorted him away from the moor while the remaining two headed for Stobsmill Toll.

Tollhouses were primarily used to collect money – tolls – on major roads. There was a keeper who manipulated a toll bar that stretched across the road, raising it to allow vehicles to pass once the toll was paid. However, tollhouses also doubled as watering holes, creating an additional source of revenue for the toll keeper, so the masons decided they would have a drink there until the others rejoined them. However, they found a drinking tent first and spent six shillings on ale and whisky before rolling out, still relatively sober, to keep their appointment with their fellow masons.

Donald Gordon, one of the masons, hammered at the tollhouse door to get in. As soon as the door opened, he tried to step inside, only to have the door slammed on his leg. When his friend and fellow mason John Syme helped him get free, the door was banged shut in their faces. Suspecting that the tollhouse was already bulging with revellers, Syme and Gordon, probably grumbling but quite peaceable, had returned to join their friends when a dozen yelling men poured out of the tollhouse. They carried a variety of weapons, including a hatchet, and before the masons could either fight or run they were under attack, with another group of youngsters joining in. Somebody in a white coat cracked Syme across the skull and he staggered, holding onto the toll bar to retain his balance as the mob surged past him and attacked the other masons.

A twenty-six-year-old mason called John Allan was hacked to the ground and lay there as a group of men kicked his prone body. Somebody shouted, 'Dundee Forever!'

Allan's brother Alexander, another of the masons, ran to help but as he held the obviously dead man he was also felled. He tried to rise but again the attackers barged him down. He heard somebody speaking, 'Don't strike him any more for he's dead!'

Leaving the security of the toll bar, Syme moved toward John Allan, but by doing so he again made himself a target.

'The bugger's up again. Have at him!'

Still dazed from the previous attack Syme could hardly resist as some of the attackers knocked him to the ground and began kicking him, their boots crunching into his head and face. A mason called John Ross saw the crowd of strangers rushing out; somebody hit him with a stick and he fell, aware that the Allan brothers were under attack but unable to help. Seeing somebody lifting his brother, Alexander again tried to rise, but his attackers returned and once more punched him to the ground. He looked up, pleading for mercy but unable to recognise anyone who was attacking him.

By that time all of the masons were injured, some severely, and the gang, still with the help of a group of younger youths, moved on to assault anyone who crossed their path. Their next target was a man by the name of Sandeman Stewart who was walking back to his home in Douglas-field. Attacked from behind, he was knocked to the ground, but before his assailants finished the job he heard somebody say, 'Don't strike that man – he doesn't belong to the band!'

Stewart saw John Allan battered down and thought he said, 'Lord I am gone. Don't strike me again,' but then, not surprisingly, Stewart ran. A young ploughman was cudgelled to the ground so savagely that it was also feared he would die, and then a man who worked in a bleach field. He also fled, pursued by a mob of youths who whooped as if he was a hunted fox. They caught him in a nearby cornfield, knocked him down and kicked him to pieces. He was left with a cracked skull and a battered and bruised body.

When the dust settled and the predatory gang had moved on, the body of John Allan was carried into the toll house before being loaded on a cart and trundled sorrowfully back to Dundee. As well as being murdered, he had been robbed, although the attackers had failed to find the pay in his vest pocket. The authorities moved as quickly as they could, with the Sheriff substitute holding an enquiry and the few constables, warrants in hand, searching for the suspected attackers.

On 21st July, large crowds of Dundonians gathered for the burial of John Allan. As he was a good worker and a quiet young man about to be married, there was a lot of sympathy for him. Despite his injuries,

Alexander Allan followed the coffin, supported on either side by a fellow mason. The others were still too badly hurt to attend the funeral of their friend, but peace officers arrested two men whom they suspected to be involved in the murder, and two days later they captured a third.

The suspects were Thomas Marshall, a mason, George Scott, a seaman and James Whyte, a lath splitter. Marshall was a known troublemaker who was suspected of being involved with the theft of a musket from a servant of Lord Duncan. He was outlawed for failing to appear at the Perth Circuit Court in the autumn of 1823. When the three accused were dragged before the bar, all pleaded not guilty, so were held in the cells while the authorities organised a proper jury trial.

When the accused finally appeared before the Circuit Court at Perth, Sandeman Stewart identified both Marshall and Scott as being with the gang, and thought it was Scott who had felled him and Marshall who stopped him from continuing the attack when he was on the ground. He also thought it had been Marshall and Scott who attacked Alexander Allan, but did not remember Whyte at all. He denied any previous knowledge of any of the men, said the masons seemed sober and, as it was a summer evening, was sure it was light enough for him to identify the men in court.

A fourteen-year-old boy named James MacKiddie also pointed out Marshall, and said he had knocked a mason down with a bludgeon. MacKiddie claimed the mason had fallen in a potato field and Marshall had walked across to look down on him. He knew both Marshall and Scott by sight, but had only seen Scott attack a man at the toll. MacKiddie's friend, Alexander Whyte, was slightly older, and he had seen Marshall and James Whyte involved in the fighting, and had heard some of the others call Marshall by name.

James Ewing had been in the tollhouse at the same time as the gang and could identify all the prisoners. He claimed to have seen Marshall and Scott knock a man down, and said the man, John Allan, was lying dead on the ground just before Marshall shouted, 'Although we are but boys we'll do for them!' He estimated there were perhaps ten 'Dundee chaps' fighting twice that number of masons, and thought the fighting was less one-sided than the others claimed. He said he had seen masons strike both Scott and Marshall.

Fifteen-year-old William Moncur was unsure how the fight began, but he saw the body of Allan on the ground with Whyte nearby. He saw Marshall with a stick and heard him say, 'Damn it for the last whup at him,' before he joined Scott and Whyte in fighting the masons.

The last witnesses for the prosecution were Mr John Crighton, the Dundee surgeon, and Mr Greig, his assistant. They had examined the body of John Allan and said that he had probably been killed by a blow from a stick to the right temple.

There were few witnesses for the defence, but Whyte's master said he was a 'decent, steady lad' while the advocates for Whyte, Marshall and Scott spoke in their favour without in the least denting the case of the Crown.

When the Lord Justice Clerk summed up the case, he did not seem to have any doubt that Marshall, Whyte and Scott had killed John Allan. In a speech that lasted over an hour and a half, he dwelled on the difference between murder, which was a capital offence, and culpable homicide, which was not. The jury deliberated for only half an hour before reaching their verdict. They thought none of the accused was a murderer, but Marshall was guilty of assault and rioting, aggravated by his carrying a stick; Scott was guilty of assault and rioting and Whyte merely of rioting. However, the Lord Justice Clerk was unhappy with this verdict. 'Gentlemen,' he said, 'I cannot admit of the aggravation expressed in your verdict . . . of the principal carrying a stick in his hand. You might as well have stated that he carried a hat on his head . . .'

Only when the fact of Marshall carrying a stick was stricken from the verdict did the judge, Lord Pitmully, pronounce sentence. Marshall was to be transported to Australia for fourteen years and Scott for seven years, while Whyte was sent to jail for a year and ordered to keep the peace for five more, with the threat of a stiff financial penalty if he failed to do so.

It was obvious that Lord Pitmully believed the jury was too lenient, but Marshall at least would not have agreed; he was reported as being sulky and ill-tempered while the others were also downcast.

One glaring question remains: Why did the mob attack the masons, who were ordinary working men with apparently no history of animosity to anybody? The only clue lies in the single slogan 'Dundee Forever' shouted out by Marshall. Perhaps he was announcing a campaign by the young men of Dundee against people he considered 'country jocks' and, in this case, he chose the wrong group. Presumably there had been an earlier confrontation between men from Dundee and those of the neighbouring countryside and John Allan was the unfortunate victim.

At the beginning of October, Marshall and Scott, together with a man named MacQuire from Cupar in Fife, left Dundee on the London smack. They would spend some time in the hulks off Chatham before being stuffed onto a ship that would transport them to the other side of the world. The affair still had some echoes, however, for about six weeks later a man named William Smith, who was suspected of being involved in the riot, was arrested for causing trouble in Fish Street, with a dire warning that the sheriff had an eye on him.

By the following year, Dundee had a professional police force and Mr Home, the superintendent, marched a strong body of men to the Stobsmuir Fair. There was a short attempt at rioting, but the police stamped hard on it. Although the reputation remained, there were no more murders at the Fair.

The Pest and Terror of All

If the gang at Stobsmuir had been murderous at least the trouble was localised and short-lived. There was another gang in the 1820s that caused mayhem for years, thieving and rioting and spreading their own brand of violence around the western suburbs of the town. That was the Peter Wallace gang, once labelled as 'the pest and terror of all'.

Already drunk and looking for trouble, they erupted from the brothel in the Scouringburn, cursing any who crossed their path and shouting obscene defiance to the June Sabbath morning. The streets emptied before them as they careened onward, pushing aside anybody bold or stupid enough to remain in their path, and battered at the door of a Hawkhill public house, demanding entrance and whisky for half a dozen thirsty throats.

They swallowed their fill of whisky, but when the landlord insisted payment they laughed in his face and displayed pockets empty of everything save holes. A man who feared neither God nor the devil, the landlord refused to back down, snatching the hat of one as partial payment, and ordered them all outside. Howling their rage, the youths lifted stones from the unpaved street and subjected the pub to a barrage that had the customers cowering for cover and reduced the windows to useless shards of glass. By that time the forenoon was advanced and the respectable or God-fearing of Dundee were hurrying to Church, turning their eyes from

© Courtesy of Dundee Art Galleries and Museums

The Scouringburn

as disgraceful a scene of blackguardism as had ever sullied a Dundee Sabbath.

Even the godly would know who these young savages were, for in a close-knit community the size of Dundee everybody knew each other. These were the Shaw brothers, James and John, accompanied by a small knot of their followers, and all were part of the gang of the even more notorious Peter Wallace, the worst young thug (although that term had not yet been coined in Scotland) to infest the streets of the rapidly-expanding town. Wallace himself was not present, for only the previous week he had been arrested and carried to gaol for attacking Lord Duncan's servant in the Hawkhill and stealing his musket. So now he lay sullenly in a cell above the Town House, listening to the vermin rustling in the straw and the moans of his fellow sufferers.

In the meantime, the Shaws and their companions played merry hell with Dundee. Swaggering to Tay Street, one produced a knife and taunted the passers-by. When a man protested they kicked him to the ground and continued their progress. The people of the Scouringburn would breathe a collective sigh of relief as the gang headed back into the centre of town, where they spent most of the day steadily drinking and becoming more quarrelsome. As the day wore on some dropped away and it was a depleted bunch that returned to the Hawkhill in the evening. Too drunk to have any caution, they continued where they had left off, shouting and blaspheming and breaking the peace of Sunday until one man, exasper-ated beyond caution, grabbed a club and left his house.

With their numbers thinned and their reactions slowed by alcohol, the members of the gang either fought or scattered, depending on their nature, but the sober citizen smashed one to the ground, faced off the rest and dragged his prisoner to the lock-up house to be secured for the night. The respectable watched and wondered. They knew that capturing one of the Peter Wallace gang was a start, but it was not enough. There were at least another nine of them, all equally desperate, and they knew the area better than just about anybody else.

As the Hawkhill and the Scouringburn were outside the town boundaries they were not patrolled by any watchman. There were no constables, so blackguards such as Wallace and the Shaws could run riot without fear of arrest or retribution. Having no peacekeepers was not unusual in many Scottish communities, for in the days before an organised police force, watchmen had to be paid for, and the people of the Scouringburn and the Hawkhill did not like the idea of wasting their money. Besides, who would pay, how much would it cost, and was the price worth the end result? In many ways, the youths who made up the Peter Wallace gang were products of their environment: they lived the only way they understood. It is unlikely that anyone knew from where they came, and even less likely that anyone cared. They grew up on the streets; either the unwanted product of a few moments of lust in a life controlled by deprivation, or the unfortunate children of early-deceased, or perhaps tragically transported parents. It is unlikely the truth will ever be known.

How they survived their infancy is also a mystery, but when they were very young boys they banded together for support and security, gathering horse droppings from the street and selling them as fertiliser to raise coppers for food. When that method of subsistence failed they turned to petty crime. Spending the nights in a smithy in the Witchknowe, they raided the local gardens, digging up potatoes, stealing apples and pears from trees and boiling the two in a pot, their only possession save for a spade. In more fortunate times they might steal one of the hens that many of the people of Dundee kept, or a pigeon from a doocot, and occasionally they washed the mess down with whisky, which they obtained by bartering with anything they sneaked through an open window or lifted from any unfortunate drunk whose pockets they rifled. They had already developed a taste for whisky, or a desire to experience the numbness of alcoholic oblivion. If they felt like bread, well, the local baker was not security conscious. On one occasion they swarmed down his chimney and lifted an entire batch of newly baked biscuits. Fagin would have been proud of them.

Their natural leader was Peter Wallace, a bold young man who, if life had afforded him better opportunities, might have made a name for himself in more profitable ventures, but in the early nineteenth century the poor were destined to remain so and authority favoured the fortunate. The others in the gang clustered around him, and as they grew older and their petty pilfering turned more serious, their names grew known and the *Dundee Advertiser* called them a 'pest and terror of all'.

There were the Shaw brothers, one of whom moved to Glasgow in his early teens. There was Alexander Gardiner, nearly as bold and fearless as Wallace in his flouting of authority. There was John Gray, a weaver who habitually carried a knife and James Ferguson, his close companion. Add the seaman, David Scott and the Stewart brothers and the nucleus of the gang was complete: a hardy bunch made desperate by poverty and violent by necessity and whisky.

From stealing fruit and biscuits, the gang graduated to more serious crimes – housebreaking and theft became common and by the early 1820s Peter Wallace led the most notorious gang in Dundee. Nevertheless in late 1822 and early 1823 a series of hammer blows destroyed their cohesion. In the absence of a proper police force, the watchmen and constables of Dundee could still act with some vigour and some of the more active members of the gang were laid by the heels and thrust into the pestilent cells of the gaol. Even worse, or perhaps better for the long-suffering citizens of the town, Peter Wallace gave up his criminal activities and found an honest job.

Dundee, and particularly the outlying districts of the Hawkhill and the Scouringburn, began to relax a little. For a few months there was peace; people could worry less about their property when they were at work and could walk the streets with more confidence. The quiet, however, could not last when the streets were not policed and youths were bored, frustrated and knew only violence and theft as a means of existence. In early spring 1823 the jail opened its doors and the young men of Wallace's gang swarmed back into the streets. They had no jobs, no permanent homes, no future and no reason to like the authority that had locked them up or conventional life that had constantly rejected them. The gang collected: Gardiner, Gray and the Shaw brothers together again, roaming the streets, breaking into houses, breaking heads, and breaking every law they could. When temptation forced Peter Wallace from the straight and narrow to the broad path he knew so much better, mayhem was as inevitable as the tide of the Tay.

Robbery was a way of life, theft from houses and shops a pastime, violence habitual, but with Wallace's astute brain behind them they soon found a novel way of making ends meet. For years there had been a virtual war in Scotland between those who illegally distilled and sold whisky and the forces of the Excise, backed often by the military. Dundee was a natural target for the whisky smugglers, having a growing and thirsty population and being within striking distance of the Highlands. One well-trodden route for this peat reek was by way of the Angus Glens, the Sidlaw Hills and the notorious smuggling village of Auchterhouse. Usually on foot and driving a packhorse, the smugglers headed for the western suburbs, congested, busy and full of hard-working and hard-drinking mill-workers. It was even sweeter that there were no peace officers on patrol, so the smugglers made hay while the sun shone. However, Peter Wallace saw his opportunity and decided to rob the smugglers.

After all, what could be easier? The smugglers could hardly complain to the authorities. The commodity they carried had a ready market and it was being taken right to the hunting ground of Wallace's gang. As the smugglers slid from the countryside with its patrols of dragoons and Excisemen, they relaxed, and walked into the ambushes set by Wallace. On one notable occasion Wallace's gang watched while revenue men and smugglers exchanged blows and calmly carried off the prize: two ankers of finest peat reek, the illicit whisky of the Highland glens.

It could not last, of course. Sooner or later even the patience of the Dundonians would break and retaliation would be harsher for the months and years of torment. The behaviour of June 1823 provided the spur. First there was the Sabbath day riot, but that was followed a few days later by a further incursion into the Scouringburn. One of the Shaw brothers wandered in, alone, unsupported and probably drunk, but no doubt sure that the reputation of the Wallace gang would defend him. As usual, he was aggressive, pushing people aside, but when he knocked a woman to the ground, the people of the Scouringburn turned on him.

A crowd gathered to help the injured woman and Shaw ran, but the Scouringburn blood was up and they chased him. Jumping over garden walls, Shaw hid in an outhouse, but the people followed, kicked down the door and dragged him out. There was a flurry of boots and fists until Shaw was subdued, somebody tied his hands with a piece of rope and he was hauled unceremoniously to the lock-up house and thrown in to await the judgement of authority. And although Peter Wallace was locked away, Dundee was not yet finished with the pestilent gang that had caused so much terror.

If the members of the gang had taken any note of public affairs they might have been more on their guard. Following the suggestion of the local Justice of the Peace, the people of the Scouringburn had held a meeting and sworn in a body of acting constables to patrol the streets and keep down predators such as the Shaws or Peter Wallace. Forty volunteers had come forward, determined to restore order to their neighbourhood, and every night they marched, eight at a time, in search of Wallace's followers.

One by one the pests were hunted down and arrested. One of the most violent was Alexander Gardiner. When he was seen in the Fish Market, a long way from the Scouringburn, a peace officer moved in at once. Gardiner did not come quietly and in the ensuing struggle he tried to throttle the constable and might have succeeded if a street porter had not run to help. Subdued and arrested, Gardiner was thrown in the lock-up house, with two porters standing on guard. Catching Gardiner, however, was not quite as easy as holding him, for while the porters remained stubbornly in place at the front of the lock-up house, some other members of the gang slipped over the back wall, forced open the door behind the sentinel's back and freed their companion. The porters apparently saw nothing.

The war against Wallace's gang continued, with skirmishes constant and victories on both sides. The Scouringburn constables dragged the streets, searching every known depraved den and filthy haunt of the gang. They started at the Witchknowe and ended at the Wellgate where they located Ferguson, grabbed him and hauled him, protesting and swearing, to the lock-up house. They entered the long, densely packed Overgate and found the second Shaw and another man, possibly Scott, in the festering sewer of Broad Close. The two fugitives, as instinctive as any hunted animals, scrambled up the side of a house, slipped over the roof and descended into Tay Street, where they jumped a fence and headed for their own territory of the Scouringburn. However, the constables were tenacious and followed hard on their heels. Shaw and Scott were both arrested in a seedy close off Small's Wynd and joined Ferguson in the lock-up house.

The gang was being whittled down, but rather than go into hiding, the remnants continued to act as if they were immune to justice. On the evening of Wednesday 24th June, John Gray and Ferguson were again on the rampage. Once more in the Scouringburn, they picked on a quiet man named Robert Petrie, punched him to the ground, kicked out some of his teeth and bloodied his face. Gray might have stabbed him to death if his mother had not made a belated appearance and hauled back her son. The drama was resolved when a group of locals came hurrying up and the attackers sauntered away, laughing as they reminded each other of Gardiner's escape from confinement.

The squeeze continued, however, and Alexander Gardiner was soon once again in jail. He had been with a group of wild men in David and Helen Mathewson's pub in the Hawkhill. The Mathewsons were probably well aware of the gang's reputation and would watch them closely. The drink had flowed freely, but the money to pay for it was less forthcoming, and when David Mathewson saw one of Gardiner's companions stealing from a wall press he immediately challenged him. The thief made a quick exit out of the nearest window. David Mathewson slammed Gardiner into a chair and warned him to stay there until he saw what had been stolen. Gardiner tried to hit Mathewson with a bottle, Mathewson blocked the blow and his daughter ran out of the pub to find a policeman, slamming shut the door behind her, but not before Gardiner's other companions slipped free.

At some time in the next few moments Gardiner thumped Mrs Mathewson, so the publican and his wife must have been relieved when their daughter banged on the door, and shouted she had brought a policeman. Mathewson opened the door, but was shoved to the floor as Gardiner's companions began a rescue mission. Everybody rushed outside, with Gardiner's friends threatening to kill the publican, but even so Gardiner was arrested and hustled into captivity. It seemed as if Wallace's gang was effectively broken. Wallace was in jail, along with both the Shaw brothers, Alexander Gardiner, Gray, Scott, Ferguson and the two Stewarts. The war had been waged and the forces of the law, ragged and as yet unorganised, had been victorious.

It was 9th October before the trials were held, and that Thursday David Jobson of Haughhead, one of Dundee's most eminent men, and David Blair of Pitpontie held the court in the Town House, the same building that contained the cells in which Dundee's most infamous pests were held. After hearing of the reign of terror the Wallace gang had put Dundee through, the Justices of the Peace were not inclined to mercy.

James and John Shaw pleaded guilty to committing assaults and riots in West Port and the Scouringburn; both were banished from Forfarshire for five years. If they were found in the county in that time they would spend three months in the cells on bread and water. The Shaws listened impassively, showing no emotion as their fate was read out to them. Exile was no light punishment, for it meant separation from friends and family and could mean destitution and the life of a beggar, for who would employ a banished stranger? As it happened John Shaw paid so little heed to the sentence that he was back in Dundee by the weekend, and got three months on bread and water for his trouble.

Scott and Gray were handed the same sentence and bore the disgrace with the same lack of fear. As they left the court they exchanged cheerful greetings with Alexander Gardiner, much to the chagrin of the massed ranks of the respectable, who hoped for repentance or, even better, dismay at the severity of the sentence. Gardiner, now twenty-three and described as a 'stout-looking fellow' was more inclined to complain than to cringe before the majesty of the court. When details of his scrimmage at the Mathewson's pub were read to him, he did not deny anything, but stated he had been kept in irons before the trial. In return he was reminded that he had already tried to escape from the authorities, and he was told he would remain in jail and in irons until the Circuit Court in Perth.

The Dundee Great Escape

If the authorities had thought about it, they might have considered putting extra guards on Dundee's most daring criminals, but by the time they realised their fault it was too late. Once confined in the upper storey of the jail, the members of Wallace's gang, together with the other assorted riff-raff of the town, contrived their escape. While Gardiner and a notorious thief named Rose Bruce industriously spun yarn, it was Ferguson who discovered that the wall of their cell was merely lathe and plaster. He hacked his way through without much difficulty to find himself in the upper lobby of the jail. There was nobody on watch, the jailer lived in Castle Street and the watchman remained in the guard-room as Ferguson casually lifted the keys from their resting place and opened the cell doors. It was the work of a triumphant moment to release Gardiner from the fetters that held his feet and then all they had to do was leave the building.

There were seven prisoners in this Dundonian version of the Great Escape: Ferguson and Rose Bruce, John Shaw and Alexander Gardiner, David Scott and two women, Robertson and Thomson, who had been imprisoned for returning to the town despite being outlawed. In the early hours of an October Sunday, while the good people of Dundee were still asleep, they entered the Town House jail kitchen, opened the window and, tying rope to the restraining bars, lowered themselves to the ground. However, things now began to go wrong.

Word of the intended escape must have leaked, for the turnkey saw the mother and sister of one of the prisoners lounging at the back of the jail and chased them away with insults and dire threats. Duty done, he retired to the guardhouse, from where he heard a scuffling noise that must have been the prisoners working their way down the wall. By the time he left his chair and peeped outside, most of the prisoners had vanished into the tangle of closes behind the jail, one was lying on the ground in obvious pain and another was by her side.

Robertson had slipped from the rope while descending the wall and had fallen heavily, and her companion Thomson had remained by her side, preferring loyalty to her friend than freedom with a guilty conscience. In the twenty minutes it took Charles Watson the jailer to come after being summoned from Castle Street, all the other escapees had vanished.

Having gone to so much trouble in capturing the wild young men of Wallace's gang the first time, the authorities had no intention of allowing them to escape. Town officers were sent to scour the streets, an express was sent on a fast horse to Patrick Mackay who was in Forfar, and everybody was put on alert for a sighting of the outlaws.

Almost immediately there were results. William Clark, one of Dundee's town officers, traced Scott and Gardiner to Tealing, a tiny village a few miles to the north, and arrested them before twelve o'clock the next day. In the meantime, Patrick Mackay was in pursuit of the others. After riding through Angus and eastern Perthshire, he found traces of his quarry and followed the trail to the west, asking questions, offering descriptions and using all the power of his official position to catch the escapees.

A reward was set for Ferguson, who was required for his promise to turn King's Evidence in another high-profile case involving a major robbery at Colonel Chalmers' house, but Patrick Mackay saved the town's finances by capturing him in Glasgow. Mackay next proved his high reputation by also putting Shaw and Rose Bruce in his bag, and while Shaw was outlawed from Dundee, the others were conveyed back to gaol. There Gardiner, Ferguson and Gray waited for the spring circuit and the decision of a higher judge; the rest just waited for the drear days to drag past.

It was always a scene of high drama when the Dundee prisoners were sent off to Perth for trial, and April of 1824 was no exception. Half the town seemed to turn out to watch the fun, support their friends or weep for loved ones who might be destined for the gallows or Van Diemen's Land. If anything there was more excitement than usual, for Ferguson had again attempted to escape, attacking the turnkey with more aggression than forethought and had been once more subdued and despatched in irons two days early. From before first light to high noon, any Dundonians not busy at work packed the High Street to witness the convicts depart, while the escorting Scots Greys sat on their tall horses, watching for any attempt at rescue.

The judges at Perth seemed to be arbitrary in their decisions. While John Gray was released with his case found not proven, Alexander Gardiner was tried for theft and housebreaking, found guilty and sentenced to seven years' transportation. There was no chance of reprieve and Gardiner would know his next seven years would be spent under a harsh regime in a land nine months' travel away. On 4th November 1824 he was one of 210 convicts transported to Van Diemen's Land. But Gardiner's fate only seemed to make the remaining members of Wallace's gang more contemptuous of law and order.

Within a few days of his returning to Dundee from his trial, Gray was suspected of stealing clothes from the bleaching green at Upper Chapelshade. As he was under sentence of banishment from an earlier case, he was taking the risk of an uncomfortable time on bread and water under the care of Charles Watson, but he was not alone. Scott was back in Dundee, and Peter Wallace had also completed his term of confinement and was roaming the streets that had given him a living but not much else. Once again, however, the authorities acted and Gray and Scott were thrown into the upper storey of the Town House. Mr Mackay was also busy, for he collared John Shaw and sent him to join his friends for a few weeks.

The next months were like a merry-go-round, with Wallace's gang returning to their old haunts, being picked up and thrown into jail. Scott was again in the cells at the end of June; Rose Bruce, likewise banished but caught robbing a house in the Overgate a few days later, also returned to the cells. No sooner was she out than in August she was back inside, having been caught in the Murraygate. Scott was next, with Patrick Mackay picking him up in early September and escorting him back to the cells. By now the authorities were tiring of Rose Bruce and banned her from the county for life, but she returned to Dundee, was spotted by Mackay and speedily locked up in a gaol which by now must have seemed like her second home. She was followed by Scott a few days later and Shaw the following week, but then Gray and Bruce came under the influence of a far more predatory personality. Peter Wallace was after bigger game than the few pennies he might find in the poor houses of the Overgate or the Scouringburn.

By November 1824 Wallace realised that returning to Dundee merely invited arrest. Instead he remained in the countryside where he was not so well known. Basing himself outside Carnoustie, a few miles north of Dundee, he may have visited Montrose on a thieving expedition, but he certainly gathered what was left of his old companions and grabbed the pack from a travelling pedlar. The pedlar, however, was not inclined to see his livelihood disappear and yelled for help. A number of country folk rallied round, helped by the fortuitous appearance of Mr James Hunter, a local solicitor. Rose Bruce and Gray were both caught, but Wallace, who had been carrying the pack, dropped it as a decoy and ran. Mr Hunter trussed Bruce and Gray to a cart and trundled them south to the gaol they knew so well.

The Legacy of Peter Wallace and His Gang

Alone once more, Wallace was suspected of robbing a shop in Forfar after neatly cutting through the window, and was also reported in Dundee; sightings and rumours were numerous, but he proved elusive until in the middle of the month he made a couple of minor mistakes. Roaming in southern Perthshire, he arrived at Dunkeld, saw an Army recruiting party and enlisted under the name of either John or Thomas Barry (his writing was not the most legible). Remembering that Wallace had already made one attempt at holding down a respectable job, and crediting him with more intelligence than his companions, it is worth considering if he was genuinely hoping to make a fresh start. Or was he hoping to grab the enlistment bounty and disappear? With a man as obviously complex and clever as Wallace, either is possible, but the evidence seems to suggest the former, for after receiving the initial advance of the bounty, he returned to Perth to be sworn in.

As he entered the magistrate's house where the ceremony would take place, two of the day patrol constables were waiting for him. One tends to imagine that the Army lost a first-class recruit, but instead Wallace's hands were tied, he was bundled into the Perth–Dundee packet boat and unloaded at the pier where he was reported as looking 'crestfallen'. Once again Wallace, together with Gray and Bruce, faced a sheriff and jury, and once again sentence was pronounced.

While the case of the Carnoustie pedlar seems to have been forgotten, on 17th March the Sheriff Depute tried them for a robbery at the shop of Mary Cowie in the Townhead of Montrose, and of resetting the proceeds, five pieces of checked cloth and a length of corduroy. Of course they pleaded not guilty. It was a nine-hour trial in front of a packed court, but it seems to have been fair, with Mr Duff speaking for the prosecution and the more than capable Mr George Kinloch for the defence, but the jury nevertheless found them guilty of reset.

All three were consigned to the Dundee gaol on a debilitating diet of bread and water until 1st August, and then banished from the county for life. If Rose Bruce returned to Forfarshire she was to be imprisoned on bread and water for ten months; if Wallace or Gray were seen again they were to endure two months in jail followed by a whipping through the Dundee streets. There was a solemn warning that 'This punishment to be inflicted as often as they are found within the county.' The sheriff also ordered that their friends could not bring them food.

Not surprisingly, the prisoners reacted with defiance. Throughout the trial they had looked with indifference at the judge, sworn at the witnesses and refreshed themselves with small beer – a mixture of beer and water. When the sentence was read, Gray, mingling insult with foul language, said that he thought some of the court authorities would make good executioners while Wallace bluntly told the sheriff to 'Go to Hell!' Battered by life and authority, Bruce told the Sheriff that the next time she stole it would be from him.

It was a Monday morning in August when Wallace, Bruce and Gray were released, and at half past eleven the next evening Wallace was back under arrest. Together with a rogue called Robert McKenzie and the notorious 'Thiefy Doig' he was charged with rioting in the Blackness Toll-house. However, in Wallace's case the court was kind. As he was arrested at half past eleven, and he was under orders to be out of the county by twelve, the judge merely ordered him to be returned to the tollhouse so he could leave the county; the others were fined five shillings each.

Despite the absence of Peter Wallace, the rump of the gang continued to annoy the respectable people of Dundee for a while. In September Scott gave the policeman John Chaplain a hard chase before he was again arrested for returning from banishment. In March 1827 Rose Bruce's luck finally ran out and she filed onto the London smack on her way to join Gardiner in Australia, but Peter Wallace seems to have vanished from history. Perhaps he found himself a steady job elsewhere in the county, or maybe he did join the Army, but he does not appear again in Dundee, at least not under his own name.

8
Not Quite a Murder

Murder is a premeditated killing of one human being by another. Murder makes the headlines as arguably the most atrocious of all crimes. But humans can kill humans without any malice and sometimes humans intend to commit murder but fail. These not-quite-murders all have their own morbid fascination.

Death by Horse and Cart

When the first motorcar grumbled onto the roads of Scotland, the authorities were quick to issue regulations that restricted their speed to the pace of a man walking with a red flag. The horseless carriage with an internal combustion engine was viewed as something terrible, a monster that would devour all pedestrians in its path, scare the milk from cows and no doubt cause serious concern in nervous women. Yet, the horsed carriages were no paragons of innocence, either. The records of the Dundee Police Court are speckled with instances of what was then known as furious or reckless driving. Then as now, there were four main causes for such behaviour: drunkenness, youth, rivalry and pure carelessness.

In a period when drinking was more of a way of life than a social pastime, it is hardly surprising some cart or coach drivers would hit the road after imbibing too much. To give a couple of typical examples: in April 1829 a well-known character known as Piper Gray appeared in the court charged with drunken driving along the Shore, where he had knocked down the stand of a fishwife. Four years previously two carters were fined ten shillings each for 'furiously driving their carts along the Shore'. Carters were frequently in trouble, possibly because they were on the road all day, probably because of the competition for trade. Children in particular tended to fall victim to the screeching wheels and iron-shod hooves of carts and carriages, but adults could also be hit and, occasionally, killed. In the autumn of 1877, such a case reached the Circuit Court.

Joseph Calder of Scouringburn was a carter; he spent much of his working life on the driving seat, negotiating the often-crowded streets of

Bustling High Street of Dundee

© Courtesy of Dundee Art Galleries and Museums

Dundee with a laden single-horse van. On Saturday 23rd June 1877 he was driving along Victoria Street when he knocked down Mary Leaden, a millworker of Kemback Street. Leaden fell heavily, fractured her skull and on 7th August she died. Calder pleaded not guilty to the charge of driving 'in a reckless and furious manner'.

There were many witnesses but as so often their evidence only clouded the issue. The first to be called was David Anderson, a baker of Erskine Street. He stated that at half-past seven that evening he saw Calder driving his van eastward along Victoria Street. Mary Leaden was standing 'in the water channel' – the gutter – with her back to the van. She was speaking to her father who stood on the pavement. According to Anderson, the van was very close to the water channel, despite the road being about forty feet across, and he was travelling at nine or ten miles an hour. Calder did not shout a warning and the van hit Leaden 'about the middle of the body'. As Leaden fell, her head smashed against the kerb of the pavement. Thinking that Calder was drunk, Anderson grabbed hold of him until the police arrived.

James Elder, who was also a baker, agreed with everything Anderson said, but added that Calder was driving recklessly and had no need to be in the water channel when the street was wide and virtually empty of traffic. A selection of other witnesses substantially agreed; Mrs Dick was watching out of her Victoria Street window and thought the wheels of Calder's van were on the kerbstone of Victoria Bridge. She also said that Calder was driving furiously while Mrs Stark of Lyon Street said it was the shaft of the machine that knocked Leaden down.

Mary's father Thomas was a hammer-man who lived in Princes Street. He agreed he had been talking to Mary when the cart hit her. Admitting she was standing in the water channel, he saw the van coming and said he tried to pull her clear but the shaft of the van knocked her over. When he visited his daughter in the infirmary she did not recognise him. However, Thomas Leaden also introduced a little doubt when he said that he, his daughter and a fourth person, a woman named Agnes Martin, had been drinking, although Mary was sober. It was the first indication that there might be some fault on the victim's side.

Mrs McKenzie of Lyon Street added to the confusion. She saw Calder's van on Victoria Street and saw it approach the father and daughter while they were talking loudly with the second woman, Martin. McKenzie said that Thomas Leaden asked Mary for money and she stepped back into the road just as Calder's cart roared up. Mrs McKenzie also said that the wheel of the van was not in the water channel when it hit Mary Leaden. Possibly more significantly, she thought the Leadens and Martin were all drunk.

The evidence of John Miller, a confectioner in Victoria Street, also tended to support Calder's case. He said that Calder was quite sober when he visited his shop, about twenty-five yards from the accident. Miller also said although he did not see the accident, he did not see Calder driving furiously.

The penultimate witness was one of the closest to the accident, and a woman who might be expected to support Mary Leaden. Agnes Martin was actually talking to Mary when the accident occurred. She admitted that they had been drinking in a number of public houses during the day and she was drunk by half past seven. According to Martin, Mary stood at the edge of the pavement and had plenty of time to see the van coming, for it was 'not driven at a furious pace'. She also said the van had hardly left Mr McKenzie's shop so there was hardly time for it so build up speed, and she reiterated that Mary Leaden was the worse for drink.

Constable William McCleary had no doubt who had taken drink. He escorted Calder to the Police Station and said he was so drunk he did not realise what had happened until the police told him. Calder claimed he was not drunk.

So the dispute lay squarely around drink. Mrs McKenzie and Agnes Martin thought Mary Leaden had been drinking and had stepped in front of the cart, while others claimed Calder had been driving furiously and Constable McCleary swore Calder was drunk. Wherever the blame lay, there was no doubt about the result. Mary Leaden had been hit by Calder's cart; she fell and cracked her head. Dr McCosh, the medical superintendent of the Dundee Royal Infirmary, confirmed that Mary had concussion of the brain and a fractured skull. She died without regaining consciousness.

Lord Craighall, the judge, gave the jury both sides of the case, and they found Calder guilty of culpable and reckless driving, but recommended leniency. The courtroom applauded when Lord Craighall sentenced Calder to four months in jail. Although drunkenness was not in itself a major crime, it is obvious there could be serious consequences. The next case was far more premeditated.

'I Didna' Shoot You'

For anybody leaving Dundee by the Coupar Angus Road, the gloomy fastnesses of Templeton Woods loom on the right-hand side. On the opposite side spreads Camperdown Park, now open to the public but in the nineteenth century the private policies of the Duncan family, descendants of the Admiral Duncan who defeated the Dutch in one of the most savage naval battles of the eighteenth century. As an area of parkland close by a large urban centre, Camperdown was prone to poaching, but in the autumn of 1842 it sprang to public attention in a case of attempted murder as cold blooded as any in the area.

Despite the advent of industrialisation, in the early 1840s agriculture was of vital importance to Scotland. Of the dozens of agricultural fairs, many were of local importance, such as the Keith Fair, the Timmer market in Aberdeen and the Aikey Brae, while the Falkirk Tryst was of national importance. Drovers would herd their cattle from the most remote Highland glens to Falkirk to sell to buyers who came from as far away as the deep south of England, but there were also many local agreements. In the summer of 1842, James Duff of Whitefield, near Kirkmichael in Strathardle, Perthshire, sold a large number of cattle and sheep to Alexander

Mackenzie, a cattle dealer from Drumhead in Glenisla, in the Angus Glens. The price came to something over a thousand pounds, which was an enormous amount of money at the time, and when Mackenzie re-sold the animals at the Falkirk Tryst, Duff followed, expecting to be paid his money.

He was disappointed. Mackenzie was charming and evasive, giving Duff excuse after excuse, eventually stating he was due to be in Glasgow in a short time. Duff listened, but he knew that Mackenzie had sold his animals at a suspiciously low price, so it was unlikely he would raise the thousand pounds he owed. He also doubted that Mackenzie was going to Glasgow so second-guessed him by taking the Edinburgh train. Farmers would rendezvous in well-known spots and sure enough Duff bumped into Mackenzie in the capital.

No doubt Mackenzie was surprised to see Duff again, but he pretended friendship and when Duff demanded he pay his debts, Mackenzie made a firm promise to settle at Blairgowrie. Duff agreed, and ensured there was not another attempt to abscond by sticking with Mackenzie every yard of the way. On the Thursday morning, both men caught the ten o'clock train from Edinburgh, crossed Fife and boarded the ferry across the Tay. At four that afternoon they arrived in Dundee and ate at Mrs Wallace's Inn at Barrack Street, where Mackenzie once again began his delaying tactics. While Duff urged him to catch the five o'clock train to Newtyle, Mackenzie claimed urgent business that took him on various errands throughout the town. Not surprisingly they missed the train and Mackenzie said they could spend the night at a small property called the Meadows of Auchterhouse, which he owned. It was only about a six-mile walk, so Duff agreed.

It was still light when they left Mrs Wallace's at about six that evening. They walked up Barrack Street and Constitution Brae, passed over the Law and from there through Dryburgh Farm and onto the Coupar Angus turnpike near the gate to Camperdown. It would probably have been better to follow the turnpike up to Auchterhouse, but Mackenzie chose a shortcut through a field of potatoes and followed a drystane dyke until they came to a break that allowed access to Camperdown Wood.

Until that moment, Duff had followed blindly, trusting to Mackenzie's knowledge of the area, but he pulled back as they entered the wood. Handing his hat to Duff, Mackenzie said he would check the route and plunged alone into the gloomy trees. He returned after a few moments, told Duff he knew where they were and invited him to follow.

They walked through the wood and onto a grassy path, when Mackenzie politely stepped aside and allowed Duff to walk in front. As Duff did so, Mackenzie pulled a pistol from under his cloak and fired a single shot before ducking away. Duff staggered, with a bullet between his left shoulder and his spine. Terrified that Mackenzie would fire again, he dropped his hat and fled, limping through the estate of Camperdown, past the eastern fields of St Mary's and came to the cottar town of Baldragon. By now it was full night and he was in pain, bleeding, dripping with sweat and exhausted, but a friendly light beckoned to him and he banged on the door for help.

The cottage belonged to a farm servant called James White and as soon as he saw the state of Duff he told Mr Patullo, the farmer. Within the hour Patullo had informed the police and sent for Doctor Cocks who dressed Duff's wound. After that, things moved swiftly. Superintendent Mackison came out from Dundee, arriving just after midnight in a flurry of horse-hooves and officialdom. Afraid that Duff might die, for Doctor Cocks had not found the pistol ball, Patullo wrote down Duff's statement of what had happened as the police began their search for Mackenzie. A quick examination of the potato field found Mackenzie's footprints heading back toward Dundee, so the police scoured the town. They arrested Mackenzie as he waited for the Arbroath train and brought him to the police office.

Denying everything, Mackenzie claimed he was innocent, until the police told him that Duff was still alive, when the colour drained from his face. When the police searched him they found £257 in bank notes as well as a deposit receipt for another £72. There was little doubt the events had happened just as Duff stated: one of Lord Duncan's keepers found Duff's hat just where he said it was, and an Edinburgh pawnbroker described Mackenzie as the man to whom he had sold a pistol.

Even so, Mackenzie said, 'You know, James, I didna shoot you.'

The jury at Perth Circuit Court, however, took a different view and found Mackenzie guilty.

Although completely different, these two cases do illustrate something of the variety of crime in Dundee. People could die because of a relatively minor misdemeanour, or could be nearly killed by a man who had planned a murder. Either way, death was always a threat.

9

'Kill the Buggers!':
Early Police 1824–1860

At first it had appeared an easy enough arrest for the watchmen of the new Dundee Police Force. It was 1825, late at night on the last Saturday before Christmas and a drunken man had been annoying people in the High Street. The watchmen arrested him, discovered he was John Gordon, a plumber's apprentice, and were escorting him to the police office when he suddenly lay down on the street and refused to move any further. As the watchmen lifted him and began to carry him away, a crowd gathered, shouting and pushing at the officers. Battering through to the police office, the watchmen deposited Gordon in a cell but when they returned to the streets the crowd was waiting, reinforced by others who emerged from the pubs and shebeens.

A shower of stones forced the watchmen back to the police office and some began to grumble that they would be better in a job with more money and less trouble. Mr Hume, the superintendent, gave them a rousing talk and ordered them back out to clear the crowd. Rather than facing them head on, the watchmen slipped out the back door, probably intending to take the rioters by surprise, and moved forward in a compact body. Immediately after the watchmen appeared, the barrage began again, with people hiding in the entrances to closes and leaning out of windows to throw whatever came to hand. This time, however, police watchmen from other parts of the town rallied to aid their comrades and dispelled the crowd.

But not for long. When the police chased the crowd from one street they reassembled in another, so Dundee echoed with the raucous cries of battle, the clatter of stones on cobbles and the crack of police truncheons on the heads of rioters. The trouble continued past twelve o'clock and into the small hours of Sunday morning, with stones weighing as much as three pounds and even a length of iron railing used as weapons. There were casualties on both sides with one police watchman, Daniel Mackay, badly injured by a stone thrown from a window in the Overgate. There were also twenty-six people arrested for rioting or refusing to go home before the police finally restored quiet to the streets.

Fifty-eight Men to Police Dundee

Although this riot was quite extreme, there was no doubt that a uniformed police force was not universally welcomed in Dundee, or indeed throughout the nation. Many believed that the police had been formed to protect the respectable from the unfortunate, or even to keep the poor under control. Having the police dressed in blue uniforms was a deliberate attempt to avoid any resemblance to the military but they were still a disciplined, uniformed body of men whose duty was to enforce laws that often seemed to victimise the underclass. With their long, tailed greatcoats, top hats and hand-held lanterns, the police were quite distinctive and were soon to be a familiar sight in the streets of Dundee.

For all the hostility of many of the population, Dundee's early police establishment was not large. In November 1824 there was one superintendant, one lieutenant, six sergeants, six men for the day patrol, six men for the night patrol, thirty-six watchmen, one turnkey to look after those arrested and one office keeper. That was a total of fifty-eight men to look after an expanding industrial city with a population exceeding 34,000. There were also the scavengers who cleared the dung piles and the lamp-lighters who fought the encroaching dark and who were on the official police establishment, but not involved in upholding the law. At that time the police office was in St Clements Lane and, without a dedicated jail, prisoners were held in the top floors of the Town House.

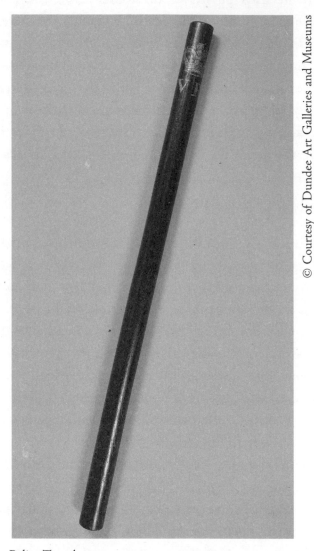

© Courtesy of Dundee Art Galleries and Museums

Police Truncheon

In those early months attacks on the police seemed to be a hobby amongst certain sections of the community. For example, on Tuesday 16th November 1824 a carter named David Morrison was fined five shillings for insulting the new police. The following week two drunken gentlemen strutted through Dundee bullying everybody in the belief that their genteel birth would protect them from justice. The Dundee police thought differently, despite being threatened with dire vengeance when they arrested the more violent of the two. The Police Court agreed with the officers and fined the drunks two guineas. That same week a man set his mastiff on a policeman walking his beat in the Seagate. In January a policeman was escorting a prisoner to the police office when a youth attacked him hoping to rescue his friend. He ended the night in a cell. Later that week the police had to tie up a man named James Wilson who had attacked them, and a carter was fined five shillings for swearing at Sergeant Thomas Hardy. The following week another gentleman was taken to court and fined for what the *Advertiser* called 'abusing the watchmen' while on Thursday 20th January in Baltic Street a man threw a stone at a watchman named David Leslie, who had to be carried to a surgeon. Also on the 20th a seaman in Seagate attacked the watchman on duty there, breaking some of their lanterns. The following week the police court seemed filled with seamen attacking the police.

And so it continued. Every time the police walked their beats they were liable to receive abuse, insult and assault and when the great Reform Riot of 1831 took place, the police office at St Clements was ransacked by an angry mob. It took a lot of courage to be a policeman on the streets of Dundee in the 1820s and 1830s.

With few men to guard the streets and no military garrison nearer than Perth to call upon, the police were very vulnerable. At the Police Court on 24th March 1825, a number of men were fined for assaulting the police watchmen, including a Chapelshade manufacturer who bit a watchman's hand. A typical case occurred in December 1829 when Alexander Gall, a man with a long record of violence, was in the company of a prostitute at the back of the Wards at about midnight on a Saturday. When James Matthews, the watchman, shone his lantern on them, Gall immediately swore and threatened to knock out his brains. Naturally Matthews answered back, but Gall grabbed his truncheon and battered him to the ground; when Matthews called for help Gall and his woman fled. Gall was later fined £2 at the Police Court.

In April of that year a man named Alexander Meldrum was accused of assaulting Sergeant Alexander Taws, who was so injured he could not work. Taws was one of the best-known of the early police, whom J.M. Beatts, in his book *Reminiscences of an Old Dundonian*, described as being 'portly'. In 1827, while still a constable, Taws was involved in an incident in Union Street when rival gangs of boys from the Grammar School and the English School were throwing stones at each other. Alexander Taws led a body of police straight into the heart of the scramash, arrested the ringleaders and marched them to the St Clements Lane Police Office.

Dismissing the Police

Despite the high hopes of the magistrates, not all the early police proved up to the job. At the beginning of March 1825 a watchman named William Stephen was fined 1/4d and dismissed the service for banging at the door of a pub in his Seagate beat and demanding drink for himself and his two companions. The following month in the Witchknowe a watchman named Raffins helped put down a disturbance by a group of weavers, but in doing so he beat one of the men so severely that Mr Dick, the police surgeon, had to dress the wound. The weaver was still bloody and bruised when he stood in front of the Police Court. In May the superintendent dismissed Raffin but took no further action. Including Raffin, ten policemen were dismissed in the four weeks between 11th April and 11th May 1825. These were David Taylor, Alexander Lesslie and James Shearer for being drunk while on their beat, William Gordon and William Middleton for being drunk and asleep on their beat, Alexander Robertson, Thomas

McEvoy and Thomas Abbott for falling asleep on their beat, David Sharp for being in a pub while on duty and finally Alexander Raffin for improper conduct. In August a policeman was jailed for the terrible crime of picking berries from somebody's garden when he was on duty. In November 1826 there was another case of police brutality when John Sharp, a Nethergate night watchman, used his staff to attack a young man, without apparent reason. With the other police as witnesses, the superintendent warned him that any further examples of violence would mean instant dismissal. The rules for police were plain: abide by every letter of the law or lose the position.

Despite these blips, the police force became established. By the middle of May 1825 there were six sergeants, four night patrols, six day patrols, thirty-six watchmen and a man who was paid the princely sum of five shillings a week to trim the watchman's lanterns. Even more significantly, the presence of uniformed police in Dundee seemed to have pushed at least some of the criminal element out of the town. In April the people of Lochee met to discuss forming their own police force as the number of undesirables coming to the village had increased. The people decided to create twenty-four constables from local men, with a six-month term of office.

Thomas Abbott, who had been dismissed from the police for falling asleep, became a weaver but was soon accused of stealing twenty spindles of yarn. He claimed he bought it from Mr Peat, the foreman of the bleach field of Turnbull and Company. Peat had conveniently disappeared but Messenger-at-Arms Patrick Mackay arrested William Stewart for buying the yarn.

In the meantime, the new force and its associates tried to prove their worth. On 12th June 1825 the Scouringburn watchman, helped by the day patrol, put out a lodging house fire. When they forced their way into the two-roomed house they found forty people inside, with piles of straw the only beds on the earth floors. It was a reminder of the conditions in which some people in Dundee had to live. In September that same year

Constable John Chaplain chased and arrested a notorious bad character named Scott, who had returned to Dundee after being banished. The uniformed men were beginning to show their teeth.

Dogs, Handcuffs and a Chewed Letter

The police were not well paid. In June Superintendent Home had suggested that the most efficient of the day patrol had earned a pay rise from 11/1d to 14/- a week. That was still not great money for men who were in the firing line the moment they stepped out the door and whose every move was watched by a critical and suspicious public. Even so, they were still allowed their idiosyncrasies. As late as August 1828, four years after the establishment of a professional, uniformed force, the Castle Street watchman took his collie dog with him as he walked his beat. It was still the watchman's job to shout the hour, and the dog helped, barking along with his master. The people of Castle Street must have wondered if it was worth the money to have a dog yapping every hour from ten at night until four in the morning.

However, the Dundee sheriff officers were equally fallible. In August, Thomas Anderson and Thomas Marshall were sent to bring in a woman who had illegally left her position in service. It was a routine task, but they took a pair of handcuffs, and fortified themselves with a few refreshments before rapping at the woman's door. Quicker witted than both the Sheriff's men, she dodged Anderson, grabbed the handcuffs and locked them around Marshall's wrists before running way, holding the keys in triumph. Two policemen carried the discomfited Marshall to the cells and left him there, still handcuffed. Presumably he was released when he sobered up.

Even so, by 1828 the Dundee police were more professional. At the beginning of December three furtive-looking men were drifting around the shops in the town centre, probing and looking but not actually buying. When they walked into Provost Brown's shop in Castle Street, he sent a message to Superintendent Home. The superintendent ordered Sergeants Hardy and Strachan to bring them in. The provost's instincts were correct, for when the sergeants dragged the men to the police office they found nine India silk handkerchiefs and a fur cap hidden in their clothes, all stolen from shops in Castle Street. As the men were searched, one, an Edinburgh cabinetmaker named John Smith, stuffed something in his mouth and tried to swallow it. Seizing Smith by the throat, Sergeant Hardy recovered a half-chewed letter.

The letter was from Smith's father, and spoke of the 'infernal police', but the name may have been an alias, as the man who chewed letters also called himself John Brown. One of his companions, known as Charles MacDonald, had an alias of Peter Jack. MacDonald was a notorious man. His father was long dead but his mother had moved in with one of the more unsavoury characters who wandered the northern counties of Scotland, living by his wits, his fists and his light fingers. Termed the 'Cock of the North', this man was well known to the authorities. The relationship between MacDonald's mother and the Cock of the North ended when he murdered her, and the Glasgow Circuit Court sentenced the Cock to be hanged. Their son continued the family tradition of lawlessness. The third man was William Cammuince and he seemed to be out of his depth among such characters.

This incident, perhaps minor in itself, demonstrates not only the sort of people the Dundee police had to deal with, but their efficiency in arresting them, and some of their methods. Perhaps they were crude by twenty-first century standards, but they were also relatively efficient. As they notched up successes, the police might have become more acceptable to the Dundee public.

The Adventures of Sergeant Jack

The *Dundee Directory* of 1829 records the names of some of these early police. It states that John Home was Superintendent of Police and the

Procurator Fiscal of Court; William Dick was Surgeon and the sergeants included Alexander Dow, Thomas Hardy, John Low and William McRoberts; Alexander Donaldson was the Harbour Sergeant and James McDougal was the keeper of the magazine. Sometimes a name reaches through the murk of time to afford brief illumination to a period. One such name was Sergeant Jack, who looms out of obscurity in a few cases in the late 1820s and early 1830s, only to fade back into the murk of history.

In January 1829 Sergeant Jack arrested a man named Alexander MacDonald, a flax dresser in Monifieth, who had stolen a silver watch. Jack also retrieved the watch. Nearly exactly a year later he arrested an Aberdeen man who had come to try his luck in Dundee, and in February 1830 he searched through the Overgate for a well-known law breaker called George Keith who had already been banished from Forfarshire. Although no details have survived, Sergeant Jack found Keith hidden in a house in Rodger's Close, Overgate, so there was either a tip-off or a thorough house-to-house search of that warren of narrow lanes and crowded houses. Either way, Sergeant Jack was doing his job in preserving the respectable of Dundee from the underworld.

Only a few months later Jack was again making the news when on one Friday in May he arrested three people under sentence of banishment. Jean Mitchell and Francis Wright were well-known as petty thieves, but Christina Scott had made her name as a hen stealer, a crime that would perhaps go unnoticed today. With nineteenth-century Dundonians far closer to their rural ancestors and rural roots than is often credited, hen keeping was quite common, both as a source of income and a dietary supplement, so hen stealing was a fairly widespread crime.

Trials and Triumphs of the Early Police Force

Even with such men, the early Dundee police could occasionally slip back to their old wayward ways. In early January 1830 an unnamed young flesher was working in Greenmarket Square when two sheriff officers and a posse of police officers grabbed him. Considering he was innocent of any crime, the flesher made a determined resistance, and the arrival of some burly shore porters to assist the forces of law and order did not make things any better. The flesher punched and wrestled and raked his boots down the shins of the porters, but eventually they dragged him to St Clements Lane and shoved him in a cell.

It was not until later that the prisoner was informed he had been arrested for being the father of an illegitimate child, a charge he denied. When the flesher's father arrived and gave his name, the police realised they had the wrong man and released him, but it was a reminder that the police were still not perfect.

Sometimes it was either inexperience or naivety that let the police down. About two o'clock on a Sunday morning in February 1831, the constable on the West Port beat came across a makeshift ladder leaning against a wall in Young's Close. The wall was one side of a small cul-de-sac with a single-storey house at the other side and no exit at the top, while the ladder consisted of a six-foot-long plank of wood with a rope attached in place of rungs. There was nothing in the close but a single water cask that stood in a corner. Realising that there was something wrong, the policeman returned to the West Port and summoned help, but re-entered Young's Close before anybody arrived. Climbing the ladder, he saw a man in the close below and called out to him.

'I'm coming up,' the man said at once, but as the policeman waited, the man jumped onto the water cask, scrambled onto the roof of the house on the opposite side of the close and vanished. Rather than arrest a burglar, the policeman found only a set of housebreaking tools, but within a day or so he had been sacked for inefficiency.

At other times, the police were very successful. In the beginning of December 1830 the watchman at the Wards found a cattle drover sleeping in an outhouse and took him to the police office. When he was questioned, the drover claimed he had spent the night with a girl who had subsequently robbed him. Drovers were good targets for thieves, for they would take a drove of cattle to market, sell them and carry the money back to their employer. They were a hardy bunch, sleeping outside beside their cattle whatever the weather, but in common with many people from the country, they were not always wise to the tricks of the town.

Making a few enquiries, the police superintendent learned that three suspicious-looking people had caught the mail coach for Aberdeen. They had given false names and sat on the roof, the cheapest, most exposed and coldest seats. The superintendent knew the mother of one of the suspects lived in Arbroath, twenty miles up the coast. Accordingly he sent the redoubtable Sergeant Dow along with the drover on the next coach. Arbroath was a small place and strangers were easily seen, so it did not take Dow long to track down the three people who had recently arrived in the town. Arresting Gersham Elder, Barbara Elder and the local bad character Alison Watt, Sergeant Dow found £2 9/- in a drawer in the Elders' house and another 20/- in Watt's. Only ten shillings had been spent, and that on women's clothing. What Watt learned next makes one wish for a time machine, or a nineteenth-century tape recorder as Gersham Elder said he had been the woman with whom the drover spent the evening. He had a very feminine voice and looks, dressed in women's clothing and confessed he was in the habit of prowling Dundee in women's clothing and performing acts that were well beyond decency. We will never know the full story.

Taking the Law into Their Own Hands

Even with the police on the streets, there were times when the Dundee public took the law into their own hands, often in indignation at some act of cruelty to a vulnerable person. As in every period, crowds of idle youths tended to congregate at certain places, and in Dundee during the early 1830s they chose the piazzas of the Town House. As this building was where much of the official business of the town was conducted, many people would feel uncomfortable passing so many youths. In February 1832 the jailer, Colin MacEwan, took matters upon himself and whipped a fourteen-year-old boy who refused to leave. Not surprisingly, people objected to a child being attacked and gathered against the jailer. For a while the situation looked ugly for MacEwan, but some police commissioners rescued him, although he was taken to court and fined £2 2/-.

While older youths congregated at street corners and outside the Town House, gangs of younger children tended to annoy the street porters. They liked to jump on the handcarts the porters trundled around the streets and get a free lift, depending on the porter's good nature and mighty muscles. However, not every porter was inclined to act as a free taxi service and in August Duncan Barland lost his temper with a girl who had jumped on his cart when he pushed it along the Murraygate. Grabbing the girl, he pulled her over his knee, lifted her skirt and spanked her soundly. When he released her, the girl ran away, howling. An indignant crowd complained and the case reached the court, where witnesses spoke of Barland's quiet character and said the girl got no more than she deserved, but the porter was fined 5/- nonetheless.

Better Equipment

In January 1835, eleven years after they were formed, the Dundee police were given better uniforms and equipment. A lot of thought had gone into the improvements, and the experiences of the watchmen were taken into account. Off came the long tails of the night watchmen's greatcoat, to be replaced by a shorter coat that was less cumbersome when they had to chase a law breaker. The hand-held lantern was also discarded in favour of one that was strapped to the body and equipped with a shutter, so enabling the watchman to approach a culprit without announcing his presence in a blaze of light.

The watchmen's hat was also improved, so it was stronger and more waterproof, with a strap that fastened under the chin. Until these alterations there had been a set pattern to attacking the watchmen. First the attacker would break his lantern or knock it out of his hand, and when the watchmen tried to pick it up, the attacker would throw the long tails of his coat over his head and thump him on the back of the head or any other vulnerable part. Now, with more efficient lanterns and stouter hats, the watchmen were slightly better protected. It was a start.

Although the population of Dundee grew year on year, the numbers of the police establishment were remarkably constant. The 1837 *Dundee Directory* states there were eleven day patrols, six night patrols and just thirty-six watchmen that year; while the 1841 issue of the same publication says that with the population around 62,000 there was one lieutenant, one sergeant major, four sergeants, one turnkey for the cells, twelve day patrols, four night patrols and thirty watchmen. According to the record of 1850, there were 70,000 people in Dundee in that year, and the police establishment had altered into something more recognisable. Under the superintendence of Donald Mackay, there was John Cameron, the lieutenant of police, two criminal officers, six police sergeants, two street sergeants, forty-three constables and one female turnkey to care for those women who were under arrest.

The criminal officer was what we now term a detective, a policeman working in civilian clothing whose primary function was to solve crimes after they had been committed, rather than the uniformed officer whose duty was more crime prevention or on-the-spot arrest. Although the British Criminal Investigation Department began in 1844 when Sir James Graham, the Home Secretary, allowed a dozen police sergeants to shed their uniforms, local superintendents throughout the country had already used plain clothed police. These men had been known as 'active officers' and were probably disliked with even greater fervour than the uniformed men. In March 1842 the superintendent had recommended Dundee should have two criminal officers. He had already experimented with two active officers, George Reid and Hope Ramsay, and was so satisfied with the results he was prepared to do without an orderly to pay them their eighteen shillings a week wages.

Those in Charge

The early police superintendents were not always successful. According to historian J.M. Beatts, the first was a tailor called John Low, who only lasted a few months. Then came Alexander Downie, who reigned from 1824 to 1825. He was an old military man who had fought in the Peninsular War under Wellington but was now retired on half pay. John Home was next, and he restored some of the faith in the police as he lasted in the job for some nine years until 1834 and had a good reputation. James Drummond followed, and then the position again became vacant.

In October 1839 the *Dundee Advertiser* placed a notice looking for a new Superintendent of Police in 1839. The town sought a man of 'superior qualifications' and offered a salary of £120 a year with a free house with coal and gas light. As well as policing, the job included inspecting the lighting and cleaning and acting as public prosecutor in the police court. Of the fifty men who came forward, David Corstorphan was selected. He was a fair choice and during his tenure there are some traces of humanity within the service. When John Ker, a policeman of four years' service, died in early 1841, David Corstorphan handed over £4 11/- to his widow. It was hardly a pension, but still a nice token for the time. Corstorphan died in late 1841.

As for his successor, Joseph Maddison, his term of office is mercifully forgotten. In 1842 there was a surge in crime in York and Maddison became superintendent of a local police force. Unfortunately he used the position to embezzle police funds, but by the time he was found out he had already been appointed superintendent of the Dundee police.

The next appointee was a Caithness man, Donald Mackay, and proved probably the most successful of the early superintendents. He had been working in Dunfermline and when he left, fifty of his friends entertained him to a farewell dinner and presented him with a gold watch and chain, so he had made an impression in Fife. Mackay remained in the position until 1876, when David Dewar took over until 1909.

'Kill the Buggers'

Regardless of who was in command, December seemed to be a bad month for attacks on the police, and 1833 was no exception. On the night of Saturday 1st December, Constable Peter Mackenzie was on his beat when somebody called for assistance. He hurried to the Witchknowe, where a man named Alexander Farquharson had been causing trouble. Mackenzie knew Farquharson had a bad reputation, so arrested him there and then. That should have been the end of the matter, but as he headed for the police office, some of the crowd moved forward. Outnumbered, Mackenzie had little chance and the mob released his prisoner, but when police reinforcements arrived they succeeded in driving a wedge into the crowd and grabbing Farquharson back.

Rather than withdraw, the crowd became more threatening, chanting, 'Kill the buggers! Kill the buggers!' There were more skirmishes; the crowd overpowered an officer and grabbed his staff and from then onward it was a running battle, with a chanting crowd around 300 strong threatening and fighting with the police. They reached the Overgate at one o'clock on Sunday morning and people stared from windows lit and unlit as the police and the mob battled for possession of the prisoner. The crowd pressed hard, knocking down the police like ninepins, and the arrival of more police only aggravated the situation.

Eventually the police gave up. With most of them walking wounded, they released Farquharson. As the crowd began to drift home, job done, the police, battered and bleeding, picked up a few they believed had been most prominent in the riot. These men appeared before Baillies Kidd and Christie at the Police Court on Monday morning and denied all the charges. They had apparently been innocently walking along the Overgate and were surprised to be arrested. The court thought otherwise: the flax dressers Peter Drysdale, John Wynd and Martin Watson, together with the weaver Colin Gallagher, were found guilty. Drysdale, Gallagher and Watson were fined the maximum £5 with an alternative of sixty days, with Wynd fined £2 or thirty days.

Incidents where the crowd interfered to rescue a prisoner were all too common. On 17th November 1835, the arrest of James Gibson, a drunken shoemaker and hawker, started another riot. When the police reached Barrack Street, Gibson bellowed for help and a crowd swarmed across. The resulting stramash saw one policeman with minor injuries, three seriously hurt, a flax dresser named John Mackay arrested and a ten-guinea reward offered for the names of the rioters.

There was another anti-police riot in June 1836 when a well-known Hilltown troublemaker named James Storier led a mob who rescued a prisoner. The police arrested Storier not long afterward. At the beginning of November 1843 a Dundee mob again rose against the police. This time the trouble started when William McCrae, an Irish weaver at Easson's Factory in Victoria Street, had attacked one of his colleagues. A policeman arrested McCrae, but as they left the factory, William's brother Samuel launched a furious attack, freed the prisoner and ran away. Picking himself off the ground and dusting himself down, the policeman sought help. The policeman guessed the McCraes would be in their father's house, and so he went there, booting open the front door, only to see the brothers escape out a skylight and onto the roof, where they danced and jeered at their pursuers. Unwilling to follow through the skylight, the police borrowed ladders from the men who worked Dundee's fire engines, captured the McCraes and brought them back in handcuffs. As usual, a crowd had gathered to see what all the commotion was about, and now attacked the police. There was the usual barrage of missiles as the police eased through Hilltown. Forced to take refuge in a shop until reinforcements arrived, the police lost control of Samuel McCrae, but grabbed a brace of bakers named Bogue and Reid in exchange. By the time they reached St Clements Lane all the police were more or less injured, one seriously, and they must have wondered if their job was worth all the fuss.

By the mid-nineteenth century there was an army garrison in Dudhope

Castle. Strangely, given the bad reputation soldiers carried, they rarely bothered the police although there were occasional incidents. One occurred in February 1844 when Private William Maxwell of the 92nd Highlanders was on sentry duty at the barrack gates. Two drunken men, Moses Taggart, a weaver from the Scouringburn, and Robert Tasker, a seaman from Chapelshade, began to antagonise, insult and assault him, but Maxwell retained his discipline and his position as sentinel. When two officers passed, Tasker turned on them, but this time Maxwell did act, fending off Tasker's punches and kicks. The police arrested both drunks and after a spell in the Dudhope's Black Hole, took them to the Police Court where they were awarded a further ten days in jail.

The next incident was potentially more serious. At midnight on 6th October 1844 a group from the 60th Rifles were causing trouble at the bottom of Crichton Street. The Fish Street watchman hurried over to quieten things down, but the soldiers turned on him. Either the 60th were unpopular or the manhood of Dundee were feeling brave that night, for several came running to help the police, whereupon the soldiers drew their swords – the Rifles' name for their bayonets. A general melee started, with the police pitting their truncheons against the swords of the soldiers, and the end result was one soldier arrested and given a week in jail. Even when they were alone, soldiers could sometimes be trouble. In October 1853, two men of the 82nd Regiment wandered along Dudhope Crescent, drunk as lords and insulting everybody they met. For some reason they took a strong dislike to a mill overseer named James McLeod. Private James Moran took off his broad belt and attacked McLeod with the buckle end, treating a policeman to the same treatment a moment later. He was rewarded with thirty days in jail.

Growing Professionalism

By the 1850s the police were based at Bell Street, where their headquarters still are. According to the 1853 *Dundee Directory*, Donald Mackay now had Alexander McQueen as First Lieutenant, Alex Mackay as Second Lieutenant and Alexander Webster as Surgeon. There were two criminal officers, one police sergeant, four street sergeants, four night patrols and a force of ninety constables, with one male and one female turnkey. The growing numbers correspond to the expanding city, but each year the police were becoming more proficient. On the last Sunday of February 1853 there was a daylight break-in at a shop in the Seagate. The owner, Mrs Wilson, was at church, and when she returned two hours later she found thieves had forced open a back window that overlooked a small court and taken her cash box.

The active officers Smith and James were put on the case. Both were experienced men and they traced and arrested the thief and found most of the money buried underground. The case was wrapped up by ten that same night. Smith and James had another success the following day when they saw three young men, McInally, Balmer and Holland, waddling around the town looking very bulky. Taking them to the police office, Smith and James had them strip-searched, to find each with several layers of clothing, all stolen from houses in Dundee's west end. Further investigation also found some pirns that had been removed from a Blackness Road factory. The three men were arrested.

By the late 1850s the Dundee police were becoming more sophisticated in crime detection. Early on a Saturday afternoon in September 1858 the manager of the Seafield Works sent a clerk named George Thomson to the bank with over £400. The temptation of such a huge sum proved too much and Thomson absconded with the money. At two o'clock the same afternoon the Seafield Works informed the police, who immediately telegraphed the police offices in the major urban centres in Scotland and England and wrote letters to the smaller towns. They also sent copies of Thomson's photograph to the main police offices around the country.

As soon as Superintendent Charles of the Arbroath Police read the letter he alerted his own officers and within an hour they found Thomson and two young women in the White Hart Hotel. A quick search found only £2, but Charles knew his own area and dug out £300 in a house in Applegate and a £100 bank note with a High Street merchant. Travelling on the midnight train, Lieutenant Neil Gunn was in Arbroath before one in the morning, took hold of Thomson and brought him back to Dundee in time for the Monday morning court sitting. As an example of the efficiency of the mid-Victorian police, the case of George Thomason would be hard to best.

The ordinary beat constable was also becoming professional. Just after midnight on Sunday 18th July 1857 the High Street constable noticed that the door to George Scott's warehouse in Tyndall's Wynd was flapping open. Gathering reinforcements, the officer forced the door and arrested a man they found inside. When they questioned their prisoner, the police found he was a ticket of leave convict called James Brown, who kept a legal grocery in the Scouringburn. He was armed with a knife and wore rubber overshoes to deaden his footsteps when engaged on his nighttime activities. A search of his house found piles of stolen property, over 200 skeleton keys, carpenter's tools, hinges, hammer heads, a jemmy and keys that fit Mr Scott's warehouse. Even more incriminating were the German silver chains and single gold chain that had been stolen from Alston's jewellery shop in the High Street and a number of cheques stolen from Smith's china shop in Castle Street. That single observant police constable had brought a notable career thief to justice, and he stands as an example of the growing professionalism of the Dundee police. However, there was still plenty crime in Dundee.

10
Thieves of the 1860s

Buried Treasure

Although theft and robbery were common throughout the whole of the nineteenth century, the 1860s spawned a clutch of thieves whose exploits rocked Dundee. Usually in their teens and early twenties, most were opportunist thieves who broke into houses and shops alike, stole any small items they could and quickly squandered what they stole. Yet very few were even moderately successful in anything other than causing trouble to their victims. Sometimes even those who appeared to escape justice could be undone by a chance encounter.

In early May 1861, a seaman named Charles Wilson noticed something half-buried just above the high tide mark on the beach near Craigie Terrace. When he investigated, he unearthed a bread rack, which he took home – seamen were not the highest paid workers and any sort of bonus was always welcome. About a fortnight later he was back, walking along the same stretch of coast but this time accompanied by his sister. It was natural that he should look in the same place, and perhaps he was not surprised that he saw something else protruding from the sand. One article was welcome, two were suspicious and Wilson, or perhaps his sister, informed the police.

Within minutes of digging, the police found an entire basket of silver plate, each one marked with the letter 'C'. There were nine silver teaspoons, twelve silver toddy ladles, two plated trays, a magnificent silver teapot, silver tongs, silver snuff boxes and wine sliders, gold studs, table spoons and mustard pots and, pride of the collection, two silver jugs embossed with a crest and the motto 'God Send Grace'. This final piece immediately identified the hoard. The police were ecstatic. They had made a major discovery and solved one of the largest household burglaries committed in the area for years.

Many people put the blame on the people of Broughty Ferry for the crime in their area. Not that they had particularly criminal tendencies. Broughty was as law-abiding as anywhere else in Scotland, but also had its share of those who lived on the shaded side of the law. Nevertheless, there was not a single constable to patrol the village and not even a watchman to cast his rheumy eyes over the fishermen's cottages and the increasing numbers of detached villas and extensive mansions of the incomers who had made their wealth from Dundee's textile trade.

As Dundee became busier with trade and the number of mills and factories increased, many of the wealthier citizens opted to leave the smoke-filled streets and head east. Here, beside the long-sweeping beaches of Broughty and backed by green countryside, solid villas sprang up. What had once been only a small fishing village was rapidly becoming one of the most desirable suburbs of Scotland. However, the good and the great were canny with their pennies and had no desire to add to their rates by paying for a police force. The Dundee policemen did not work outwith the perimeters of the burgh, so Broughty was wealthy and Broughty was unprotected.

For a man such as Thomas MacMillan, the houses of Broughty were an open invitation. He was a professional thief, a man who had already served time for burglary and who had returned to Dundee. At the beginning of June 1858 he selected a victim.

Archibald Crichton was not as stupendously rich as the jute barons, but he was certainly not poor and the manner in which he displayed his wealth could have been termed ostentatious. He was also gregarious, and on the last Wednesday in May 1858 he held a magnificent dinner party in his semi-detached villa in Douglas Terrace. To impress his guests, he used his silver plate dinner service, each piece of which was engraved with the letter 'C' to prove he owned it. When the dinner was over and the guests departed, the servants washed the silver dinner service but did not put it away; that would wait until Thursday morning.

Thomas McMillan, however, had other ideas. He had only to wait a short time before the last weary servant extinguished the last light in the house, and another few moments to ensure everybody was safely in bed. In Dundee he would be a suspicious character, lurking around an obviously prosperous street in the wee small hours of the morning, but without police or watchmen to challenge him, he loitered undisturbed. When he judged it safe, MacMillan walked warily to the rear of Crichton's house

© Courtesy of Dundee Art Galleries and Museums

Jute Factory Workers

and quietly opened the window of the water closet. Presumably he had already reconnoitred the house and knew exactly which window was best, but the water-closet window was small so he had to squeeze through. Once inside he lit a candle and by its flickering yellow light moved immediately to the silver, ready-washed and neatly stacked as if waiting just for him.

It was the work of only a few moments to remove the pieces, stuff some in his pockets and others in a bag, and then climb back out of the window and escape into the silent street. Experienced in his profession, MacMillan must have guessed the value of about £150, about two years' wages for a skilled artisan, and he would know that no normal Dundee fence could handle so much stolen property, particularly as it was all clearly marked with the letter 'C'. Accordingly, he selected a piece of beach above the high tide mark, stored it in his memory and buried most of the bulkier items. It would be safe there until he came to dig it up once more. Keeping some of the smaller items to prove the value of his haul, he returned home.

There was pandemonium in the Crichton household when the theft was discovered. Despite the Broughty disinclination to pay extra rates for their own police force, Archibald Crichton had no scruples about calling the Dundee police. Constable MacGregor left his normal beat to travel to the Ferry. He noticed the open window, reasoned there might be two people involved, and set about catching the thief. First he notified the police offices in Aberdeen, Edinburgh and Glasgow, and then printed notices describing the missing silverware and forwarded them to police superintendents around the country. After that the police began asking questions and seeking out their informants.

The Victorian police depended on informants. Many of their successes were due to their maintaining a network of people who lived on the fringe of the underworld, who knew what was happening and who were quite prepared to welsh on their comrades. This case was no exception. It was a colleague of MacMillan who gave the police his name, and told them exactly where he would be found.

In the meantime the good folk of the Ferry were rocked by another burglary. This time the station house of the Edinburgh and Perth Railway had been hit. The thief, or thieves, had struck early on Sunday morning, smashing a pane of glass, opening a window and removing the cash box, with about £1 3/- inside. As the Ferry folk pondered the price of a police force, MacMillan and the constables played out their own personal drama.

MacMillan had decided to take a small sample of the silver to Glasgow to find a fence, but when he entered the railway station the police were waiting for him. Snapping on the handcuffs, the officers hustled him down to the police office to be searched. When they found several small pieces of Mr Crichton's silverware, some of it hammered flat for easy storage, MacMillan could not deny the theft. He admitted who he was and did not struggle when the police took him to the Procurator Fiscal's office and stripped him naked in case they had missed anything the first time. Indeed they had; between his underwear and his skin they found an impressive collection of silk handkerchiefs, stolen from a shop in Montrose the previous month. It was Wednesday 7th June, less than a week since MacMillan had gloated over his silver future.

When the police asked MacMillan where the rest of the silver was, he told them nothing. He remained cool, even when he was called to the bar of the Circuit Court, and when the judge sent him back to jail he still gave nothing away. He listened when people spoke of the police searching for the silverware, but said only that it was hidden in a place it would never be found. The thought of a small fortune in silver waiting for him must have sweetened the long, lonely, drab days in confinement, and he might well have been released to dig up his hoard like a latter-day Treasure Island, had it not been for a wandering seaman and his inquisitive sister.

Others were more typical thieves, petty criminals after petty gain and caught out by their own mistakes. In one case a thief was caught out simply because he changed his drawers.

Captured by his Drawers

It would have seemed like any other Friday morning to Peter Reid. He had left his work the previous evening as normal, and was now returning to open up, as he always did. Unlocking the door, he stepped inside the shop and stopped in shock. Where he had left everything neat and tidy, ready to start business, now the place was a mess, with all the drawers hanging out and their contents strewn across the floor. He looked for a second, and then ran further inside, seeing the shambles and the wide-open back window and realised he had been robbed. It took only moments to send for his boss, John Earl Robertson, and before long the police were present, working out exactly what had happened.

There had been at least two burglars: John Norrie, a millworker of Blackness Road and James Gormally of Hawkhill, and perhaps they were helped by James's brother Owen. All were between thirteen and sixteen years old and they had already had a busy time. On Tuesday 16th January 1866 they had broken into a shop in Yeaman Shore and stolen £1 from David Clark, pork curer. The following Tuesday they broke into the Overgate premises of Grandy and Scott, ironmongers, and found 12/-. Next was the night of Thursday 1st February when they broke into Durham and Sons, the High Street stationers, where they stole a handy pair of scissors, printer's types and the quite sizeable sum of £3 in cash – more than many working men earned in three weeks.

Now they were busy again. James Gormally and John Norrie were in the High Street, and they knew exactly what they were doing. The houses were quite low there, so they entered Mint Close that led northward behind Reform Street, climbed up a lamppost, and stretched onto the roof of a house. Their target was the shop opposite; it was the work of a few moments to remove a pane of glass from the cupola, but either the rope they had brought was too short or they thought it too dangerous to attempt entry that way so looked for something easier. They found a back window, forced it open, clambered down the rope and entered Spence and Company in Reform Street, one of Dundee's leading drapers, hoping for rich pickings.

Despite their youth they were experienced burglars and had come prepared with matches. By their light they saw a desk opposite. Forcing the drawer open, they looked at the pile of money for only a second before scooping it into a bag. It was mainly copper but with a sprinkling of silver. In total there was about £3 15/- in value, the change ready for the following day's trade, which made quite a bulky package. With the cash bundled

© Courtesy of Dundee Art Galleries and Museums

Reform Street

up, they ransacked the remainder of the shop, hauling open all the drawers, peering in presses, and generally ensuring they had missed nothing. With money being their only object, they did not really concern themselves with the stock, but stole a few small items that they could use themselves.

As well as a coat and a vest they found in a small room, they took a pair of men's drawers each and Gormally, no doubt to the accompaniment of ribald comments, dragged off his own threadbare, tattered and much-used drawers, dropped them on the floor and pulled on the new pair in exchange. Norrie slid on the other pair of drawers but did not leave his own: perhaps he had none to leave. Placing the money into three handkerchiefs they dragged a drawer to the back window, put a pair of ladders on top, slipped outside and escaped down the outside wall. Perhaps because they would look conspicuous wandering through Dundee with clinking copper coins, they hid the bags on top of a chimney high on the roof and returned home, with Gormally keeping the coat and vest.

Next day Peter Reid discovered the robbery and the police were called. Immediately discarding the missing pane of glass in the cupola, they found the forced back window and the scuff marks of feet on the wall down which the intruders had climbed. They knew by the size of the footprints that at least one of the intruders had been a boy, and they conjectured that he had entered the shop first and had then opened the door for an older accomplice. They also commented on the way the place had been searched for money, with little else taken.

Armed with the clue of the discarded drawers, the police began a systematic search for the burglars. Moving through the streets, wynds and closes of Dundee, they questioned all the most obvious suspects and searched those who could not give an account of their actions on the nights of the break-ins. Usually when shops or houses were robbed, the police would check the pawn shops for the stolen articles and often found the thief by reading the name on the pawn ticket, but that was not possible when only money was taken. Their best chance of success was to trace the few items of clothing that had been stolen.

While the police were searching, James Gormally was busily recovering the money. Teaming up with Norrie again and roping in a shoemaker named Robert Williamson, he returned with them to the Mint Close. Gormally climbed up a water spout – drain pipe – and recovered the bags of money. They divided it between them, with Williamson clutching about five shillings in copper and Gormally seemingly keeping all the silver, about 12/6. Norrie returned to his lodgings, where there was a man named William More. With no privacy in such places, More remarked on Norrie's new drawers and said he might have been better to buy himself a shirt.

'I've plenty of money,' Norrie said, then he told More about the theft and passed over some loose change. With More for company he bought a shirt from a pawnbroker.

On 5th February the police made a breakthrough. Detective officers Stirling and Ferguson were walking down the Vault when they saw Williamson, who they already suspected of being a fence. As they arrested him, John Norrie appeared. He stared at the detectives for a second and then turned and ran. While Stirling held Williamson, Ferguson chased, caught and arrested Norrie. Taking both men back to Bell Street, the police questioned and searched them. When they saw Norrie's brand new drawers, they knew they had their man. They also knew Norrie's associates so waited outside the Gormallys' house until they returned and snatched them up.

On 6th February Norrie and the Gormally brothers were questioned and remitted to the Procurator Fiscal, but before the case came to trial Owen was released for not being involved. Norrie confessed everything and was sentenced to five years in a Reformatory; James Gormally appeared before Sheriff Ogilvy and a jury on 14th April. Although he pleaded not guilty, both Norrie and Williamson identified him as being the principal in the robbery.

Gormally's father tried to defend him, saying he wanted his son to learn a trade. He claimed James was working at a mill and attending night school. He also said his son was a quiet lad and had never been out all night before. Sheriff Ogilvy, however, did not agree. He already knew the Gormally clan, having had others of that name standing before him, so ignoring the father's appeals, he sent James Gormally to gaol for fourteen days, and then ordered him to Rossie Reformatory for the next five years.

That should have been the end of the Reform Street robbery case. However, James Gormally was not a youth to submit to authority so easily. A Reformatory was intended to be exactly what the name suggested; a place where wild young men were reformed, a place they entered as thieves and blackguards and emerged with better characters, ready to take their places in the ranks of the respectable. Five years of such training did not appeal to Gormally, and on 27th May, he escaped and once again appeared before the sheriff. Three months in jail and he was free to prowl the streets again, while John Norrie remained behind the walls of Rossie Reformatory.

An Unsuccessful Career Thief

While it is possible to feel sympathy for criminals whose circumstances have left them with little choice but to steal to survive, others deliberately choose theft and violence as a way of life. David Crockatt was one of the latter. He was a career thief who led others astray and did not hesitate to use violence when it suited him. Probably worse, by Victorian standards, he also denied his own mother. Crockatt was not one of the shifting unemployed who lived by their wits; he seems to have avoided crime, or at least avoided being caught in criminal activity until a relatively late age. He had a respectable job in a mill and lived in Temple Lane, which was a decent address in a hard-working quarter of the town. It seems his lifestyle was of his own choosing. In his own way he was an example of the pointless, profitless, utterly shiftless criminal class which infested Victorian cities and which still exists in the sordid underbelly of society.

It was in February of 1868 that the then sixteen-year-old Crockatt first came to the attention of the police. Along with fifteen-year-old John

Hutcheson, he appeared at the Dundee Sheriff Criminal Court on a charge of housebreaking. On 28th January the two youths had climbed onto the roof of Mr Anthony Carrick's farrier business in Gellatly Street, removed a few slates and lowered themselves inside to see what they could steal. Both pleaded guilty but Crockatt claimed that they had not originally planned to steal anything. He said they had been chasing a pigeon and when the bird fluttered inside the building they had taken off the tiles to follow it. According to Mr Douglas, who defended them, they were good boys really; he apologised profusely for their poor behaviour.

Not quite so sure about their innocence but obviously willing to afford them the benefit of the doubt, the sheriff gave them a further fortnight in jail to augment the two weeks they had already spent waiting for trial. Crockatt was hardly released when he was back in trouble, and again pigeons figured.

On 17th March a millworker named Alexander Bennet appeared before Provost Hay at the Police Court. Bennet claimed to be twelve-and-a-half, although his father said he was fourteen. He was charged with stealing five pigeons from Mr C. Kerr's dovecot in Broughty Ferry Road two days previously. Co-accused was David Crockatt, who Bennett's father said was the instigator who had led his son astray. Unfortunately, Crockatt failed to appear, so the police searched him out and dragged him to court. When he pleaded guilty the judge ordered him fifteen stripes of the birch.

The weals must have still been throbbing when Crockatt next appeared before Provost Hay, this time charged with stealing a fourteen-pound tin of strawberry jam from the confectionery workshop of John Low and Sons in New Inn Entry. Once more it was a low-level crime and once again he had acted with another boy. This time Neil Stevenson of Blackness Road was his companion, but like Crockatt, Stevenson had already been twice convicted of theft. Provost Hay remitted both to the Procurator Fiscal, and Crockatt was sent to prison.

Perhaps the experience sobered him, but Crockatt was quiet for a while. Then, in August 1868 he was suspected of being involved in a break-in at David Colville's grocer shop in South Union Street. Rather than a few pigeons or a jar of jam, this time there were eleven shillings in cash and a dozen postage stamps. It was still small-scale stuff, but these persistent robberies were what spoiled a decent community. The police knew there were at least three young men involved; they caught William Mackay and John Lindsay and after a jury found them guilty they were sentenced to eighteen months in jail.

Whether Crockatt was guilty or not, he slipped out of Dundee to live in Edinburgh for a few months, and when he came back in November he probably thought the dust had settled. Nearly as soon as he set foot back in his native streets he was arrested again. However when they began to question him, the police found themselves in difficulties. The youth they had arrested claimed he was not David Crockatt, but somebody called Miller. There was a cure for that, though, and the police knocked on the door of Crockatt's mother, dragged the poor woman to the police office and presented her with their suspect.

But there was still confusion. Although Mrs Crockatt agreed that she was looking at her son David, the young man refused to acknowledge her, and continued to say he was Miller. Even when Mrs Crockatt collapsed into tears and embraced him, the man denied her. It was only when he realised that the police would not believe him that he also began to cry and admitted he was indeed her son.

For the next year or two, Crockatt was a frequent visitor to the courts and nearly a resident in Dundee jail. Shop breaking was his speciality, and as the records only speak of the crimes for which he was officially accused or tried, it is difficult to judge how successful, or otherwise, he was. He was in the Police Court in August and before the bar of the Sheriff Criminal Court in December, both times on charges of house-breaking or shop breaking. The Sheriff Court found him guilty of the break-in at David Colville's South Union Street grocer's shop and awarded him twelve months. For that year Dundee was free of him, but he was released in December 1869. Within the month he was back in trouble again, accused of breaking into O'Farrell's pawnbroker's in North Tay Street on the Tuesday night or Wednesday morning and stealing £3 in silver and copper coins. By now Crockatt was living at Dudhope Crescent, a handy hundred yards or so from the prison where Provost Yeaman ordered him detained until the judges of the Spring Circuit Court could decide what best to do with him.

For the best part of four months Crockatt remained confined in Dundee Jail, but at the beginning of May the Circuit judges rolled into town. While the prisoners remained in their bleak cells the Lords Deas and Jerviswoode held a lavish levee in the Royal Hotel before driving to the Sheriff Court Buildings in a horse and four with a military escort and all the pomp and ceremony that the Victorians did so well. To assist the learned judges, Mr H. Moncrieff acted as Advocate Depute, while a Mr Smith would defend Crockatt. It was a splendid array of wigs and gowns that surveyed the ragged accused with their prison pallor and knowledge that these well-fed, well-bred men had the power to imprison them for a terrifyingly long period because of a relatively minor crime.

The charge was simple: theft by housebreaking. The method was also simple: Crockatt was accused of bending the iron stanchions that protected the back window of O'Farrell's pawnshop, forcing open the inside wooden shutter and entering to steal £2 7/- in silver and fifteen shillings in copper. He pleaded not guilty and probably hoped the jury would ignore his four previous convictions for theft.

George O'Farrell, the pawnbroker, was first to give his evidence. He said he left the shop at about nine o'clock on the night of 18th January and next morning he had been robbed. His money had been removed from the cash drawer and the central bar of the back window had been drawn apart, and with the Victorian love of detailed statistics he added that rather than their normal five and a half inches apart they were seven and a half inches apart. The window had been raised and the front door was locked. So far there was nothing new; all Mr O'Farrell had done was confirm he had been robbed by somebody coming through the back window.

Now he gave his only evidence to implicate Crockatt. He said he had seen Crockatt looking in the window on the 17th, just as he was putting money in a box. With the window being four feet tall, Mr O'Farrell claimed that a boy could have got in. At that point at last some of the jury must have looked at Crockatt. He was a short, slight man and after months on prison fare it is unlikely he was carrying any excess fat.

It was perhaps a mistake for Mr O'Farrell to add that a police officer had put his head through the gap, for Mr Smith, defending Crockatt, turned the statement to his advantage, using humour against the pawn-broker.

'And is an officer's head as large as a boy's body?'

If he said it was as large, O'Farrell might have been accused of ridiculing the police. If he said it was not, he would be damaging his case. Instead he tried to bluster by saying:

'I don't know but he looked in between the bars.'

As the audience laughed, Mr Smith must have known he was a small step closer toward creating a bond of sympathy between Crockatt and the jury.

The next witness was less easy to manipulate. Peter Duff was a criminal officer, a detective, and his evidence could have been damning. When he searched the pawnshop he had found part of a buckle and when arrested, Crockatt had two half crowns, two shilling pieces and eleven pence halfpenny in copper – nearly eight shillings altogether, which was quite a decent sum for a man not a month out of jail. One of the buckles on Crockatt's braces was also broken, and although he claimed to have broken it at home, the broken part exactly matched the piece Duff had found. Possibly even more damning for a respectable Victorian jury: Crockatt was known to have the character of a common thief.

A blacksmith agreed that the two broken parts belonged to the same buckle, 'because no man could make the same buckle joint'. Nevertheless, when pressed by Mr Smith he agreed he had seen that type of buckle before. It therefore was not unique.

The Police Surgeon, Doctor George Pirie, said when he examined Crockatt on 18th January he had an abrasion on his shoulder. The sort of mark somebody might get by scraping against a hard surface. Although Doctor Pirie did not say Crockatt might have scraped himself squeezing between two iron bars, the inference was obvious.

Catherine Crockatt, the already-denied mother, said her son was not at home on the night of the robbery. Crockatt himself claimed to have stayed overnight with a man called Michael Downs, but Downs disagreed. On the surface there seemed to be quite a pile of evidence against Crockatt, but it was all circumstantial. A broken buckle that could have belonged to anybody, a half-seen glance through a window, money in his pocket, a scraped shoulder and a lie as to his whereabouts. The jury were not overly convinced and a majority found the case not proven.

David Crockatt was free to go and steal again, which he did. Either he was a compulsive thief or just a man with an overwhelming confidence in his ability to evade justice, but within a week he was back under arrest. On this occasion he was suspected of having broken into John Milne's grocer and spirit dealer's shop in the Lower Pleasance. Once again there was little subtlety in the robbery; the shop had two windows, one larger than the other and both protected by wooden shutters. The thieves had simply torn out one of the planks of the shutter outside the small window, hauled back the restraining bolts and pulled open the window. They had stolen the till, with between fifteen shillings and a pound in change, and escaped out the same window.

A mill watchman saw three men emerge from the window and alerted the police, who arrested two men that same night. One was Neill Stevenson and the other was David Crockatt. When the police searched them they both had money and Mr Milne's sister, who also worked in the shop, claimed to identify one of the coins. She said a customer had handed it to her only the previous day.

Once again Crockatt's luck held, for although he was remitted to the Procurator Fiscal, he was not charged for that particular robbery either.

Nevertheless, while a more sensible or cautious man would have kept out of trouble for a while, Crockatt seemed hell-bent on thievery. On 13th May another shop was broken into and once again Crockatt was arrested. This time there were four others also accused: Neil Stevenson and Peter McDonald of Scouringburn, Donald Fraser of Ash Lane and John Johnstone of Cherryfield. Again the thieves had escaped with petty quantities: half a pound of tobacco, four pounds of cheese and three shillings in copper coins, but the amount was irrelevant, the repetition was what mattered. Now Crockatt was thrust back into Dundee Jail to await the autumn sitting of the Circuit Court.

The Dundee Circuit Court did not meet until 5th September, with the Lord Justice Clerk and Lord Cowan presiding. The police had been busy, and while some of their original suspects had been released, others had been arrested. Now Crockatt and Stevenson had Peter McFall and John Johnstone as co-accused. They stood charged with breaking into David Munro's shop in Lochee Road on 13th May and as expected, they pleaded not guilty.

David Munro gave his statement first. He said he left his shop between nine and ten o'clock on the night of Thursday 12th May but about three on Friday morning a policeman woke him with the news he had been robbed. There had been no subtlety in the break in: the door had been forced open by bursting the bolts and the money drawer torn out. Between three and five shillings had been stolen, and a purse that held a halfpenny, which he called a cent. That small coin was important, for Munro had kept it for years, never having seen one quite like it before. Some cheese and tobacco were also missing.

Constable Ward had seen all the prisoners together with young Donald Fraser in the Scouringburn. As soon as they noticed him, one had sworn and said, 'Here's that bugger. We'd better shift – he knows us,' and they disappeared up Milne's West Wynd. About half-past one Ward saw them again in Douglas Street, and quarter of an hour after that they were in Smellie's Lane, about 300 yards from Munro's shop. By that time Constable

Ward had joined up with Constable McIsaac, and the sight of two policemen sent the suspects running down Blinshall Street.

As the youths tried to hide in the shadows, the police followed. Constable Ward heard somebody curse and say, 'It's no' fairly divided,' but then the suspects passed beyond the bounds of his beat and he had to leave them. When he passed Munro's shop just before one o'clock the premises were secure, but when he returned at three the door had been burst open.

There was a whole raft of police constables involved. Constables Cuthbert and Forbes followed the suspects; Constable McIsaac arrested Johnstone and Fraser and Constable Abbott arrested Crockatt. Constable John Graham arrested McFall in Brown Street and later raided Neil Stevenson's house, hauled him out of bed by the hair and dragged him to Bell Street. When Crockatt was arrested he wore no stockings, but Abbott found one in his pocket and the second, with a piece of tobacco inside, at the spot where he was arrested. McFall had two shillings and sixpence in his pocket. The police also found a piece of cheese in the Lochee Road.

The criminal officers Henry Ferguson and William Bremner said the prisoners were all common thieves and, according to Bremner, whenever Crockatt was released from prison he haunted the streets of Dundee in the company of 'famous thieves'.

As the prisoner least hardened by crime, the police leaned most heavily on Donald Fraser, but it was more likely his mother's influence that made him co-operate. When he spoke at the trial he admitted knowing all four of the prisoners, and agreed he had been with them on the night of 12th May. According to his account, the evening had started innocently in Barrack Park, 'where we lay till about one o'clock'. After that they wandered up Lochee Road but when they passed Munro's shop Peter McFall said, 'We'll try this ane.'

Fraser was ordered to keep watch while the others broke in. He said the whole operation took about ten minutes and Peter McFall was out first, carrying money in his bonnet. Crockatt was next, saying, 'Here's tobacco, lads,' and he was followed by Stevenson with the cheese, while

Johnston came out empty-handed. As soon as they left the shop they began to run down Lochee Road, with Stevenson already discarding the cheese. The police followed them up Blinshall Street and then they separated. Fraser said that he and Johnston were in Brown Street when they were arrested.

Neil Stevenson's mother gave a slightly different story. She agreed that her son had gone out on the night of the 12th, 'to get some fun', he had said, but he was back before eleven and she saw him in bed beside his brother Nicholas before she locked the door at twelve. She was up at five to waken Nicholas and Neil was still there and 'he rose because I bade him get a job of work'. When he said the police had chased him she told him to stay in and lock the door, and she was at work when a girl told her he had been arrested. Her third son was already in prison for 'capering in the street'.

The defence council for McFall called up a man named Henry Goodwin who claimed that he was with McFall in a public house until eleven o'clock, and after that they walked to Goodwin's house together. Only then did they meet Fraser, who was with two girls. By this time it was twenty to one in the morning and Fraser asked McFall to give him a dram. Pulling out a bag of coppers, Fraser boasted he had plenty money. When a couple of policemen came into view Fraser gave the money to McFall and walked rapidly away.

The jury were not convinced and found all four prisoners guilty. The Lord Justice Clerk said, 'It is with the greatest possibly difficulty' he did not sentence Crockatt and Stevenson to at least seven years' penal servitude. He added that they had 'little knowledge what a sentence of penal servitude is' and they 'have very little notion what it entails upon the person subjected to it'. Instead he sentenced Stevenson and Crockatt to eighteen months' imprisonment. The others were given lesser sentences, and McFall shouted, 'Cheer up, boys; I'll be back on Sunday.'

The others replied, 'Cheer up,' but only quietly. Even without penal servitude, eighteen months in a Victorian prison was not a cheering prospect.

When Crockatt re-emerged at the beginning of March 1872 he was still only twenty years old and had spent most of his late teenage years in jail. Perhaps he had some intention to reform, but possibly his experiences had embittered him against society in general and the police in particular. It is equally possible he had a natural truculence that made it impossible for him to conform to even the slightest show of authority.

On 18th March 1872, Crockatt strolled around the Scouringburn area with a couple of prostitutes. About two in the afternoon they stopped to talk in a close at the top of Brown Street. The two policemen who challenged them might have genuinely believed they were blocking the passageway, or they might have been suspicious that Crockatt, a known thief, had something illegal in mind. Either way they asked all three to move on. The prostitutes obeyed but Crockatt refused, claiming he lived there. Although Sergeant William Carnegie knew that was a lie, he still gave Crockatt time to leave. Again the police asked him to move on, and again Crockatt refused, and when Constable Robb took hold of his arm to escort him to the pavement, Crockatt slipped his feet between Robb's ankles and punched him in the chest, knocking him down.

The result was inevitable. Carnegie and Robb put Crockatt under arrest, Crockatt resisted fiercely with fist and boot but was outnumbered and, after eighteen months on prison rations, outmuscled. He appeared before the Police Court on Thursday, with Bailie Chalmers and Superintendent Donald Mackay glowering at him. As usual, Crockatt pleaded not guilty. After hearing the evidence, Mackay asked if Crockatt had anything to say. He said no, there would be no point in speaking after the police had given their evidence. Mackay probably agreed. He said the police had acted in a 'prudent and gentle manner', and their conduct deserved the highest praise. Bailie Chalmers gave Crockatt another sixty days, the maximum he could award.

Crockatt threw him a look of contempt. 'That's not much,' he said.

That same year, David Crockatt committed his last recorded crime.

After four years of shop breaking and jail, he branched out into something different.

John Littlejohn was a lapper who lived in Charles Street. Sometime after midnight on Sunday 26th May he was walking up Dens Brae on his way home from work. He had just reached Bucklemaker Wynd when two men jumped on him. While one held him down and clapped a hand over his mouth to keep him quiet, the other went through his pockets and robbed him of what little money he had. Both attackers ran when a couple of late-night walkers arrived. One of the newcomers, Peter Gilligan, chased and brought down the smaller of the attackers, David Crockatt. When the police came, Crockatt resisted, but he was dragged once more to the police office.

On Monday 27th May David Crockatt of Dudhope Crescent appeared at the Police Court and Bailie Petrie remitted him to the Procurator Fiscal. He was ordered once more to appear in the Circuit Court in October. As usual, Crockatt pleaded not guilty and following the usual pattern, Littlejohn gave his evidence first. He named Crockatt as one of his attackers, and added that, while on his way to the police office, Crockatt had begged not to be identified or he would get ten years.

The other witnesses told the same story. William Duncan, a packer, saw Littlejohn being attacked, and shouted for Peter Gilligan to help. He had chased the second, taller attacker but had lost him. 'But' he confirmed, 'the little one is the prisoner.'

There could be no doubt about the verdict, and as Crockatt predicted, he got ten years of penal servitude. After he was sentenced he gave a mocking bow and said, 'Thank you, your lordship,' but the world heard no more of David Crockatt. Possibly the rigid, inhuman conditions of the crank – that diabolical wheel prisoners had to rotate 14,400 times a day – and the solitary system broke his spirit. It is difficult to feel sympathy for David Crockatt, for he was certainly not a pleasant person, but to have only five or six weeks' freedom in fourteen years surely argues about not only a failure in his own sordid life, but also a failure in the entire social system.

Crockatt was only one of a host of petty criminals in the area. Although Dundee, as the largest town in the area, was the centre of most illegal activity, the surrounding countryside could also be wild. Lying to the north of Dundee, the county of Forfarshire, now Angus, is one of the most fertile areas of Scotland. It includes the fruit-growing Strathmore and some of the finest farms as well as some of the most interesting castles and houses to be found anywhere. The northern portion of the county consists of an area known as the Angus Glens, which is in reality the southern hills of the Highlands. To the south is the low, fascinating range of the Sidlaw Hills, crossed by the whisky paths of the smugglers and allegedly recently used for dog fighting matches. Forfarshire was a frontier land between city and Highlands, town and country. Such areas do not breed quiet men and not everybody in this apparently peaceful countryside was law-abiding.

Armed Robbery at Auchterhouse

In the nineteenth century, many people did not consider poaching a crime, particularly when the game laws were intended to preserve the property of the landowner against the rural poor. Poachers were often somewhat ambiguous figures. Although some may well have been rural Robin Hoods, and most were just after the odd rabbit or two to supplement a meagre diet, others operated on a larger scale and would probably have been rogues wherever they lived. Such a man was James Robertson, a man of many addresses but who seems to have lived most often in Blairgowrie in Strathmore.

In the early morning of Wednesday 10th January 1866, somebody burgled the farmhouse of James Playfair at Kirkton of Auchterhouse. The house stood alone in the southern shadow of the Sidlaw Hills and James Playfair lived with his brother. There were also a handful of female servants inside the house. About a quarter of a mile away was the farm steading where the male farm servants lived, for in a period of high rural illegitimacy, young single men and women were often kept apart or under the watchful eye of respectable authority. The farmhouse was typically Scottish, a stone-built, uncompromising building of two stories that unflinchingly endured the winds and frosts, glaring from its tall windows over fields that stretched toward Dundee and the Firth of Tay. The Playfair brothers slept on the upper flat, with the servants on the ground floor, and on the Tuesday the brother was absent on some business. Not long after midnight, something abruptly woke Playfair from his sleep.

By the flickering light of a candle he saw three men in the room beside him. They all wore different disguises, and all had blackened their faces so they would not be recognised, but there was no mistaking the pistol that one thrust at Playfair's head. With a threat to shoot the farmer unless he complied, the intruder demanded to know where the money was. As Playfair stared, a second intruder raised an axe and said he would kill him if he tried to waken the servants or offer the slightest resistance.

Faced with two armed intruders and with a third hovering nearby, it is unlikely that Playfair had any intention of resisting. He obeyed at once, saying that his money was locked in his wardrobe, and showed where the keys were kept. The intruders did not relax; while the two armed men ensured Playfair did not resist, the third man, quieter but just as efficient, took the keys and opened the drawer of the wardrobe. He took out £84, which Playfair had put there temporarily until he carried it to the bank. He also lifted a gold watch.

Without searching any further, the three intruders gave a final chilling warning that if Playfair shouted out or warned the servants they would return and murder him in his own bed. Having seen the pistol, the axe and the determinedly disguised faces, Playfair thought it best to do exactly what they said. Only when the intruders were well clear of the house did he rush downstairs and waken the women. Once the alarm was given, the male servants stuffed powder and ball into a fowling piece and began to search the grounds and surrounding fields. However the intruders had not wasted the long minutes gained by their threat. The servants found no trace.

An inspection of the house was slightly more fruitful. Playfair worked out that the intruders entered the house by the parlour window. Once inside they had lighted their candle before climbing the stairs to the bedroom. They must have moved very quietly as they passed the door of the servants' bedroom without waking them, both going upstairs and coming back down. Such an action suggests that the intruders were men of iron nerve, and possibly hints that at least one of them might already know the layout of the house. Either way, the robbery had been well-planned.

With the initial search completed and with nothing to show for their trouble, a group of male servants travelled the six miles or so to Dundee. Knowing there were armed men hiding in the dark winter night, the journey must have been a bit nerve-racking, and the servants would have been glad to arrive at the gas-lit streets of Dundee. It was four in the morning when they reported to the police, and while the local constables came out immediately, Inspector Adams did not travel to Auchterhouse until after dawn.

News of the robbery spread quickly amongst the farming folk of the area, and they were all willing to give their meagre information, advice and suspicions to the Inspector. He spent the entire day in the area, asking questions, searching for clues and listening to all the rumours.

It seems to have been the case in the Victorian period that either the police made a quick arrest, or they did not make one at all. In this case, it was the former. Rather than the beloved country plods depicted in poor-quality films, the Forfarshire police asked all the correct questions, added what they learned to what they already knew of the wild men of the fields and glens, they set out after an obvious suspect.

The robbery had been committed in the very early morning of the Wednesday, and by the Saturday the county police had made their arrest. The robbery having been so well-planned and so expertly executed, the police knew they were not looking for a novice, nor probably a stranger to the district, for in rural areas any stranger would be immediately noticed. Instead they concentrated on local men who had a history of crime, and that shortened their list considerably. Then they investigated the whereabouts of such people, and the list shortened some more. One name stood out. James Robertson.

James Robertson was a bad man with a list of offences that stretched way back. Sometimes he lived in Arbroath, sometimes at Green Tree by Blairgowrie on the fringe of the open country that stretched to the Angus glens, but just recently he had blessed Dundee with his presence. He was a poacher of note, being known throughout Forfarshire as well as in neighbouring Perthshire. However, although he had frequently been caught and accused, he had a bad habit of sliding away just before the local sheriff required his presence at the bar, so many of his convictions were made in his absence. The robbery at Auchterhouse only gave the police another excuse to search him out, for there were a number of warrants issued for him for offences against the Day Trespass Act and a cell lacking his presence. Arresting him, however, was not so easy for he was a will-o'-the wisp character, with no fixed home. But this time the police were determined.

They paid a call to his lodgings in Dundee and were not overly surprised to find him not at home. They made enquiries, and found he had been absent on the previous Tuesday night as well, which was what they had suspected and, probably, hoped for. Now that their suspicions were justified, all they had to do was find him. Whatever his skills as a poacher and his ability to plan and execute a clever robbery, Robertson was less adept at hiding his success. A few more enquiries and the police knew he had been back in Dundee on the Wednesday, but by the Friday had left. They followed the paper trail to Forfar and toured the public houses.

On Friday evening the police found their man. Rather than hiding in some obscure corner or skulking in disguise, James Robertson was in a Forfar public house, drinking with a fine set of poachers and local ne'er-do-wells. While other men might have tried to blend in and look incon-spicuous, Robertson had donned full Highland dress, with rings gleaming on his fingers, pins on his plaid and a silver-mounted sporran. Like a true Highland warrior, he fought back hard when the police moved in, but he was outnumbered and overpowered. While some of the police dragged his battered body to the police office, others searched the area where he had been sitting. It did not take long to find Playfair's gold watch beneath Robertson's chair, and someone in the pub told them he had been showing it off to his comrades.

With such damning evidence and a history of poaching and trespassing, there was little doubt that Robertson was guilty. The judge gave him five years, and it is unlikely that many people in Forfarshire really regretted his absence. He was certainly a colourful character, but unlike Robin Hood, he spent the proceeds of his robberies on himself, not on helping the poor.

11

Crimes Against Children

Although the Victorian apprehension of youth crime is mirrored in today's society, children were every bit as likely to be victims as perpetrators. While some crimes, such as computer hacking or witchcraft, are period-specific, others are common to every era. Some criminals may invoke sympathy, particularly when the passage of time paints a gloss of romance over what was probably a pretty sordid reality, but others have always been seen only as vile. Child abuse of any type is arguably one of the most heinous possible crime and one which seems to have been relatively uncommon, or at least seldom reported, in Dundee. However, in 1880 there was one particularly shocking case, made worse by the fact that the abuser was also the child's mother.

'I Do Not Care if the Child is Dead'

Mary Ann Henderson was a twenty-six-year-old widow. She had been married to Thomas Henderson, a labourer, but he had died when she was only nineteen, leaving her with a one-year-old daughter, also named Mary Ann. Like so many desperate young mothers before and since, Mrs Henderson turned to her mother for help, and she, Mary Ann Hutton, took in the child. That situation lasted for six years, with young Mary

Ann Henderson living with her grandparents in Milnathort, Kinross-shire, and her mother elsewhere. It must have come as a shock to the child when her mother took her back and, after a short spell in Milnathort, relocated to Dundee. By that time young Mary Ann was already deteriorating, with sores breaking out on her body, and the change from a small town to a bustling, busy industrial centre must have been incredibly traumatic for her.

However, things were about to get worse. About three years before, Mrs Henderson had had a romantic fling that left her pregnant, so in 1880 she had two children to care for. There was Mary Ann Henderson, now aged eight, and a toddling two-year-old. For some reason, Mary Ann Henderson took a dislike to the daughter she barely knew, and nearly as soon as they arrived in Dundee, she began to treat her with abominable cruelty. It was not difficult for a young, active woman to find work in Dundee in the 1880s, and when Mrs Henderson was not working at one of the many mills, she was busily sewing sacks at home.

Nobody will ever know exactly when the beatings began, but in April 1880, when Mrs Henderson and her children lived in Session Street, she attacked young Mary Ann with a broom and a leather belt, striking her on the head, back, arms and other places. Catherine Murray, who worked in a mill, lodged beside the Henderson family, and witnessed the cruelty. She saw how well the little girl looked after the toddler, made herself busy about the house and sometimes sewed sacks to bring in some money, but nothing she did could please her mother.

When the case eventually came to court, Catherine Murray described how Mrs Henderson called her daughter horrible names and said she did not like her. Even when Murray asked, Mrs Henderson did not say why she disliked her daughter, but used the heavy navvy's belt whenever the inclination took her.

In May of that year Murray accompanied the family when they moved to a house in St Peter Street and the beatings continued. As well as striking her with a broom and a leather belt, Mary Ann also knocked down and kicked her daughter. On one horrific occasion she stripped the girl naked and tied her to a bed before slapping and striking her with her hands. Tiring of this, Mrs Henderson whipped the underweight, sickly child with a rope's end, leaving her bruised, wealed and bleeding.

'I do not care,' Mrs Henderson said, 'if the child is dead.'

Living in the house next door, Mrs McGee said she saw Mrs Henderson beating Mary Ann with a besom, knocking her down and kicking her when she was on the ground. She also said that the child was kept constantly busy sewing sacks and if she ever looked up she was 'sure of a leathering'.

All Catherine Murray's attempts to intervene were fruitless; she could do nothing to protect young Mary Ann. According to Murray, the beatings took place mainly at night when the neighbours were in bed, and without any reason. Murray also said that Mrs Henderson was a very passionate woman who disliked everybody and who certainly never listened to the opinion or advice of others.

By August they lived in Miller's Land, Mid Wynd, and things continued as before, except now Mrs Henderson added a poker to her arsenal, striking Mary Ann on the head. Murray had moved out. Mrs Samson, who lived next door, knew everything that occurred as the wall between the two houses was so thin that, in her own words, she 'could hear the sound of a thread being pulled through a sack'. She said she heard young Mrs Henderson 'skelping' Mary Ann 'nearly every hour of the day'. When Mrs Samson tried to protect the girl, Mrs Henderson said she had a 'right to do what she liked' with her own child and anyway, 'she didna sew enough sacks'. Mrs Samson also thought Mary Ann had caused no offence.

Martin Hogan, another neighbour, said the opposite. Backed by his wife, he said he had never heard any noises from the Henderson household and to them the child looked perfectly all right.

The assaults continued until 11th November when Murray happened to meet young Mary Ann in the street. The child's face and head were cut and she was in such a pitiable state that Murray could not stand by and do nothing. Taking Mary Ann away from her mother, she looked after the child for a few days, contacted her grandmother and packed her off to Milnathort. Although beating children was the norm in the nineteenth century and Dundee was as hard and violent an industrial town as any, there was also a streak of genuine kindness that burst through at unexpected moments.

When the case came to the Sheriff Criminal Court Mrs Henderson pleaded not guilty, so everybody concerned, including the beleaguered child, had to appear.

Dr Pirie, who had examined Mary Ann, confirmed her body was covered in bruises, caused either by somebody's hand or some other blunt instrument. Her arm was in a particularly damaged state so she had to support it by a sling. The doctor thought the girl had been subjected to violence for a long time. However, Mrs Henderson said she hit her daughter because she stole things from a shop, spoke back to her and threw a sack at her.

Young Mary Ann still had a bandage around her head where her mother had struck her with a poker. Not surprisingly, she was extremely nervous when faced with an array of adult authority, but the sheriff proved his compassion by asking the child's grandmother to comfort her in the witness room. Only when Mary Ann was more controlled did he put her through the ordeal of answering questions.

Young Mary Ann's version of events did not differ much from that presented by the adults. She said her mother took her from her grandmother, moving first to Leith and then to Dundee. Her life was spent looking after the 'bairn', sewing sacks and being attacked by her mother who 'was aye bad to her'. Mary Ann had learned not to cry, for that just encouraged her mother to more violence. Despite what her mother claimed, she said she never threw a sack at her and never stole anything from a shop. The court must have been very quiet when the eight-year-old told the sheriff that her mother said she did not like her and said, chillingly, she would 'cut her up and get her out of the road'.

Once Mary Ann had given her evidence the sheriff again showed kindness, asking the grandmother to take her home. The child was not to be in the court when the verdict was given. She was no longer to face the woman who had abused her.

The jury had no doubt about Mrs Henderson's guilt, and the sheriff sent her to jail for a full fifteen months. To young Mary Ann, however, the best result must have been the sheer relief at being back with her grandmother.

Parents' Horrific Crimes

Mary Ann Henderson's case was disturbing enough, but at least it had a fairly satisfactory ending, at least for her. Elizabeth or Lizzie Urquhart, two years old and even more helpless, was not so fortunate. On Sunday 25th February 1883 her naked body was found stone dead in a tenement flat in Hilltown, murdered by her father.

David Urquhart lived in a two-storey tenement a stone's throw from Victoria Road. The building stood alone, hidden by those that front Hilltown and with only a single road passing it, on its way to a contractor's stable. The memory is long gone now, swept away within a half-forgotten improvement scheme but even in Urquhart's time it was a place of dilapidation and decay, the resort of the despairing and defeated. Here, in an attic virtually bare of furniture, Urquhart and Isabella Meffan lived as man and wife and brought up their three children. There was Davida, aged four, Elizabeth or Lizzie, aged two and the twelve-month-old Alexander.

It was about August 1882 when the Urquhart family arrived in Hilltown. Urquhart was a labourer, seldom in regular employment, working when there was work, or whenever the mood took him. Isabella Meffan, known as Mrs Urquhart, was a spinner, and on the occasion when both were at work the children were locked in the attic and left to their own devices. That suggests that there was no family to help or to witness anything that occurred in the house.

© Courtesy of Dundee Art Galleries and Museums

Tenement in Dundee

Urquhart was about thirty-three years old. He was an Arbroath man, straight-backed, about five foot nine with brown hair, a moustache and a small scar between his eyebrows. A member of the Forfar and Kincardine Militia, he habitually wore a dark silk cap, a dark brown coat out at the elbows, white moleskin trousers, brown shirt and militia boots. In 1880 he spent eight months in Perth Jail for assault, but a week before the murder he had been labouring at the docks.

The neighbours knew the Urquharts as an unhappy couple who argued a lot, while Urquhart showed no kindness toward his children and was said to be especially cruel to his two-year-old daughter, Lizzie. Only a few weeks before he had struck her so severely that her arm was sore days later. He was also found bathing her in water so hot that she screamed. At some earlier period Davida also suffered a broken arm. Urquhart had other punishments for his children, including making young Lizzie walk up and down the room carrying half a brick because he caught her licking jelly.

On the Saturday evening, Urquhart came home about half-past seven. He was at least partly drunk. His wife and children were sitting on the floor, for there was not even a stool in the house, and no fire. February in Dundee can be cold, and an attic flat with neither insulation nor heating is an uncomfortable place at best, but rather than coal, clothing or firewood, Urquhart had bought a bottle of whisky. He shared the whisky with his wife, allowing her three nips, and then they began to argue.

As so often when drink was involved, the argument became heated and Mrs Urquhart ran from her violent husband. Obviously terrified, she jumped over the banisters of the stair, landed on the landing eight feet below and fled to her friend Mrs Cleary for sanctuary. Urquhart watched her go and returned inside, slamming the door emphatically.

There were sundry bangs and noises from the flat for a few moments, as if Urquhart was chopping wood, and shortly after he came knocking at Mrs Cleary's door.

Mrs Urquhart, who had been sitting at the fire nursing a sore head and moaning, was scared, so Mrs Cleary hid her in a closet, but Urquhart only borrowed the key for the well outside, filled a pail with water and returned the key with a polite 'Thank you'. About ten that night Mrs Urquhart asked Bridget Mulraney, Mrs Cleary's sister-in-law who lived in the same house, to go upstairs for the coal pock. She obliged, but the house was in darkness with not even a fire to give light. Urquhart told her shortly there was no pock. Hearing the baby cry, Bridget asked, 'What's wrong with the bairn?'

'It's hungry,' Urquhart told her, and asked, 'Where's Isa?'

'I don't know,' Bridget said.

'You know brawly where she is,' Urquhart said. With the house so dark, Bridget could not see him, but she heard his voice distinctly.

'No,' Bridget denied, obviously scared to tell him.

Her fear was justified by Urquhart's next statement: 'When I get her in the morning I'll kick the belly out of her.'

Borrowing a basket from Mrs Cleary, Mrs Urquhart spent two pence on a basket of coal and left it at the door of her house. She did not go up alone, for Mrs Cleary accompanied either for physical or moral support, and a neighbour's boy carried a lantern in the dark stair. The house door was locked so Mrs Urquhart left the basket outside and returned to Mrs Cleary's house.

After that small excursion, the night was quiet. It was not until half-past eight on the Sunday morning that the tenants in the flat below heard Urquhart moving around, together with a strange knocking sound that they could not recognise. Telling themselves that Urquhart was probably chopping wood, they ignored it and continued with their lives.

In the meantime, Mrs Urquhart was awake. When she heard footsteps on the stairs outside she said, 'That'll be Dave,' and asked Mrs Cleary to 'look out ... and see what road he takes'.

Afraid of Urquhart, Mrs Cleary refused. She lit the fire instead, tidied up the fireplace, watched Mrs Urquhart sit beside it and suggested she should go back upstairs and feed the children.

'I'm afraid to go up,' Mrs Urquhart said, 'for he'll kick me.' Nevertheless, a few minutes later she took off her boots and crept upstairs. She was back immediately, crying hard. 'Lizzie's killed,' she said, and asked Mrs Cleary to go back with her. Still afraid, Mrs Cleary refused, but ran outside to search for a policeman. She found two.

Mrs Urquhart was correct: Lizzie, two years old, was dead and naked in her hammock. She lay on her back and her body, face and head were battered, bruised and damaged. There were long scars on her body but little blood; the purpose of the pail of water was now revealed. A later medical examination showed a damaged nose, abrasions around the eyes and on the forehead, bruised lips and ears, a bruised chest, groin, legs, back, buttocks, damaged spine and bruised arms. However the cause of death was a rupture of the liver that had caused a haemorrhage. Lizzie's father had probably kicked her to death.

There was a bloody shirt crumpled on the floor, blood spots on the floor and wall, and more on the shakedown on which the other two children lay. They were filthy and nearly naked, and young Alexander had a cut and sore face, but they were alive. The house was one of the poorest the policemen had ever seen. There was no furniture and the household possessions consisted of a couple of plates, a pail, a large bowl half filled with bloody water, and half a slice of bread. Four-year-old Davida said that after her father had beaten her sister he had lain down on the shake-down bed and said, 'She is dead now.'

Kindly authorities summoned a cab to take Mrs Urquhart and her remaining children to the poorhouse while the police began the hunt for Urquhart. The photograph taken when he was in Perth Prison was copied and circulated throughout Scotland, together with details of the clothes he was wearing when he left Hilltown. Although many of the police were on court duty, and others busy monitoring the roads for the cattle being driven to market, by noon on Sunday most were actively searching for the murderer. Some patrolled the roads out of the town, a detective took the train to search in Urquhart's old Arbroath stomping grounds but they found not a trace. People began to murmur he had committed suicide but the police continued their search. It seemed, however, that Urquhart had escaped.

When Isa had left him on the Saturday night, Urquhart was drunk. According to some of his friends, he was basically a kindly man, but drink altered his character so he became 'clean dark'. Perhaps he was enraged with Isabella, perhaps he was frustrated at his inability to find steady work, perhaps he saw his children as a burden, but for whatever reason he took out his anger on Lizzie. He kicked her on the face and the chest, he kicked her on the stomach, and he grabbed her and smashed her against the floor until she was dead. It was then that he fetched a bucket of water, washed her and laid her in bed.

When he woke on Sunday morning, Urquhart realised he had murdered his daughter and ran from the house. Passing through the town, he headed north by the Arbroath Road and hid out in a farm outhouse near Whitehills. When a baker followed him and told the police, they either disbelieved him or had no spare men for they took no action. When darkness fell, Urquhart ventured out, but after a few days without food he returned to Dundee to give himself up.

Just after ten on the morning of Tuesday 27th February, a man interrupted the sitting of the Police Court with the news that Urquhart was in Bell Street. Inspector Lamb hurried out of the court, arrested Urquhart and brought him into the court, where he sat, head down, until he was escorted the few yards to Dundee Jail. When the trial took place in the Dundee Circuit Court in April, Urquhart barely spoke and the jury found him guilty of culpable homicide. Possibly the most chilling evidence came from Davida, who said Urquhart had made Lizzie walk back and forward carrying a brick while he kicked her. The judge gave him twenty-one years' penal servitude.

Urquhart's case was of simple brutality, but there were different levels of parental cruelty to children. Helen Shaw was a drinking woman with two children, renowned for standing at her door in Polepark Road, swearing, cursing and annoying her neighbours. She had a boy just entering his teenage years and a girl of four, both of whom she treated abominably. She had a habit of locking them in the house while she spent the night drinking, to return in the early hours, hammer at the door and demand entrance.

One night in February 1865 she came back drunk and swearing, barged into the house and threw her four-year-old daughter, completely naked, into the morning. Luckily the neighbours took her in, looked after her and called the police. Shaw was given thirty days in jail in a case which shows callous unconcern and the kindness of a neighbour, both of which Dundee knew well.

Before the advent of the Welfare State the unemployed or unemployable would experience hunger and deprivation. The margin between security and the gutter could hinge on a single unguarded remark to an employer, and the difference between death by exposure and the comparative comfort of a night's shelter was only a few pennies. In these circumstances, the desperate and the unscrupulous would do anything for money. One of the most heartless crimes was child stripping.

Child Stripping

On Sunday 6th August 1852 a four-year-old child and her older brother were on the Lochee Road on their way to church in Dundee, with their parents walking a few moments behind. When a woman beckoned and held out a sweetie, the little girl followed her into a close, whereupon the woman, a factory worker named Isabella Shaw, robbed her of her valuable silk overcoat. The parents only found out when they reached Dundee, but the police were quick to trace and arrest Shaw, who was rewarded with sixty days in jail. Shaw's theft may have been a one-off, but Catherine Kidd seemed to have made a habit of child stripping. In the summer of 1856 she haunted the streets of Dundee, enticing young girls into dark closes, where she stripped them of all their clothes to leave them naked and upset. When the police caught up with her she was sent to the Circuit Court in Perth, to be handed a hefty eighteen months in jail.

The Saddest Crime of All

If there was one crime above all that typified the nineteenth century, it was infanticide, the killing by a mother of her own child, often accompanied by the concealment of pregnancy.

In April 1841 Catherine Symon of Dundee, a worker at John Brown's Mill, was taken to the Circuit Court at Perth, charged with murder. According to the prosecution, she had carried her infant child to the water dam between the Tay Foundry and the Arbroath Railway near the foot of the Trades Lane and thrown it in, either alive or after she had strangled or suffocated it. The evidence was overwhelming: Janet Low of Windymill in the parish of Murroes was present when Symon gave birth to a child at the house of her friend, Mrs Nicoll, and gave the baby a pinafore. Low saw Symon place the baby in a cart for the short journey to Dundee and a few weeks later identified the pinafore on a child's body taken from the water. Helen Nicoll, who had known Symon for eight months, agreed on all points.

The story was sordid but not atypical for the period. Catherine Symon was not a pretty young teenager but a stout, plain-looking woman of twenty-eight. She belonged to Errol in Perthshire but lived most of her life in Dundee. Symon was not particularly bright and was already the mother of a six-year-old child. In January 1841 she gave birth to another baby, a girl who she chose not to name. The baby was born on the Monday, and on the Thursday Symon bundled her, a pile of clothing, eight shillings in cash and two pecks of meal into a cart for the journey from Windy-hill back to Dundee.

Finding lodgings in a house in the Scouringburn with a Mrs Balbirnie and her mother, Symon stagnated, doing nothing. After a month Mrs Balbirnie offered to look after the baby to allow Symon to find work, but Symon refused the offer. Knowing Symon was 'a bit dumpish' about being short of money, Mrs Balbirnie applied to the Kirk for help and Mr Sydie, a Kirk Elder, stumped up 1/6d. There was another lodger, Agnes Cowan, who constantly nagged at Symon to get the child's father to provide money, but Symon said the father refused to accept responsibility. She claimed the father was a mill foreman named David Anderson but when he was asked, he neither denied nor accepted the fact.

Two weeks later, Symon left the lodgings, carrying her daughter with her. The girl was reported to be plump, well cared for and healthy, but was still known only as Symon's child: she still had no name. Moving to the house of Euphemia Wannan in the Hawkhill, Symon remained there for a few days before she left, saying she was taking her daughter to the house of her friend Mrs Anderson in Temple Lane. When she returned alone, Wannan was uneasy and went to check on the baby, but Symon had given her the wrong address. Later, Mrs Anderson told Wannan she had not seen Symon or the child but by that time it was too late.

A seaman named John Robertson and James Gilchrist of the Harbour Police found Symon's daughter in a pool of water near the foot of Trade's Lane. The child was wearing a night dress with two caps on her head and was quite dead. Euphemia Wannan identified her, with Mrs Balbirnie and Agnes Cowan identifying the clothing while Sergeant James Low of the Dundee police found other articles of the child's clothing among the straw in Symon's bed.

Mrs Anderson said that Symon had certainly been in her house that January, but had not left her child there. There was never any doubt about what had happened: Symon had already told her sister she had drowned the baby and when Sergeant Low asked her what had happened to her child she told him quite candidly she had 'put it into the water'. When the case came to trial a majority of the jury found Symon guilty, but, as was usual in Dundee, they asked for mercy. The Victorian Dundonians had a strong streak of compassion, even for child murderers, and although the term post-natal depression had not yet been coined, the city was family orientated enough for people to understand the concept. Nevertheless, Lord Mackenzie donned his black cap and pronounced the death sentence. Symon was to be hanged at Dundee on the morning of Wednesday 26th May.

Hanging was not popular in Dundee and three separate petitions for clemency were sent to the Queen. On 21st May, five days before the proposed execution, Lord Normanby announced that the hanging was suspended until the Queen's pleasure was known. As it happened Her Majesty was pleased to grant a reprieve and Symon was transported for life instead.

Symon's case was unusual because the details are known, but infanticide was frighteningly common in Victorian Dundee and often the mother was not found. Such an action was euphemistically known as 'child exposure'. However, Dundee was no worse than other cities of the period. In September 1886 there was a Parliamentary Return of women held on commuted capital sentences for infanticide. There were twenty-seven in jail, with five sentenced in 1884 and four in 1885; others had been languishing in jail for years, with one unfortunate women held since July 1865.

There were many instances of infanticide in Dundee, such as the box found near Magdalen Yard in April 1824, with the body of a week-old baby inside, or the body of a newborn girl found in Park Place in January 1862 and taken to the Dead House at the graveyard. At the beginning of October 1840 the body of a two-month-old boy, described in the *Advertiser* as 'a fine male child' was found wrapped in rags in a close in Dudhope Crescent. In April 1859 a decomposed baby was found, again at Magdalen Green, but as usual there was no indication who the parents might be.

Sometimes it was obvious that the child had been killed before it was abandoned, such as the girl found in Doig's Court in February 1841. This unfortunate baby had never been washed in her young life and had been strangled to death. Sometimes there was a strange logic with the mothers, and they left their dead babies in the Howff graveyard so it was at least in the proper place. Such a case happened in March 1830 when the watchman at the Howff finished his time searching for Resurrection men and found instead the body of a young girl, tossed over the railing at the north-east corner of the ground. The doctors who examined the baby said it had been violently killed. Just as bad was the case of the newborn boy who was found beside a path in the Howff in November 1834. The baby was wrapped in worn cotton and had been battered to death but again the mother was never found. On 20th January 1842 another newly-born boy was found in a common stair at Anderson's Buildings, Meadowside. Once again an investigation discovered that the child had been beaten to death before the body was dumped.

There were also occasions when a mother must have been so desperate she would do anything to rid herself of her child, or possibly rid her child of the terrible burden of life. About seven in the evening of 1st April 1849 the superintendent of the Victoria Lodging House answered a knock at the door. There was an Irishwoman there, with a six-week-old child in her arms. Nearly dropping with tiredness, she stated her husband would join her shortly. Inviting her in, the superintendent suggested she sit by the kitchen fire. The woman accepted, but after a few moments she asked another woman to hold her baby while she left to buy something for her husband's supper. Just before she left she gave her child something to drink from a small bottle.

When a couple of hours passed and the woman did not return, the superintendent called the police. They launched a painstaking trawl through all the lodging houses and places of refuge in Dundee but failed to find the missing mother. In the meantime the child became sick, altering colour, and gradually wasted away. Despite everything the lodging house matron could do, the baby only lived until one o'clock in the morning. The Irishwoman was not traced.

Each case concealed a tale of harrowing human suffering, with a mother incapable of looking after her child, not knowing how to cope with a baby or suffering a terrible loss. In June 1824 after a woman dropped the dead body of a child in a shop doorway in the Overgate the police arrested her. She was taken to the police office and questioned, when she admitted the child belonged to a relative. It had been stillborn, the mother asked her husband to bury it but he refused and nobody knew what else to do but dump the body and run. The father in this case was not unique. In May 1836 a gaggle of boys were playing beside the building works in Reform Street when they found a small coffin. When the coffin was opened at the Howff, the body of a stillborn child was found. The police made their investigations and discovered that the death had been perfectly natural and the mother had given her husband money to have the child properly buried, but instead he had dumped the body and drunk the money away.

When a mother was found guilty of infanticide, the penalties were widely differing. While Symon's original death sentence was commuted to transportation for life, in October 1842, Christina Robertson was given three months for exposing her newborn child in Anchor Lane. The child died. In December the same year Margaret Elder of Broughty Ferry was given thirty days in jail for exposing her baby daughter. In April 1853

Ann Smith, a millworker, dumped her seventeen-month-old child on the road between Stobswell and the Churchyard of Mains. This child was lucky as it was rescued, but Smith was given eight months in jail. Two years later Mary Chaplin, also a millworker, deserted her illegitimate child. The child was rescued and taken into the orphanage, or in the words of the time 'became a burden on the parish'. Chaplin was merely fined.

Burdens on the Parish

It was not uncommon for abandoned children to be rescued. At the beginning of January 1821 a gamekeeper at the Lundie estate of Lord Duncan found a tiny baby abandoned among the bare whins in a ditch. Only a small piece of blanket protected the child from the bitter winter cold. Whipping off his coat, the gamekeeper wrapped it around the baby and ran to the nearest house, where the lady kept it warm and fed it as best she could. Lord Duncan ensured baby clothes were provided while an abortive search began for the mother.

There was a similar case in late March 1834 when a watchman at the West Harbour Wall heard a dog whining somewhere nearby. When he searched for the animal he found a baby boy among the stones. Dressed in a blue-and-white cotton frock, the child was very much alive so the watchman carried him to a wet nurse he knew. A similar situation occurred at three o'clock on a July morning in 1837 when the Cowgate watchman found a baby girl in the Sugarhouse Wynd. Once again the watchman rescued the baby and found a wet nurse, while the Kirk session took care of the costs.

Sometimes these cases betrayed both the worst and the best of human behaviour, as happened with Jane McKenna in 1866. McKenna lived at Burnside, Lochee with her two illegitimate children. She worked as a weaver, earning 7/6d a week, and one day she simply upped and left without a word to her children or anyone else. The children might have starved if a kindly neighbour had not realised they had been left alone in the house. She took them to the Liff and Benvie Poorhouse, and the parochial board began a search for the mother.

They found her in Alyth, living with a fellow weaver named John Fitzcharles, and McKenna was charged with child desertion. Even in front of the bench, McKenna was quite blasé, claiming she paid 2/6 for lodgings and could not afford to feed and clothe her family. Giving her the maximum sentence of sixty days, the sheriff also advised her she could claim parish relief, but rather than gratitude, McKenna shouted that the sheriff 'could keep her children ... they would never cross her threshold ... never till she died'. Although he was the father of both children, Fitzcharles still pleaded not guilty to child desertion because he had a sore leg. The sheriff was not impressed and added hard labour to his sentence of sixty days.

On other occasions it was an outraged wife who pointed the finger at a supposed child murderer. In February 1863 a ploughman at Pitmannies near Coupar Angus found a dead baby in a field. The boy had been strangled with a cord. The mother was unknown but the police began to suspect a good-looking woman named Isabella Wright who had lived in the Hawkhill. She had vanished shortly after having a baby and rumour said the clothes on the dead child were the same as her son had worn. Although a police search failed to find Wright, she walked on ground too dangerous to escape for long. The father of her child was a married man, and as well as cheating on his wife he argued with his brother, which was a fatal combination. The brother told the wife about her husband's affair, and pointed out Wright's house at Lower Crofts in Dundee. The wife told the police, and Inspector Adams knocked on Wright's door. She was not there, and nor was she at her work in Blackscroft. Not yet defeated, Adams followed the cheating husband instead, and saw a young and excited woman meet him in the Seagate. They spoke for a while and entered a public house, where Inspector Adams arrested Wright for suspected child murder.

The cases mentioned are only samples; there were so many more they beg the question: Why were so many women desperate to get rid of their own children? The case of twenty-eight-year-old Euphemia McGrigor may give one answer. In June 1841 McGrigor lived with her mother in St Mary's Close, Nethergate. She had no husband but two children, which made her a fine target for some supposedly religious people. Eventually the constant harping of these moralists had their effect on McGrigor, and she took a knife and cut her throat. Luckily somebody saved her life, but her attempted suicide shows just how bad the pressure was for unmarried mothers in the respectable nineteenth century.

There is no doubt that infanticide is a terrible thing, but the moralists were certainly not blameless. Children will always be at risk from stressed, deranged or unscrupulous adults, but luckily in Dundee there was also a strong streak of kindness behind the poverty, and people who wanted to help.

12

Did the Punishment Fit the Crime?

When considering prisons and punishments of the nineteenth century, one is apt to think of Dartmoor, transportation to Australia or a convict in striped uniform languishing in solitary confinement. All these preconceptions are correct, but they only make up part of the picture. The nineteenth century was a period of penal reform, when people seriously considered how to best solve the problem of crime.

Transportation and the Lash

In the early decades of the century the erratic nature of sentencing was noticeable. While some hardened criminals were let off with relatively mild sentences, first offenders were often treated with utter severity. For example, in the Circuit Court in Perth in September 1834 the judges Lords Moncrieff and Medwyn sent James Bell to Australia for seven years for stealing a pewter teapot and a few bottles from a house in Perth Road and an urn, a jug and a handful of coppers from a shop. The judge marked Bell as a thief by habit and repute: he was also just ten years old.

Yet on Friday 14th January 1825 the mature James Douglas had to undergo a much shorter sentence. He had to parade through the main streets of Dundee with placards on his back and breast informing the world he was a resetter of stolen goods and the town drummer announcing his presence to the entire world. A crowd watched as he walked, with a lugubrious face but a steady gait. Less than a fortnight later he had reason to celebrate, for his name was announced again, this time on banns of marriage as his engagement to a woman of considerable wealth was proclaimed.

In the early decades of the century punishment could be visibly corporal. At twelve noon on Friday 4th October 1822 around 10,000 people crowded the High Street to watch a double public flogging. Dead on noon a cart stopped at the piazza of the Town House, as two prisoners were brought down from the cells. Both John Miller and William Storrier were shirtless but with broad hats tilted to conceal their faces, they were fastened to the cart with a rope around their waists and then the public executioner flourished the official cat o' nine tails.

As the crowd jeered, the cart trundled on a slow traverse of the town, stopping thirteen times for the executioner to lay three stripes across the back of each man, so they received thirty-nine lashes, the Biblical forty less one, and were then dragged back to the Town House cells. But their ordeal had only just begun, for like young James Bell they were also transported to Australia. In their cases, however, the punishment was more justified, for they were accused of assaulting fourteen-year-old

© Courtesy of Dundee Art Galleries and Museums

The Town House

Mary Miller on the road between Dundee and Glamis. The original accusation had included rape, but as this was a hanging offence, a benevolent prosecutor, John Hope, struck that part and pushed only the assault. In a trial held behind closed doors, both men were sentenced to thirty-nine lashes and fourteen years' transportation.

There was another whipping in Dundee on Friday 14th May 1824. The culprit was a hardened and unpleasant man named Webster. He had appeared before the Perth Circuit Court in 1821, charged with assault and intent to rob. The judge awarded him a year in jail and five years' banishment from Scotland, together with the promise of a public whipping if he returned before his time. But in May 1824, Webster was back in Dundee. Together with a comrade, he burst out of a public house and began kicking passers-by. He resisted arrest, and was sentenced to be flogged.

There had been a public whipping in Arbroath recently and the authorities retained the Edinburgh executioner who had performed the punishment. They also recruited scores of special constables to help control the crowd, but their presence did nothing to stop the pickpockets to whom such gatherings were a bonanza. Although the gathered crowd would not realise it, they were witnessing history, for the Police Act, passed that year, marked the end of public whipping. Transportation, however, was to continue.

Transportation was no light punishment, but the ultimate step of banishment. In Scotland, offenders could be banished from the town, the county or the country for various periods of time, depending on the seriousness of the offence. Banishment was not a new punishment but had been common for centuries. Even banishment to a colony was not new; in the early seventeenth century many outlawed Borderers were banished to Ireland. Cromwell sent captured Scottish prisoners of war to the American colonies and Caribbean islands as slave labour, and many Americans could trace their ancestors to a convict, military, religious or political prisoner of the seventeenth or early eighteenth century. Other equally unfortunate convicts could be forcibly recruited into the army, to fight the wars the Stuart kings waged for their English kingdom.

When the American Revolution and the emergence of the United States closed that particular destination, the British government looked for other lands to contaminate with their undesirables. The re-discovery of Australia by James Cook proved a godsend. To the British authorities, here was a huge, virtually empty land a long way off and in need of cheap labour.

There is a myth that those transported to Australia were innocent poachers and articulate political radicals. There is a counter myth that only the truly hardened offenders were transported; the truth is somewhere between the two extremes, but probably slanted more toward the latter. Scottish courts were reluctant to send first offenders to New South Wales or Van Diemen's Land and even the notoriously hard-hearted English courts did not automatically banish wrongdoers on a whim. According to Robert Hughes' book *The Fatal Shore*, over half the English convicts were repeat offenders, with around eighty per cent being thieves.

Being separated from home, friends and family was surely a terrible punishment, but there were some who seized the opportunity of a fresh start in a new land to make a name for themselves. Others, of course, survived their time and merged with the population of Australia, or returned to Britain, while there were some who were too truculent to knuckle down and joined the ranks of the bushrangers who infested the bush and highways. These 'demons' as they were known – the word was a shortening of Van Diemen and had nothing to do with supernatural evil – often earned a reputation for savagery.

As early as 1837 a government select committee met to discuss the whole question of transportation, and recommended the alternative of keeping the culprits occupied with hard labour in British prisons. As there were not enough prisons to hold all the convicts, the government compromised, ending the transportation to relatively mild New South Wales, but continuing to the hell hole of Van Diemen's Land, Tasmania. Sometimes the convicts did not even reach Australia. In September 1833 the convict transport *Amphitrite* was wrecked on the passage from Britain. Among the dead were Mary Stirling, Janet Kennedy, Mary Dakers and

Mary Clark from Dundee. They had left the Tay on 9th August.

Transportation was used with surprising frequency, and most Circuit Courts sentenced some Scots to lengthy periods of exile. For example, the Perth court of September 1824 ordered the thief Janet Angus to Australia for life, and the spring court of 1825 sentenced Margaret Macdonald to seven years' transportation for passing forged bank notes. Both women waited in Dundee jail until July 1825 before being shuffled in chains to the docks to begin the long voyage to Woolwich and then to the other side of the world. As well as petty thieves and forgers there were killers. In March 1836 a carpenter named John MacIntyre was transported for seven years for murdering his wife. He punched her, kicked her and threw her against a wall and then to the ground.

And age was no bar to transportation either. James Bell was only one of many Dundee children sent to Australia. In May 1835 Circuit Court Lords Mackenzie and Medwyn looked across the bar at fourteen-year-old James Morris. He had stolen around 4/6 from Mungo Shepherd's shop in the Overgate, but because he had twice before been convicted of theft, he was given seven years in Australia. Despite his youth, Morris was not overawed by the sentence but faced the judge squarely. 'Damnation to you!' he responded.

Other children were not so truculent. In September 1830 two boys, Dugald Wright and William Croll went on a crime spree. First they broke into the garret owned by Alexander Guid and removed a handkerchief. Then they took a variety of articles including two silk gowns from the attic of James Ogilvy. Still not satisfied, they broke into John Scott's shop on the Shore and removed what they fancied. The pair were caught, held in jail and appeared before the Circuit Court in April 1831. As William Croll was a known thief, the judge sentenced him to fourteen years' transportation, but he showed mercy to first offender Wright and awarded him only seven years. Perhaps it is not surprising that Wright cried as he stood at the bar; both he and Croll were under ten years old.

An equally sad case occurred at the Perth Circuit Court of April 1842 when William Cuthbert and Isobel Cuthbert, father and daughter, stood accused of incest. William Cuthbert failed to appear and initially Isobel denied the charge, but when it was proven she had given birth to two children by her own father she pleaded guilty. The older child was nearly three, the younger just eighteen months, and the judge sentenced Isobel to transportation for life. One wonders if she could have denied her father's attentions, and if she was perhaps better off in Australia than living in obviously sordid conditions in Scotland. Was she a three-times victim, twice by her father and once by the court?

To give the courts their due, most of the people transported were thieves 'by habit and repute' and so were not people who would be pleasant neighbours. Sometimes the people of Dundee would be heartily pleased to see the back of those sent to Australia. In the autumn Circuit Court of September 1856, the judges, Lords Cowan and Ardmillan, presided over eighteen cases, one of which was that of Frederick McDiarmaid. He was a ticket-of-leave convict, which meant he had been released from jail early, but he stood accused of housebreaking. The evidence was against him and he was found guilty of breaking into the draper's shop of James Spence in Reform Street and stealing various items including thirteen pairs of gloves, four shirts, three parasols, five pairs of stockings and £3 in copper coins. Because of McDiarmid's previous convictions the judge was not inclined to mercy and sent him to Australia for fifteen years.

In some ways McDiarmaid was unlucky in his timing. In 1846 transportation was suspended for two years, with those convicted instead being confined in solitary confinement for eighteen months. Possibly disorientated by that experience, they were then used as forced labourers either in Britain or abroad in Gibraltar or Bermuda before being released on licence, ticket-of-leave to any British colony. In 1852 Tasmania, the much-feared Van Diemen's Land stopped accepting transportees and Western Australia, where Sir Edward du Cane ruled with an iron fist, became the destination of transport ships. In 1867 transportation ended for good.

Banished from Dundee

More simple banishment was quite common, usually accompanied with the threat of imprisonment if the culprit was caught returning to the town. For example, when the Sheriff Court found William Higgins guilty of theft they sentenced him to the severe punishment of three months in solitary confinement, including thirty days on a diet of bread and water, and then banishment from the county for seven years. In October 1825 when the troublemaker James Reid was found drunk in a stable near the harbour when he was already banished, he was taken to the even less comfortable jail. The convict David Scott, banished from Forfarshire in 1825, was caught in Dundee in October 1825 and again at the beginning of February 1826 and both times thrown into the Town House jail.

Despite the threat of jail, many of those banished returned to Dundee, either because they wanted to come home, or because there were more lucrative opportunities in the town. When William Higgins was banished in early 1825, he moved south but was caught disembarking from the Fife ferry in July. The police court had no sympathy with his story that items in Dundee were cheaper than in Fife, and ordered him to jail. It may just have been coincidence that he had returned at the same time as the Stobs Fair, that happy hunting ground for pickpockets and thieves.

During the 1820s, many unsavoury people infested Dundee, but few were worse than Janet Cassels. She was a thief, a troublemaker and a known prostitute who haunted the low lodging houses of Couttie's Wynd, but on 12th September 1827 she excelled herself. Cassels was working in Elizabeth Muat's brothel run when she took a dislike to a prostitute named Jean Adam. When she saw Adam at the other side of a glass door Cassels lifted a table knife and thrust it right through the glass, stabbing Adam in the arm and the face just below the eye.

When the case appeared before the sheriff later in the year, Cassels was as respectable looking as possible and declared, 'I am not guilty, please, your lordship.'

Although the sheriff took the unusual course of being judge and defender, he still found Cassel guilty and told her she was lucky she was not at a higher court on a much more serious charge. Immediately Cassel's politeness ended and she reverted to type, 'Go to hell, you bugger. I hope to God I'll be tried before the Lords next time and not before yon old damned sheriff.'

Those words were only the beginning of a tirade that continued as the sheriff sentenced her to two years' banishment from Forfarshire, with the warning that if she returned she would be put in prison and sustained only on bread and water for two months. Patrick Mackay, the Messenger-at-Arms, was given the unenviable task of taking her by post chaise out of the county and into Perthshire.

The very next day at twelve o'clock the watchman at the Witchknowe hauled her into custody again. Rather than show remorse, she declared she preferred to be in prison in Dundee than exist outside the county. She was released in January 1828 but a week later was once more arrested and returned to her former lodging. The same thing happened again, and again, she held true to her promise not to leave the town.

The policy of near starvation, when a convicted offender would be sentenced to a period on bread and water, was sometimes imposed as an extra punishment or for a repeated offence. For example in July 1825 a rootless, shiftless man by the name of David Wilson stood before the Police Court. As it was his ninth appearance he was given thirty days on bread and water. Cassels, on the other hand, was given a longer period for her more serious crime.

The Living Hell of Penal Servitude

Penal servitude took the place of transportation. Perhaps the prospect of remaining within the British Isles was preferable to being sent thousands of miles away, but the new punishment was no sinecure. The initial 1853 Penal Servitude Act was for a four-year period only, but with no colonies willing or able to take convicted, ticket-of-leave criminals, a second Act in 1857 ordered that the period of servitude should be exactly the same as it had been for transportation: seven years or more. Penal servitude started off with a tough regime, but co-operation by the prisoner could earn better conditions in what was termed the Progressive Stage System. There were four stages of servitude and once sentenced the prisoner was thrown straight into a nightmare of work and hardship from which he or she had to labour to crawl up the ladder. The first stage was a daily regime of ten hours of muscle-tearing, back-breaking, and mind-numbing class one hard labour. Much of that time was spent at either the crank, shot drill, or the treadmill. The crank entailed turning a handle to rotate a box filled with gravel, hour after agonising hour, 14,400 times a day. The treadmill was an ingeniously revolting contraption where a convict was forced to walk on a never-ending series of steps, rather like a hamster on a wheel. Those who used it knew it as the shin-scraper or cock-chafer, which vividly demonstrated the secondary effects the procedure could have. To engage in shot drill was to stand in a line, endlessly lifting and carrying heavy cannonballs.

Even when the prisoner returned to his cell there was no real rest. Night after night he or she slept on bare wooden planks, alone and silent. No communication with either prisoner or warden was permitted, so there was no means of redress and nobody to whom the prisoner could complain or even vent steam. Protests led to cramped days handcuffed in an unlit punishment cell, frustrated violence could end in a whipping, either by the birch or the cat. The longer the sentence continued the more chance of breaking the spirit of the prisoner. It was not surprising that some descended into insanity.

If the prisoner behaved and attained enough marks, he or she could rise to the second stage, with slightly easier labour and a mattress to sleep on five nights a week. He or she could also earn a few pennies and had the privilege of exercise and education on the Sabbath. The third stage saw the lighter labour continue, while the convict enjoyed a mattress six days a week; wages rose and library books were allowed. The fourth and final stage must have seemed like paradise, with wages of perhaps two shillings a week, a mattress every night, the luxury of letters home and the incredible joy of a twenty-minute visit. To a man or woman living in utter solitary silence, a letter or a visit would be a reminder they were not alone; they were part of the human race, they mattered. But the road to such salvation broke many.

Penal servitude was undoubtedly a savage system, intended to punish and with the consequential effect of destroying people who were often the most vulnerable in society and embittering those who had the mental strength to survive.

Birching the Boys

For much of the nineteenth century there was no special provision for the young. Children who broke the law were treated much the same as adults. Even when they were not transported, they could be sent to an adult jail, to endure the same conditions. In 1851 a Police Bill gave a different slant to the treatment of young male offenders who appeared before the Police Court. These were children accused of petty crimes, the day-by-day, opportunist crimes that often were more mischievous or plain thoughtless than malicious. For such offences a child could now be flogged rather than sent to jail. The same bill restricted the sentences police courts could inflict on adults from sixty to thirty days, and maximum fines were reduced from £5 to £2.

It was May 1852 before the Dundee Police Court used its new power of corporal punishment when the aptly-named Baillie Spankie ordered a boy to receive twenty strokes and two days in the jail. The boy was a worker in Kinnaird, Hill and Luke's Mill at Burnside, Lochee and he had vandalised a pump. All work had to stop for hours, so causing the mill to lose production and possibly costing the workers some wages. At this time, and for some years afterward in Dundee, the boys were punished with the tawse, a long leather strap with the striking section divided into two or three tails. The tawse was inflicted across the bare buttocks. Schools and some parents in Scotland used a similar instrument.

From that date on, sentences of whipping became fairly common in the Dundee Police Court. At the end of November 1852 Sheriff Henderson ordered a housebreaker and regular offender named Alexander Robertson to eight months in jail and thirty stripes. A week later Sheriff Henderson awarded George Gray, another boy with a record of housebreaking, six months and thirty stripes. In August 1853 the court awarded ten days and twenty stripes to two very young children named Alexander Piper and James Irwan. They had committed the shocking crime of stealing apples from a garden in Greenfield Place. Strangely, nobody seemed to question why they had been allowed out at two o'clock on a Sunday morning, and how they got their hands on the false key that gave them access to the garden.

A false key got another bunch of boys in trouble in February 1854. Seven youngsters aged from ten to fourteen used a false key to enter the stateroom and cabin of the schooner *Mary and Rose* in Victoria Dock. Once inside they took everything that was not nailed down: a sand glass, kitchen forks, spoons and four-dozen laxatives. When they reached the Sheriff Criminal Court in early March, Sheriff Logan treated them to a long lecture about their youth and probable future and awarded them painful sentences. Twelve-year-old John Connor, who had already been in trouble with the police, was awarded four months in jail, with ten weeks at hard labour as well as one whipping of thirty-six stripes. Frances Gillan, a youth of fourteen, was given four months, with ten weeks at hard labour and the others, Robert Page, aged twelve; Hugh Money, aged thirteen; Owen Gillan aged thirteen; James Stewart, aged ten and eleven-year-old Owen Morgan were given three months, with eight weeks at hard labour, plus twenty-four stripes.

Although the judicial flogging of children was to continue until 1948, the instrument and number of strokes altered. By an Act of Parliament of 1862, the tawse was replaced by the birch rod. The law stipulated that nobody could be birched more than once for the same offence and in Scotland children of fourteen and under could only suffer twelve strokes. Offenders of sixteen and over could not be birched for theft or for a crime against a person or property. In time the Scottish Home Office drew up more precise regulations that commanded a birching was to be severe enough to ensure the recipient dreaded any repetition. The birch rod was a bundle of twigs tied together at the handle. Two policemen would hold the boy down on a wooden bench while a third applied the birch, normally in the police cells or courthouse.

There is no doubt that birching was a savage punishment, but it was seen as advantageous to the reformers of the period. It cost next to nothing, it frequently saved boys from being exposed to the worse abuses of an adult prison and at an age when pubescent boys often turned to crime to gain the reputation of being men, a birching across the bare bottom treated them instead like naughty children; unlike a spell in jail, it was not an experience of which they could boast.

Yet for all the efforts of the authorities, sentencing still remained something of a lottery. In June 1863 Owan Gorman entered a grocer's shop in the Overgate and stole 1/7 and three farthings – less than eight pence in today's currency – and was jailed for nine months. In October that same year Thomas Reynolds indecently assaulted a child in the Overgate and was given only fourteen days. Yet when Mark Devlin, a weaver, raped a fourteen-year-old in February 1835 he was hanged. His was the only execution for rape in Dundee that century and one of the few executions in the city, but his case was a reminder that behind all the judges and prisons there waited always the shadow of the noose.

13

Dangerous Women

The Rule of Margaret Nicoll

'Give the bugger law!'

Every city has some places that could have been made specifically for crime, and the Little Close in Dundee was one such. It ran between Blackness Road and the Hawkhill, a narrow, dark and airless passage, stifling hot in summer when flies feasted on the sundry dung heaps, slippery and chill in winter when fog and frost beset the traveller. At all seasons it was dark, and with so little elbow room that two people could not pass each other unless one pressed against the wall. About half-way down the close, the gable end of a single house formed part of the wall, and in here lived a family who terrorised the lane and the fear of whom deterred travellers from using this passageway unless in full daylight.

There were four of them: James Greig and his wife Helen, her brother James Nicoll and their sister Margaret Nicoll. Of them all, Margaret Nicoll was the worst. She was the mainspring of the group, a woman who constantly abused her neighbours with words or violence and who had appeared before the Police Court on a number of occasions. Yet although the Nicolls controlled the house, the Little Close and much of the neighbourhood, they did not own the house, nor were they even the tenants. Margaret Nicoll was the servant of the owner, an unmarried man who seemed not to care what she did, and she had brought in her relatives to rule her employer's house. From that time onward Margaret Nicoll was the real Mistress of the house.

On Saturday 5th October 1833 John Murray, a rope maker, was walking along the Close when he heard Margaret's voice. 'Now, Greig, give the bugger law!' and two people attacked him. It was half-past ten at night, and as dark and miserable as October can be, but Murray defended himself so effectively that he beat Greig off and even made Margaret back away.

'It's all a mistake,' Margaret assured him, and offered to take Murray into her home to treat his wounds. More trusting than worldly, Murray agreed, and stepped inside the house, only to once again hear the words, 'Give the bugger law' and the whole pack of Nicolls attacked him. Helen Nicoll cracked him over the head with the large house key, temporarily dazing him. He struggled free, crashed against the gate, burst it open and fell into the Close, followed by the howling mob. When a man loomed through the dark, Murray must have felt some relief, but it was Greig returning and they grappled together, until another rush from the Nicolls pushed Murray back. For a moment he thought his life was in danger, with one of the assailants attempting to 'Burke' or smother him, and he was about to be overcome when another traveller, James Macintosh, appeared and piled in on his side. Between the two they rushed Greig and Helen Nicoll along the close and handed them to the police.

The next morning Greig made his confession and put all the blame on his sister-in-law, Margaret Nicoll. Both he and Helen were sent to jail for sixty days and the police made a quick raid on the Nicolls' house, arresting Margaret as she worked in the garden. Her arrest was something of a public spectacle, as all her neighbours turned out to watch, together with many of the decent people of the Hawkhill and Overgate who had suffered at her tongue and hands. She was also given sixty days, which was the maximum the Police Court could impose. Bailie Christie also warned the police to keep a close eye on 'that abominable establishment' before somebody was murdered in the close.

Female Pugilists

When Lord Cockburn said, 'What a set of she-devils were before us!' he was referring to the Dundee women who were dragged, often kicking and swearing,

Looking Towards Overgate

before the bar of the Circuit Court. Margaret Nicoll was only one of a long line of Dundee women who were at least as dangerous as their menfolk, and they pepper the annals of nineteenth-century crime in the city. Often they took out their aggression on each other, as in the case of the face-to-face battle of two women at Dallfield Walk in April 1824, when one used a poker to batter her opponent into bloody submission. A similar case occurred in April 1830 when Elizabeth Savage attacked Rose Montgomery in her house in the Hawkhill. In this instance the women had shared a single man, and when he chose to marry Montgomery, Savage lived up to her name and responded by attacking her rival. When this case came to court, Montgomery shouted at her ex-lover, calling him a 'jackdaw' and vowing to torment him at every opportunity. She was still screaming and threatening when she was dragged away to the cells.

Elizabeth Savage had some justification for her assault, as her trust had been abused and her man stolen from her, but in the case of Williamina Thomson, the only reason was theft. Thomson was a young woman, still in her teens, and on 16th June 1878 she ambushed Ann Banks. Mrs Banks was a much older woman, perhaps in her fifties, and she was walking through Watson's Lane in the early hours of the morning when Thomson came up from behind her and asked if she knew a good place for a dram. When Mrs Banks said she did not know, Thomson put an arm around her neck and wrestled her to the ground. Kneeling on her breast, Thomson slapped Mrs Banks' face and rifled her pockets. The spoil was really not worth the effort: three farthings, a snuff box and a small bottle with a gill of whisky. When Mrs Banks screamed for help, a flax dresser named Charles Lamb ran up and demanded to know what was happening.

'Come, come,' Lamb said. 'What are you doing?'

'Mannie,' Thomson said. 'It's my mother, and I'll learn her not to go about and spend my money!' She explained that her mother had gone off with her father's wages and there was no food left in the house.

Lamb nodded. It was not an uncommon situation for a wife to squander her man's wages on drink and he had no intention of interfering in a domestic squabble. He left, and as soon as the echoes of his feet faded, Thomson rolled off her victim, landed a hefty kick and told her to go home.

Thomson was not the cleverest of thieves. After her failure to steal a respectable haul, she remained in the same area, so when Mrs Banks complained to the police, Thomson was arrested and hauled into the police office. As well as Charles Lamb, a weaver named Elizabeth Kennedy had witnessed the assault, and when her case came to trial in September 1878, Lord Mure sent Thomson to jail for eighteen months.

Sometimes women banded together and hunted in pairs. Such an occasion occurred at the end of August 1837 when Ann Smith and Ann Craig assaulted Agnes Stewart and Euphemia Menzies in Dudhope Crescent and tore their clothes to shreds. It was also known for one woman to attack two or more, which is what happened in April 1884 in one of Dundee's less than salubrious lodging houses. These places were for the poor, the dispossessed, desperate travellers and those without hope. Anybody who used a lodging house would not expect luxury, while even comfort and cleanliness would be an unexpected bonus. However, lodging houses did offer shelter from the worst of the weather, they provided some sort of a bed and maybe a fire and the lodgers would hope to spend the night without being assaulted. Sometimes all these comforts were not received.

At about one in the morning Sunday 21st April 1884 the Gillespie family knocked on the door of Catherine Falconer's Lodging House. There were four Gillespies: Mr and Mrs Gillespie and their two children, and Catherine Falconer showed them into a double-bedded room. There was already another couple in the room, with Mr Jones, an Englishman, lying in bed and his young wife undressed, and sitting beside the fire. Within a few moments the two wives had fallen out, and with Mrs Jones being drunk and aggressive, the argument escalated into a full-scale fight. T he Englishwoman jumped at Mrs Gillespie, knocked her down, grabbed her hair with both hands and began to bite into her shoulders and back, screaming, 'I'll eat you alive!'

The two husbands tried to haul Mrs Jones from her prey, but without any success, and Gillespie ran downstairs to fetch the landlady, who appeared with a servant named McCauley. Between the four of them they dragged the drunken Englishwoman from Mrs Gillespie. Mrs Falconer told McCauley to find out the cause and end the dispute, but Mrs Jones was still agitated and, grabbing a poker, she attacked the inoffensive servant. After that, the police were called and the cursing, near-demented Englishwoman was dragged to the police station. She was fined 30/- with an alternative of fifteen days in the jail.

Women Assaulting Men

Women did not just confine their aggression to other women. They also attacked men. Sometimes they followed the example of Mrs Jones and used a poker, as Hopeton Watt of Peter Street did in February 1843 when she attacked the starcher John Robertson. At other times they did not have to use anything at all, as in the case of Janet Miller of Scott's Close in March 1879. She had met James Peebles, a labourer, in a Fish Street pub, but their conversation soon became an argument and Peebles left. Miller was not keen to let him off so easily. She followed him into an eating-house and attacked him, punching furiously so he staggered out of the shop into the street and fell in the gutter, where she kicked him savagely as he lay helpless. The Police Court gave her ten days in jail to think about her exploits. Sometimes women used whatever was in their hand, as in the case of millworker Jane Hall of Rosebank Road who attacked two seamen, James Connel and Charles McKenzie, with a tin flagon. She hit them both on the head or the face and then, to finish off her day, smashed a window in Cochrane Street. When her trial came, she pleaded guilty, but said she was so drunk she could not remember a thing. She was fined £1.

Sometimes a girl attacked a boy by mistake, as in September 1883 when Betsy Steel from Union Street in Maxwelltown visited the theatre in the old cattle market. Her mother had warned her not to go to such places, but Betsy thought she could look after herself. She took her knitting with her, so she did not completely waste her time. As she was watching the performance a girl in the row behind her repeatedly pulled her hair. Eventually Betsy lost her temper, pulled out the needle from her knitting and thrust it toward the annoying girl. Unfortunately she missed and hit a completely innocent boy instead, nearly taking his eye out. The case went to the Police Court and Betsy was only admonished, but her mother promised 'to take care of her', which sounded very much like a threat.

On other occasions, the woman knew exactly what she was doing and attacked a man with cold-blooded efficiency. On the night of 12th August 1874 Mary Webster acted in such a manner when she attacked and robbed the auctioneer Charles Grant in St Andrews Street. Charles Grant really knew little about it. He was on his way home to Seagate when somebody came up behind him, cracked him over the head and knocked him into the gutter. A Good Samaritan found him there and took him home, and only then did he realise he had been robbed of a gold watch and chain.

As in so many of these cases, there was a witness. Elizabeth Soutar of St Andrews Street had been in her house about eleven in the evening when she heard a sound like somebody falling down. When she looked out of her ground floor window she saw a man lying on the ground and Mary Webster loosening his clothes. Webster looked up, saw Soutar and said Grant had fallen as she was passing, and then she walked away. However, she returned in a few minutes and stole Grant's watch, with Soutar still watching.

There was even more damning, if slightly contradictory, evidence from the local beat policeman. Constable Robertson saw Webster slide between Grant and the wall of the street, knock him down with a single blow behind the left ear and then bend over him as he sprawled on the ground. When Robertson shouted, Webster ran, but the policeman was the faster and caught her with Grant's watch chain held tightly in her hand and his watch in her pocket. Once she was caught, Webster pleaded for the mercy she had not herself shown, asking him to release her for she might be charged with murder, but once Robertson had checked on Grant's condition and sent a messenger to fetch Mrs Grant, he wrestled Webster to the police office. Once she was taken inside, she swore and shouted at the police officers.

The jury had little doubt as to Webster's guilt and Lord Ardmillan sentenced her to eighteen months in jail. At least in her case the victim, innocent as he was, survived to complain about the assault. On some occasions a man died at the hands of Dundee's dangerous women.

Mary Ann Stirling was no different from hundreds of other Dundee women. Hard-working, she lived with a man to whom she was not married, and who liked his drink. On Sunday 16th April 1876 her man, John McCartney, a marble polisher, came home more than a little drunk and hauled her out of bed. Not surprisingly, the couple began to quarrel. The words grew more heated, they shoved each other and McCartney punched Stirling in the face. She fell back, her nose bleeding. Rather than cower or plead, Stirling lifted a brick and smashed him over the head, finishing off the job with an axe, or so the prosecution alleged. She denied that, saying that the brick had been enough. And it had, for McCartney's skull was fractured, and although he was rushed to the infirmary, he died six days later.

In her defence, Stirling explained that it had been dark; McCartney often hit her when he was drunk and she had been afraid he might go too far. In the event, it had been she who had overstepped the mark. At the Circuit Court Lord Young showed surprising leniency, giving her only six months, and as she had been in jail nearly that length of time awaiting trial, she was soon back out on the streets.

Female Footpads

Much more premeditated was the case of Helen Morrison and Ann McGuire. These two did not act in sudden anger or out of self-defence, or through drink, but were cold criminals. On 20th October 1879, when Mary McLauchlan was working in a mill, Helen Morrison forced open the locked door of her house at Blackscroft and stole a pair of boots and a shawl. She would probably have taken more, but millworkers did not have much to steal. On the same day, about one in the afternoon and along with the equally unpleasant Ann McGuire, Morrison waited near the Sawmill Gate of Camperdown on the turnpike road from Dundee to Coupar Angus. As Mary Anderson, a seventy-year-old widow walked past on her way to Lochee from her home in Woodside Cottage, Birkhill, they jumped on her, grabbed her neck and threw her to the ground. As Mrs Anderson lay there confused and helpless, Morrison and McGuire knelt on top of her, punched her in the face and chest and stole her purse with a little over sixteen shillings in silver and copper.

'We've got the money!' McGuire said, and they walked away, leaving Mrs Anderson still lying on the ground. Realising they were both a little drunk, Mrs Anderson dragged herself up and bravely followed toward Birkhill. Twice they turned and ordered her to go back where she was going, and Mrs Anderson did so, until she met a local farmer, George Turnbull, driving a cart along the road. Mud-stained, confused and with a badly bruised face and aching ribs, she poured out her story.

In a manner that seemed natural to the people around Dundee, George Turnbull did not hesitate to help. As soon as he heard Mrs Anderson's story, he whipped up his horse and searched for the thieves. A young girl called Susan Milne told him they had just passed her. Turnbull found them at the New Gate, walking toward Birkhill, but as he approached they hauled themselves over a hedge and ran into a wood. Turnbull followed, demanding to know why they had attacked Mrs Anderson. Morrison admitted they had asked for money, but claimed Mrs Anderson had not given them any, but Turnbull angrily repudiated that, and asked what they had done with it. As McGuire handed over six shillings, Morrison swore at her, saying by giving up the money they had shown themselves guilty. Obviously a man of some resolution, Turnbull hauled both the women to the local policeman, Constable Charles Jarren of Birkhill Feus.

Eventually limping home, Mrs Anderson sent her servant to tell the police what had happened, but by that time George Turnbull had virtually wrapped everything up. Constable Jarren called Mrs Anderson to the police station, which doubled as his house. When she arrived McGuire and Morrison were already there, and together with Jane Jarren, the policeman's wife, Mrs Anderson searched them. When Mrs Jarren found two of her rings and more money, Constable Jarren charged Morrison and McGuire with the assault, although Morrison gave her name as Sarah Connor. When Constable McArthur found Mrs Anderson's purse discarded beside a hedge, there was little further to say. Both girls, eighteen-year-old Morrison and sixteen-year-old McGuire, appeared at the Dundee Spring Circuit Court and were given eight months in prison.

Dundee has often been called a woman's town, partly because of the huge part women played in the jute industry. Unfortunately, it was also a town where women could be at least equal to men in the field of crime. In some ways, Lord Cockburn's statements were correct.

14

Mag Gow, Drink and Dundee

In February 1834 the Dundee Police Commission issued the following statement:

> There is hardly a crime committed or a riot perpetrated but what may be referred to the intemperate use of ardent spirits and that mostly in the night-time.

That statement, from a very responsible body of men with vast experience of conditions in Dundee, must count for a great deal. Yet the Police Commission was not the first to make that damning claim. As early as 1824, when illicit distilling was a major problem in Scotland, the *Advertiser* claimed that 'cheap whisky' was to blame for much of Dundee's crime. There is no doubt that Dundee had a large number of drinking places. For example, in September 1843 the *Advertiser* claimed there were 500 licensed premises in the town and ten years later there were 555, which was an estimated one pub for every 144 people, plus an unknown number of shebeens, the unlicensed drinking houses that sold raw whisky straight from the glens.

In May 1854 the Public House Act regulated drinking hours and closed spirit shops on Sundays, which had an immediate effect on Dundee's behaviour. In areas such as the Overgate the number of drunks dropped, and crime figures fell considerably. In the twenty-four Sundays between 15th May and 24th October 1853 there were 414 people arrested for drunkenness or disorderly conduct in Dundee. In the corresponding period in 1854, there were only 201, a drop of over fifty per cent in the single year following the Act.

Crime statistics, in common with all others, can only tell part of the story. A casual glance at the statistics for Dundee for any year in the high Victorian period would see scores or perhaps hundreds of people committed to prison. This figure would automatically draw a mental picture of a city filled with desperate criminals, a place to avoid. However a slightly more detailed examination would reveal a different reality. Although Dundee had its share of murders and culpable homicides, assaults and daring robberies, the majority of the crimes were minor, and often committed by a small number of repeat offenders. One of these incorrigibles was a woman named Margaret Gow, who appeared before the courts on an astounding 260 occasions in a life ruined by drink. In the modern world she would be recognised as an alcoholic and be offered as much help and guidance as possible. In the Victorian age, alcoholism was not recognised as a disease, but considered a character failing, and Gow spent much of her life within the stark confines of Dundee jail.

The Incorrigible Mag Gow

The daughter of a journeyman tailor and theatre owner known as Fizzie Gow, she must have had a decent upbringing. Her first few dozen offences barely merited a brief mention alongside other petty offenders. It was in July 1856 that Gow began to be noted, when Sheriff Henderson awarded her six months for assault. Five years and many prison visits later, Margaret Gow, or Mag Gow as she was familiarly known, made her first major milestone.

On 28th May 1861, Margaret Gow made her ninety-ninth appearance at the Police Court, charged with disorderly conduct at the Fish Market. After pleading guilty, she said she regretted her actions and if their Honours let her off this time she would never demean herself again. Surprisingly, when dealing with a woman with such a disreputable record, the clerk of court spoke up for her. Saying that she was an industrious woman, he added the Fish Market was a bad place for her and she should keep away from it. As Gow was a fish cadger and lived in Fish Street a few yards from the market where she worked, that might have been difficult, but she promised to leave Dundee for her father's house in Errol. The Bailie took her at her word and, after delivering an admonition, dismissed her.

To give Gow her due, she must have tried to be good as it was nearly four months before she was back in court on a charge of disorderly conduct in Whitehall Close.

Bailie Ower faced her and accused, 'Margaret, you've been here a hundred times.'

But Gow was always ready to defend herself with a mixture of good humour and surprised indignation that she should be so harshly treated.

'I've done very little,' she said, 'to be here a hundred times.'

When Bailie Ower reminded her of her pledge to leave Dundee and live in the country, Gow replied that she had been living in Errol but she came in to pay respects to a friend who had died. The Bailie asked what pledge she would give Mr Mackay, the Procurator Fiscal and Superintendent of Police, to be let off again.

'I can't say what pledge I would give,' Gow replied, 'for I've said so much already.'

It was an honest reply and once again she was set free, after she promised to behave herself.

Despite the Baillie's forbearance, only two nights later a police constable found Mag Gow in Whitehall Close, shouting loudly and kicking at house doors. Next morning she was once again before Bailie Ower.

'It's awfu that I cannae get past that close without being disturbed,'

Gow complained, until the Bailie wondered what she was doing there at one o'clock in the morning. Gow explained, very politely, that she had been looking for somebody; Whitehall Close was full of cheepers – illegal drinking dens – and she thought he would be in one.

'You have been taking too much drink of late,' the Bailie told her, and sentenced her to twenty-one days in jail.

By April 1862 Gow's score was up to 104 when she was given another forty days for disorderly conduct. It was on this occasion that the *Courier* branded her an incorrigible, which was probably no less than the truth, although she seemed always to have an excuse for her actions. By mid-July her score was 107 appearances, with a dribble of a few shilling fines here and a few weeks in jail there. As her name and fame spread, Gow became a target of interest and mischief from the rootless, shifting youths who infested the streets of Dundee.

As Gow's drunken stagger from the streets to the courts to the jail and out to the pubs continued, even the tolerance of the Dundee bailies was stretched beyond tolerance. In January 1866 the police picked up the drink-sodden quartet of Helen Ramsay, Thomas Halley, Nicholas Lamb and Margaret Gow. The record of the women was unimpressive: it was Helen Ramsay's 143rd appearance at court and Gow's 146th between them they had been in the Police Court twenty-one times that year alone. Bailie Hay told them exactly what he thought. He said that they ignored any advice from the court, they had no self-respect and they lowered the character of the town and increased the crime statistics. With surprising insight into what was more likely a medical condition rather than criminal intent, the Bailie said there should be some other remedy for their type of case. He closed by fining them 2/6 each or taking two days in jail.

The Bailies' rebuke was as useless as the constant jail sentences. In May of that year Gow was poured into a wheelbarrow and trundled to the police office, and next day she got another seven days or a five-shilling fine. It was her 151st appearance in court. She was out for a few days and then found drunk on the street. When she told the Bailie she had declared herself teetotal he suspected her sanity and adjourned the case until she was examined by two doctors. The doctors declared her sane so the bailie gave her a week and the golden advice to turn a new leaf.

As always, Gow gave a polite reply, promised to behave and within weeks was back, as dishevelled and repentant as ever. When Bailie Foggie showed mercy and allowed her to walk free so long as she kept away from the drink in future, Gow agreed, saying she would keep him up-to-date with her life if they met on the street. Bailie Ritchie asked for the same promise in January 1867, and Gow was reported as saying, 'A' richt, Bailie. Thank you.' Less than a week later she stood before Bailie Greig.

'Well Margaret,' the Bailie said, 'this is most extraordinary conduct – do you hear me?'

'I hear it,' Margaret replied.

'It is a pity to see you here so often,' Bailie Greig said, and gave her another seven days.

But there was no humour and little pathos when Gow appeared before the Procurator Fiscal in June 1867 and was handed a hefty twelve months for assault. Perhaps it was hoped that such a long dry spell would cure Gow of her love affair with alcohol, but she was only out for a few weeks when she was found drunk in Hilltown and made her 180th court appearance. In September that year she was charged with being drunk and disorderly in the Scouringburn. In November the Overgate had to endure her drunken presence and in December she chose to bless the West Port with her antics and faced a new bailie in the morning.

'Hello, Mr Nicoll,' Gow greeted him like a friend, 'I never saw you here afore.'

When it was pointed out that this was her 187th appearance Gow laughed it off. 'Oh that's no very muckle yet.' She explained that she was walking down the West Port and the police arrested her because there was a gaggle of children around her. 'Mister Nicoll has kent me a' my days,' she added, perhaps a little tongue in cheek, 'and he never saw me the waur of drink.'

Bailie Nicoll did not agree. 'I really hope we have seen the last of you here,' he said. 'I think you would be better under the care of the jailer altogether.'

And that was another seven days in jail for Margaret Gow. Her appearances before the courts continued, with an admonition followed by a few days in jail, and Gow constantly protesting repentance and promising to behave. Her total increased: 188 in January 1869, 190 at the beginning of February and 191 a fortnight later.

This time Gow was accused of fighting with Jane McDonald and she had a black eye to prove it. The three police who had arrested the pair claimed they were creating a great disturbance in Shore Terrace but Gow disagreed, saying she was 'always very agreeable and happy with Mrs McDonald'. The Bailie sentenced McDonald to ten days and, saying he wished he had the power to send Gow somewhere she would be taken care of, awarded her sixty days.

'Well, that's no' fair, sir,' Gow said.

No sooner was she released than she was back again, this time for assaulting Ann Barber and her son Robert in an Overgate close. With the case handed to the Procurator Fiscal, Gow had to wait until the Dundee Sheriff Criminal Court met in October to state her case, and for once she was as much victim as perpetrator. For some time now her notoriety had attracted crowds of young boys who teased her both while she worked at selling her fish and when she refreshed herself in one of Dundee's many public houses.

On this occasion Gow had tried to escape her tormentors by running to Crichton's Close in the Overgate. However the boys followed her, calling her names and showering her with horse dung as she sat on a step. According to young Robert Barber, she was muttering to herself but when he came close she twisted his nose and punched and kicked him, whereupon he ran crying upstairs for help. His mother rushed to avenge him, shouted Gow had 'better not strike a bairn belonging to me', and ran for the police.

The arrival of the constables encouraged Gow to more violence and as Ann Barbour searched for witnesses to her son's assault, Gow seized her hair and punched her on the eye.

By this time in her career, Gow had collected nine convictions for assault and as usual she pleaded not guilty. The defence concentrated on the group of young boys who had harassed her, claiming that they had been thrusting horse dung into her mouth and 'smashing her with their bonnets'. Robert Barber was possibly one of the group. Her defence, Mr Paul, called a surprise character witness in Bailie Stewart, who stated that Gow's father was a very respectable man. He also said that Margaret Gow was 'addicted to taking a dram now and then' and added the boys 'attack her even when she is sober'. Even more interestingly, Bailie Stewart had personally tried to have Gow put into a home where she would have regular work, decent food and would be free from the temptation of the public houses. Finally he mentioned that Mr McQueen, the Governor of Dundee Gaol, thought her a willing and obedient worker.

The jury found Gow not guilty of attacking young Robert but guilty of assaulting his mother, and Sheriff Smith gave her thirty days above the five months she had already spent in jail.

'Thank you, My Lord,' Gow said politely. 'Thank you, gentlemen.'

But in January 1870, liberated again, Gow was found drunk in Powrie Lane and had her 197th appearance in court. She was back in jail in March for another ten days, marked up her 200th appearance in May with another two days, when the police thought she was 'using most disgusting language', and returned again in June for a breach of the peace in the Greenmarket, when Bailie Nicol gave her sixty days.

She was hardly out when she got drunk in the Scouringburn and appeared before Bailie Cox, who let her off on condition she signed the pledge. However Gow made her 205th appearance in December 1870 and her 218th in September 1872. Once again she was charged with disorderly behaviour, leaving her barrow in the Scouringburn while she toured the pubs, danced, sang and jumped about, to the entertainment of a gathered crowd. Despite police warnings to move, her capers continued, and despite her plausible explanations to the bench Bailie Maxwell gave her thirty days.

'Oh, sir,' said Mag Gow in real or pretended horror. 'Thirty days, thirty days! Oh dear.'

Exactly the same behaviour in Polepark Road in March 1873 saw her in jail for forty days, despite her story of a group of men robbing her. In June she was back for another sixty days for disorderly conduct and breach of the peace in the Overgate. She was out for a few hours and bounced back like a drink-sodden yo-yo, with thirty days and a promise to join the Good Templars. Next month it was the same story and another sixty days for disorderly conduct in Forebank Road and Ann Street.

The years rolled on and Mag Gow continued her descent. November 1874: sixty days for breach of the peace in the Greenmarket. February 1875: sixty days for cursing and swearing in St Margaret's Close. April 1875: sixty days for breach of the peace in the Overgate. She was out for a day and back in for breach of the peace in Tyndals Wynd: sixty days. She was given another sixty days in September; sixty more in January and the same in April, July, September and November.

By November 1877 Gow had made over 250 court appearances but when she appeared before Bailie Robertson that month she was obviously unwell and rather than sending her back to jail, the bailie ordered a doctor examine her. Doctors Pirie and Miller did so and said, not surprisingly, that she had signs of mental aberration. This time the heavy doors that banged shut on her were those of the lunatic ward of the Dundee Poorhouse.

Nevertheless, Margaret Gow still managed to re-enter the public eye. In July 1878 both wards of the poorhouse were taken on an excursion to Perth. As they walked in procession to Craig Pier and the packet boat, crowds gathered to see the famous Mag Gow, with the brave thrusting out to shake her hand or give her money. Sensible of the possibility of disorder, the police called a cab and placed her inside. As so often before, a gaggle of boys followed, cheering. Gow's last appearance was in 1885 when the poorhouse allowed her a day's liberty, but she was unable to restrain her old impulses and drank herself into a stupor.

Tightening Drinking Laws

Margaret Gow was only one of a huge number of people in Dundee to whom drinking was a way of life so, naturally, much of Dundee's petty crime centred on the public houses. There were probably hundreds if not thousands of instances throughout the nineteenth century, but most followed the same sordid pattern of ordinary people causing trouble through drink. For example there was a brawl in a pub in the Overgate on Sunday 17th September 1821. When the town officers arrived they found most of the combatants were women and arrested four sorry-looking specimens, heavily marked with the bruises and cuts of battle.

Drunkenness was prevalent throughout the century, but the 1820s seem to have been particularly bad. For example, one week in June 1824 a group of drunkards wrecked a Hilltown pub while five drunks destroyed another pub in the Nethergate. In November that same year William Shand was fined for causing trouble in a pub and on the same day the Excise Court was crowded with people charged for selling whisky and ale without a licence. Even worse was the number of people who infested the town selling what they claimed was smuggled brandy and whisky but was in reality a compound so vicious it could literally kill the drinker.

In late summer 1841 the Superintendent of police ordered that all pubs should be empty by twelve at night, which was another step toward a more regulated system. Many publicans, not surprisingly, disagreed. Some young gentlemen thought it daring to visit the mildly dangerous pubs of Dundee's less savoury areas, but not all came away unscathed. In April 1843 two gentlemen spent some time in the Red Lion, one of the Overgate's less appealing places of refreshment. The men regretted their daring shortly after when a couple of local ladies robbed them of most of their money. That same year there were 500 places in Dundee where drink could be bought and some councillors hoped to cut that number by half.

Lord Cockburn had commented on the behaviour of Dundee women, and some of the Police Court figures bear this out. For example, in Bailie Moyes' first appearance as a judge in the Police Court in December 1843, seventeen of the twenty-seven people who appeared before him were women and most were accused of drunkenness and riotous behaviour.

Sometimes the publican was heavily involved in the trouble, as in November 1845 when Patrick Devlin was playing cards with a weaver called Taggart in Devlin's Overgate pub. They argued, Develin first ejected him then attacked him in the street. He was promptly arrested. When the case came to the Police Court, Develin was fined but vanished before the fine was paid, so his licence was revoked.

By the 1850s the laws against unlicensed public houses were being tightened. Known colloquially as 'cheeping shops', or more commonly as shebeens, these places were scattered throughout the town; they often sold raw illegal whisky, often caused a disturbance to the immediate neighbourhood and cost the town valuable revenue. In order to end this practice, the finance committee of the Dundee Police Commission paid women 2/6d to find the cheeping houses and act as a witnesses when the case came to court. Bailie Spankie and Bailie Jobson disagreed with this procedure, with Jobson saying that only the lowest type of women would take such a position.

With spies and entrapment not popular the courts tried other methods to stem the tide of drunkenness. In January 1861 Margaret Downfield from the Overgate pleaded guilty to being drunk on the Sabbath. When she said she had abstained for the past fourteen months, Bailie Ower set her free on the condition she took the pledge of total abstinence. To ensure Downfield kept her word, the Bailie handed her to Mr McLean the Temperance Missionary.

Despite numerous Acts of Parliament, drink remained a major problem in Dundee, as in most places in nineteenth-century Britain. The police and courts continued to hunt for shebeens, which, if anything, increased after the 1859 Forbes Mackenzie Act that furthered official control of public houses. During the 1860s Dundee held special courts purely for shebeens. In one court held in May 1861 Margaret Gilbert, Jane Morris, Mrs Low and Harriet Macdonald were jailed for six weeks for having a shebeen in their Peter Street house, while Peter Bock and Ann Lindsay of Fish Street, Henry Coleman and Catherine Crow of Pullar's Close,

Rodger's Close

Murraygate, Lewis and Bridget Devlin of Chapelshade and Mary Brymer of Seagate were fined £7 each. In June 1863 Isabella Forbes or Smith was given six months or a £30 fine for having a brothel and shebeen in Couttie's Wynd.

The Public House Act of 1862 did not alter the opening hours for public houses, but restricted hotels to only serving drink to genuine travellers on Sundays. The police were given new powers that allowed them to enter any premises purely on the suspicion they may sell alcohol. A fine of 40/- or two days in jail could be imposed on anybody who refused to leave a pub when the police ordered, and a 5/- fine or 24 days in jail for anybody found drunk.

In the Police Court held on 8th May 1883 a carter named Francis Johnston and his wife Bridget pleaded guilty to selling whisky without a licence from their house in Miller's Pend. Bailie Bradford fined them £7. The following month Francis Reilly senior from Horsewater Wynd was charged with the same offence, but many people in Dundee in the late 1880s knew that the largest shebeen in Dundee sheltered behind a facade of respectability; the Kincardine Literary Club hid many secrets. In 1885 Dundee had 448 premises licensed to sell alcohol, with 229 pubs, 211 licensed grocers and eight hotels. There was also Ballingall's Brewery at the Pleasance and the Albert Hotel and Brewery. Some of these establishments could bear comparison with anywhere in the country and many were filled with character. Russell's Royal Hotel in Union Street had been upgraded in mid-century and boasted the best billiard room and smoking room in Scotland. The Eagle Inn, opposite Horse Wynd at 42 Murraygate was a coaching and a carrier inn, while the John o' Groats at the Cowgate had the alternative name of Heaven and Hell. It stood at the corner of St Roques's Lane and was situated immediately below the Wishart Memorial Church. Yet despite all the efforts of government and the police, the Dundee drinking culture continued to blight the lives of far too many of the citizens. Drink and crime marched hand in hand through the streets of the industrial city.

15

The Bonnet Came First: Family Disputes and Other Acts of Violence

Domestic Disturbances

The bonnet came first, flipping from the window to land on the bottom step of the Bell Street close. The crutch came next, clattering down the common stair to rest accusingly on the cobbles. Finally the owner appeared, yelling as his wife, Margaret Finlay, helped him out of his house and down the stairs to the street below by hauling him by the hair of his head.

Husband beating was not uncommon in nineteenth-century Dundee. In this case in March 1866, Mrs Findlay had accused her husband of being too friendly with other women. He had slapped her for her suspicions and she had retaliated with interest. The bailie at the Police Court found her guilty of assault, said her conduct was 'very unbecoming, especially as her husband was a cripple' and gave her five days in jail or a five shilling fine to help her mend her ways.

Perhaps spouse beating is one of the hidden crimes; for once a man and a woman enter a marriage they retreat behind the curtain of matrimony. Nobody except themselves knows the full truth of their lives, or the pressures and tensions that cause a union, once based on mutual affection, turn to anger and violence. Having said that, there were few secrets in nineteenth-century Dundee with the majority of its citizens living in overcrowded tenements separated from their neighbours only by a thin partition wall. People knew if a marriage was troubled by the voices coming from next door, and in a town of one- and two-roomed houses, disagreements that started inside were often continued in the common close or in the street outside.

Sometimes arguments were very public indeed, and it is difficult to feel anything but sympathy for the individual in the dock. In August 1893 Helen Hackney of Gray's Square, Hospital Wynd, stood accused of assaulting her husband Charles and another man named Edward Quin. When Mrs Hackney appeared in court she was described as a 'slatternly looking woman with a voluble tongue' and it seemed that it was to this tongue that her husband most objected. As she stood facing the judge at the Police Court, she called her husband an 'outlaw'.

As the couple were questioned, some of their story emerged. There was a history of unhappiness in the marriage, with years of bickering. On this occasion Helen had attacked Hackney, so he pushed her outside, whereupon she struck both him and Quin with a key. Hackney said she 'annoyed' him wherever he went, and because of her he had already been imprisoned for fourteen days.

At that point Mrs Hackney proved the power of her tongue by screaming the fourteen days in jail were for deserting his children to live with another woman in Monifieth, and now he was not only living with another woman, but she had eight children. It is not difficult to imagine Mrs Hackney's anger as she loudly informed the judge, the court and the world at large that her husband had also taken their two children to a 'bad house' from a Thursday night to a Saturday and he was keeping low company with the even 'bigger blackguard' Edward Quin.

Uncaring of her audience, Mrs Hackney continued to scold when Quin was called upon to give evidence. She finished her work by telling him to go and get a job. 'You cannae work and you winnae work. Go awa', ye scoondril!'

When all the evidence was completed, the Bailie obviously sympathised with the bitter-tongued but obviously hard-used Mrs Hackney and only admonished her.

Although Dundee women were more than capable of standing up for themselves, most cases of domestic abuse concerned husbands assaulting their wives. Sometimes the end result was tragic. By February 1870 Charles Taws already had two convictions for assault but his third and last was his worst. He came home to his house in James Street, Maxwelltown, punched his wife, burned her face with a candle and began kicking her about the body. She died nine days later but Taws only got five years' penal servitude for assault. John McIntyre, a Dundee carpenter got seven years transportation at the Circuit Court at Perth in April 1836 when he kicked and punched his wife Allison, and dashed her against a wall. She died of her injuries.

© Author's Collection

Seagate

Other cases were equally brutal but received more attention, possibly because they had elements of drama that was lacking in the sordid murders of Mrs Taws and Allison McIntyre. The attack on Julia Ann Hutcheson was one such.

Julia Ann had not long been married to the baker Robert Hutcheson when they moved into a top flat in Seagate. On Saturday 29th December 1883, eighteen months into their marriage, Robert Hutcheson got drunk, staggered up the four flights of stairs, charged into the house and began to shout at Julia Ann. After calling her every name he could think of, he told her he did not care if this was her last Saturday. He was obviously savagely angry and followed up his verbal assault by punching her face and head. Julia Ann backed away but Hutcheson kicked her legs, grabbed her by the throat and threw her to the ground. As she lay there, rolled into a ball for protection, Hutcheson picked up a washing board and cracked it against her back. Rather than lie still and be assaulted, Julia Ann struggled to her feet and ran to her neighbour, Thomas Rhynd.

Neighbours in nineteenth-century Dundee seemed to have an open door policy, with keys and locks not used, for Hutcheson followed into Rhynd's house, grabbed Julia Ann by the hair and dragged her screaming back to her own house. It is unclear what his intentions were, but he thrust her into a chair, knelt on her and tried to tie her hands together. Fighting free, Julia Ann dived for the door but Hutcheson grabbed her again and dragged her to the window. Holding her firmly, he opened the window and threw her onto the roof outside.

'You haven't got another hour to live!' Hutcheson promised, and for a while it seemed as if his prophesy was correct.

Four stories up on the steeply sloping slates of a tenement roof on a dark December evening, Julie Ann would have been terrified. Grabbing the gutter of the window, she lay there, calling for help as the Seagate traffic rumbled past far below her. It was about an hour before Constable Alexander Scott appeared, opened the window and eased her back into the house. By then Julia Ann was shivering with cold, terrified, battered, sore and bleeding from the mouth, but her husband was completely unrepentant, claiming she had gone onto the roof of her own free will. Sensibly, Constable Scott guided her away from Hutcheson and into the house of another neighbour, Mrs Fisher, where Julia Ann was examined and found to have bruises and injuries on her face, legs, hands and other parts of her body. Even when the case came to the Sheriff Court on 15th January she was so weak she had to sit while giving evidence.

Sheriff Cheyne listened as Hutcheson denied he had ill-treated his wife, claiming she had hit him with the washing board and then climbed out the window herself. When he heard the testimony of the neighbours and the police, the sheriff had no difficulty in deciding that Julia Ann was telling the truth. He gave Hutcheson sixty days with hard labour.

Domestic assaults were so common throughout the century that even to list them would take many pages. Some of the cases were sickening in their brutality, all were sordid, many were drink-related and probably most were caused by a combination of stress, frustration and alcohol. A few examples out of the hundreds will be enough to give a flavour and an idea of the extent.

In July 1824 a drunken man began to wreck his own home in Dallfield Walk. When his wife tried to stop him he attacked her instead, but the noise they made drew a crowd who saved the woman and carried the man bodily to the lock-up house. The following month an Irishman from East Port came home drunk at two on a Sunday morning to find his wife waiting up for him. Although she was heavily pregnant he beat her so badly she nearly died. In December a man protested he had the right to beat his wife because she was having an affair, a story she emphatically denied. That same month a painter called George Ingram attacked his wife with an axe and an iron bar. Despite her severe wounds he was only fined.

January 1825 started the same way with a flax dresser named Alexander Kidd fined seven guineas for assaulting both his wife and another woman who tried to protect her. It continued with Mrs Clark of Tindall's Wynd running to the police office with a claim her husband threatened to murder her. The court bound him over with a £10 penalty for his future good behaviour. That month a woman who lived in the Wellgate was thrown into the Town House jail for six days on bread and water for attacking her husband. The same Police Court fined a labourer 5/4, not for assaulting his wife, but for beating up an old woman who tried to protect her when he was hitting her.

And so it continued: sordid tragedy week after depressing week. In February 1826 a scavenger named John Hughes was charged with two assaults on his wife but dismissed as there was no evidence. In March a seaman named Innes was found guilty of a brace of assaults on his wife; in August 1826 a carter who lived in the cesspit of Couttie's Wynd was fined for assaulting his wife. In one court at Christmas 1828 there were seven cases of wife beating, in another in October 1829 there were three.

The 1830s followed the same pattern with, for example, a case in August 1837 when a flax dresser named James Whyte attacked his wife Elizabeth Wilson and her sister Sarah in his Small's Wynd house. He spent the next thirty days in jail. A month later another flax dresser named William Cruden hit his wife Elizabeth Pert with a besom. Cruden was jailed but it was neither his first or last offence. In 1839, when the couple lived in the Upper Pleasance, Cruden was released from jail and came straight home. When Elizabeth saw him she ran out of the house and tried to hide with a neighbour, locking the door behind her. Forcing his way in, Cruden found her and, with no provocation at all, attacked her. He was arrested again and faced the judge at the autumn Circuit Court, who finished Cruden's wife beating career by sending to Australia for seven years.

This decade also saw the case of Robert Bain, the Overgate weaver who on a July Friday in 1835 arrived home drunk and demanded tripe. When his wife said she had none, he changed his order to whisky, but again the cupboard was bare so he attacked her. She tried to escape out of the window but he hauled her back in and kicked her up and down the house, making so much noise that the neighbours called the police.

When he stood before the court Bain faced his bandaged and bruised wife and said she had attacked him with a poker and her wounds were self-inflicted.

'It must have been a very soft poker,' said the judge, and gave Bain sixty days.

The 1840s were no better, with, for instance, the shoemaker Robert Stewart of Fish Street fined twenty shillings in July 1840 for coming home drunk, pulling his wife out of bed and kicking her. Then there was Thomas Cadger the flax dresser and George Crabb the carpenter who

Looking Toward Dudhope Castle

both appeared at the Police Court on 8th June 1843 for assaulting their wives, and the ugly case in October 1843 when a hawker named Connor stabbed his wife Helen several times.

The pattern did not change as the years passed. Most cases were men attacking their wives, but there were always a few when the woman was the aggressor. There was another serial wife beater in the 1860s when Alexander Peebles, a weaver, seemed to specialise in attacking his wife. In 1862 and again in 1863 he appeared in court for punching and kicking his wife, the second time ending in jail for thirty days.

Often the punishments seem ludicrously small when the nature of the assault is detailed. In September 1873 James Hendry of Albert Street in Lochee was given thirty days in jail for wife assault. He had come home, locked the door and pocketed the key, punched his wife Sarah in the face, cracked her over the head with a walking stick so the stick broke, hit her again and dragged her around the house by her hair. Unable to escape by the door, Sarah had to open the window and jump into the street. Thirty days seems very little for putting his wife through such an ordeal. On other occasions the court probably got it right. On Christmas Day 1874 John Fox of Miller's Pend, Scouringburn, attacked his wife with an axe, inflicting wounds on her head and shoulders. The judge and doctor at the Criminal Sheriff deemed him insane and ordered him detained in prison at Her Majesty's pleasure.

Wives, too, were capable of extreme violence. In July 1857 Margaret Hurley of Highland Close, Overgate took a knife to her husband John and sliced off part of his nose. Although a doctor sewed it back on, he remained disfigured for the rest of his life. On 11th September 1866 an elderly couple from the Beach in Broughty Ferry fell out, possibly over another woman. Mrs Mooney took a knife, cut her husband's throat and slashed him across both temples. As Mooney's daughter and a neighbour jumped to save her father, Mrs Mooney tried to cut her own wrists. The knife was wrested from her but she ran away. A doctor attended to Mooney and the police caught Mrs Mooney after a chase through the streets of Broughty.

The Price of an Affair

Third parties and extra-marital affairs were responsible for quite a few domestic disputes. For example, in 1872 Euphemia and Archibald White of Arbroath separated. They had eleven children, but married life was not always smooth. Archibald was a drinking man and when his bouts became increasingly obnoxious, Euphemia left him. The children had always supported their mother in the marital disputes, so accompanied her when she moved to Dundee.

Despite their differences, the Whites remained on relatively friendly terms, with Archibald doing his bit to bring up their children. One by one the children left home to create their own lives until only the eldest daughter, Charlotte, remained. Things jogged along peacefully until March 1875, when Euphemia met another man and then her behaviour altered. She began to drink, and then she emptied the house of chairs, bedclothes and everything else she could wrap her hands around.

When Charlotte informed her father of her mother's behaviour, Archibald followed Euphemia to her home in Littlejohn Street, by Dudhope Crescent. Rather than persuade her to return, Archibald began to reclaim the family's possessions, but Euphemia would have none of it. Lifting a carter's whip that happened to be lying around, she thumped Archibald on the head with the handle and threatened to kill him if he carried anything away.

Charlotte did not see the assault and this time did not take anybody's side. She was so sick of her drunken parents she wanted to leave them both and move in with her siblings. When the case came to court, Bailie Edward found it not proven but said both parents should be proud of their daughter Charlotte for telling the truth and remaining sober and hard-working.

In the case of Michael Bourke of Bog in Lochee, it was mother-in-law trouble that caused him to assault his wife. That was in October 1886 and he had argued with his wife, who retaliated by throwing a boot at him, while his mother in law skelped him with the lid of a kettle. Bourke retaliated by hitting them both, but Sheriff Campbell Smith did not show any sympathy. Bourke had already appeared in court nine times for assault, so the sheriff gave him four months.

It was sometimes the case that a husband who abused his wife also turned his drunken anger onto his children. James Couper, a labourer from Hilltown was one such. He was in the habit of coming home drunk on Saturday nights and throwing his two sons out of the house. One Saturday in August 1882 he also threw out his wife. Somehow she returned back inside and spent the night hiding under the bed, but the two teenage boys remained in the passage outside until six the following morning. When the case reached the Police Court Couper was fined 15/-.

Mothers could be just as unpleasant to their children as fathers. Mrs Burns lived in a single room in an attic in Miller's Pend, four floors up and facing onto the Scouringburn. She was a respectable woman who earned a precarious living sewing sacks, and was busy with her needle on a Monday afternoon in June 1889 when she heard a girl screaming. Within seconds there were feet rapidly pounding up the stairs and a young teenager burst through Mrs Burns' unlocked door and begged for somewhere to hide. When Mrs Burns saw a drunken woman chasing the girl she closed the door, locked it from the outside and stood guard to protect the child. Rather than withdraw, the drunken woman attacked Mrs Burns. A neighbour, Mrs McGinnes, tried to help but the woman slapped her across the face. Meanwhile, the girl, hearing the commotion, opened the skylight window and climbed onto the roof. Four stories above the bustling streets and too terrified to move, she clung to the slates.

The sight of a young girl balanced on the roof attracted a crowd, who pointed to her and gave advice, but eventually Constable Jack appeared, rescued her and arrested the drunken woman. It had been a domestic quarrel between the drunk, Margaret Carr, and her daughter. While the mother was locked in jail for fifteen days, the child was sent for sanctuary to the poorhouse.

Assault Outside the Family

Violence, of course, was not just confined to family disputes. Sometimes only the victim was found, as happened at the end of March 1824 when a man was found lying bleeding in the Nethergate. His arm was broken and there were extensive injuries to his back. He died a few days later without anybody ever knowing what had happened, but it was suspected a gang of footpads had assaulted him. A few days later four men attacked a lone man near the Butterburn on the Strathmartine Road. One of the attackers was captured but the others escaped. Such attacks on travellers were fairly common throughout the century.

Sometimes the attackers escaped with valuables, as happened at the end of November 1824 when a brace of men and their dogs set upon a countryman in the Fairmuir, knocked him down and rifled his pockets. They escaped with his watch and a packet he had been carrying. At other times the reward was hardly worth the risk, as in the assault just off Crichton Street in September the same year when four men attacked a lone pedestrian at two in the afternoon. After a brief scuffle they ran off with his umbrella and his hat, closely pursued by a large crowd.

Although the image of Victorian violence is usually coloured by images of Jack the Ripper or the garrotting scares of the 1860s, the range of perpetrators was quite wide. Dundee was no exception. For instance in November 1853 in the Overgate, a broker's wife drew a butcher's knife on her servant and stabbed her on the arm and the neck. Sometimes assaults by the supposedly respectable members of society were utterly brutal, as in the case in August 1855 when a druggist named John Smith attacked his wife Janet Smith. Although she was pregnant, her husband cut off her clothes, punched her head and face, grabbed her hair and dragged her across the floor of their Princes Street house until her body was a mass of bruises and cuts.

The Use of Weapons

Weapons were common in the assaults that marred Dundee's streets. Wives smashed bottles over the heads of their husbands, men clashed pokers on their wives, belts were wrapped around fists and the buckles used to smash teeth and noses, sticks were common and in the 1860s, a time when many Britons looked over their shoulders in fear of garrotters, there was a rash of knuckleduster crime in the city. In December 1863 a sixteen-year-old apprentice mechanic named Alexander Raffan was arrested for using iron knuckledusters on a plumber named James Rose; he got sixty days for it. Another favoured weapon was simpler: a stone contained in a handkerchief. This was the weapon used by William Murray, a weaver, when he attacked James Fenton in Lochee's Ann Street. He got thirty days and came out in February 1866. Fists and boots were normal, but Mary Weir broke the mould when she attacked Mrs Christie in Constitution Road. After punching Mrs Christie in the face, Weir drew a razor and slashed her across the neck.

However, Robert Cunningham probably deserves the accolade for the most unusual weapon. He was a man with a bad record of violence, with seven convictions for assault, three of which were on police constables, but he was also had a bad leg and in March 1884 he used his crutch to attack two policemen on Victoria Road. Sheriff Cheyne had little belief in his promise to reform if he was treated leniently and gave him four months.

Overall, Dundee could be a violent place, but compared to other cities, it was relatively peaceful. There were few really violent professional criminals and the organised gang troubles that infested places such as Manchester and Glasgow were notably absent. Drink or domestic disputes seem to have been the root of most of the assaults, and in most parts of the town the streets were comparatively safe.

16

The Later Years

A Policeman's Lot

A Victorian policeman's life was never easy. He worked long hours, walked many miles, mixed with the worst people in the country and had to follow strict rules. The police had one week's holiday a year. By the 1860s his uniform and equipment was fixed and would remain constant for the remainder of the century. He had a cape with a strap; a staff or truncheon that fitted in a long inside pocket, a belt, one pair of leggings, two great coats and two dress coats, uniform trousers and two reinforced hats, leather neck stocks that gave some protection against possible strangulation, cleaning materials, a rattle, a lantern and a pair of handcuffs.

The truncheon he carried would be painted and decorated. There are a number of these items held in the McManus museum in Dundee. One is of turned wood with the top and bottom section painted black and nicely varnished. On the top is a painted crown with the letters VR in blue, red and gold and a number, presumably of the officer, at the bottom. At 658 mm long and 34 mm diameter, it is quite a formidable weapon. An earlier version is similar in size, with the top and the lower two-thirds again painted black and a gold and red crown at the top together with

W IV R. These truncheons served both for protection and as a means of identification: warrant cards were not issued until much later in the century.

Handcuffs were carried in the pocket and were probably of the 'D' pattern, so called because they were shaped like the letter 'D'. They were worked with a large key that screwed into either edge, but the procedure took some time, and once locked they could not be adjusted. If they were too large for the prisoner, he or she could slip free. If too small, they painfully constricted the prisoner's wrists. Again, there is an example in the museum at Dundee, together with the much less elaborate 'shangie', a 330mm-long article with a wooden handle and length of rope that was looped around a single wrist of the offender. The rattle was a large wooden device used to summon help if required; it was carried in a coat pocket and remained in use until whistles appeared in the 1890s. The lantern, of a bull's-eye pattern that could be used to direct a narrow beam of light, could also burn the policeman's fingers and often left a film of soot on his uniform and face.

In 1861 the average height of a Dundee policeman was five foot nine and three quarters; tall for a town where bad living conditions dramatically curtailed growth. That same year saw a number of promotions within the force as Lieutenant McQueen became governor of Dundee Prison and 2nd Lieutenant James Christie took his place as lieutenant; others also took a step up as James Cathro moved from Sergeant Major to 2nd Lieutenant, John Hills from Sergeant to Sergeant Major and William Ruxton became a sergeant. For those at the top, there were also good rewards, with Superintendent Mackay having a salary of £50 a week from 1870. The police were now established and accepted as part of Dundee society.

Policing Dundee

During the 1860s the police continued their successes. In May 1862 there was a theft of two silver watches in Blairgowrie and the thief jumped on a train to Dundee. The local police telegraphed the force in Dundee, who caught the thief as he arrived at the station. In June 1863 Constable Wales made a bit of a name for himself by tracing a thief. About half past two on the morning of Tuesday 23rd June he was walking past Doig's Entry in the Overgate. Hearing something suspicious, he entered the close and followed a paper trail of letters until a man rushed past him and into the Overgate. Wales chased him, joined by a dozen eager Dundonians.

© Courtesy of Dundee Art Galleries and Museums

Doig's Entry

At that time there was a quarry in Lindsay Street, and as the suspect ran, he threw a screwdriver into it. Wales caught him a minute later. With the suspect safely in custody at the police station, Wales returned to Doig's Entry and found a portable writing desk still with some letters inside. Some were addressed to Mr Robert Fleming, Airlie Place. Together with Inspector Rennie, Wales examined Fleming's house. A window catch had been forced, a desk opened and a rosewood writing desk stolen. The man Wales arrested was a seaman from London who called himself Thomas Williams.

Wales' success was just a drop in a flood of crime that threatened to engulf the whole country. While the government passed more severe penalties for violent crime, in December 1868 Dundee reeled under a rash of assaults and robberies. There was a man garrotted and robbed outside the Royal Lunatic Asylum, and another attacked in South Lindsay Street, a robbery at Shaw and Baxter's factory in North Tay Street which ended with the place being set on fire, a couple of robberies in the same night in Long Wynd and a burglary at a spirit shop in Perth Road. The police were more efficient, using the telegraph system, and in 1873 obtaining a prison van to transport the criminals, but the criminal element also knew every trick.

As well as the opportunist thieves and drunken brawlers, there were bad men who lived their lives on the dark side of the law. Alexander Dow was one of these. He claimed to come from Arbroath but drifted from place to place as the fancy took him. His first criminal appearance was before the court in Aberdeen in June 1861 when he was given three months for theft. The next year the Aberdeen sheriff gave him eighteen months, which either taught him caution or put him on the right side of the law, for it was not until May 1867 that his name next appeared, when he ended in jail for just sixty days. By April 1868 Dow was operating in Dundee, where the Circuit Court welcomed him with an eighteen-month sentence. He was hardly out before he was back in again, this time for police assault. In October 1871 he haunted the crowds that gathered at the grand opening of Balgay Park, but the police caught him stealing a gentleman's watch and he was back before the judge. With his long record he could not expect any mercy and the April 1872 Circuit Court awarded him seven years' penal servitude. Dow must have been a hard man to survive this nightmare and come back for more, but in 1882 he appeared before the High Court of Justiciary in Edinburgh and gained yet another seven years.

Despite his record, Dow was released early on a ticket-of-leave but rather than try to keep straight, he returned to the only way of life he knew. More a thief than a man of violence, Dow liked to ply his pick-pocket trade in the railway stations. His *modus operandi* was to board a busy train, get off further down the line and mix with the crowd and see whose pocket he could dip before returning to a different carriage in the same train. At that time the train would be of the corridor type, rather than the long, open-plan variety that are used today. Perhaps old age and repeated confinement were catching up with him, or maybe he was never really adept at his job, but a Ladybank policeman saw Dow with his hand in a lady's pocket.

Grabbing Dow, the policeman thrust him into a carriage and searched him but found nothing. Certain that Dow was a thief, the policeman held him secure until the train reached Perth, where he was bundled out and arrested. When Dow was again unsuccessfully searched, the police had the carriage thoroughly taken apart. When they removed the door an upended it, a purse fell out; Dow had managed to slip it inside. The judge at Perth Circuit Court gave him eighteen months.

When he finished that term, Dow was retained in jail to finish the seven years from which he had been released. When he eventually returned to the world, he again reverted to thieving. In 1891 a Dundee detective arrested him at the Martinmas Feeing Market and in 1892 he was back in the city. In May of that year Dow found a drapery auction in the Hawkhill and stood at the back of the crowd as the largely female audience hoped for a bargain. He had just lifted a fat purse from a Lunan

Bay fisher wife when a detective put a heavy hand on his shoulder and arrested him. Maybe Dow was a career criminal, but the police had career officers who also knew exactly what they were doing.

Compared to the other cities of Scotland, Dundee was very lightly policed. In 1880 Edinburgh had one policeman for every 532 citizens, Glasgow one to every 535, Aberdeen one to every 758 and Dundee one to every 967, but the authorities decided to add another six men to the force. Perhaps it was this slight reinforcement that brought down the crime rate in Dundee.

Throughout the 1880s police crime statistics saw a constant downturn that indicated they had succeeded in making the city a safer place in which to live. However, there were still enough incidents to make the honest citizens wary. Drunken assaults and common theft continued, and sometimes the theft was not quite so common.

Safe to Steal

In the 1880s, the Hawkhill was a busy place. The name covers both an area of Dundee and a long street that runs from the West Port in a roughly south-westerly direction until it meets the Perth Road at a Y-junction known as the Sinderins. As was common to most of the old-established streets in Dundee, there were a number of smaller streets, wynds or closes running at right angles from the Hawkhill. Along the front of the Hawkhill, and often situated at the corners where the main street met the wynds, there were a selection of public houses and shops. One of these shops, at the corner of the Hawkhill and Miller's Wynd, was owned by David McGavin, who lived in the flat above. At about half-past seven on the night of 6th February 1888, McGavin said farewell to his final customer of the day, turned off the gas, locked the door and carried the keys upstairs to his house. As was normal in such corner sites, the shop had two doors, one in the Hawkhill and the other in Miller's Wynd.

Seven hours later, at half-past two in the morning, Constable James Glen woke McGavin with the bad news that the shop door was gaping open. Not bothering to dress, McGavin rushed down the stairs and found both the Miller's Wynd door and the back door open, and a quick examination found a skeleton key still in one of the locks. An investigation inside proved even more disturbing, with the counter drawer pulled right out and the safe, where McGavin's money and papers were held, missing. He estimated there had been something in excess of twenty pounds in cash, as well as his title deeds. As the purpose of having a safe was to deter thieves, McGavin had possibly expected a burglar to try and break in, but he had no idea that somebody would steal the whole thing. The revelation came as a shock.

Constable Glen had checked McGavin's shop at half past ten the previous night and found everything secure, but when he returned four hours later the door in Miller's Wynd was open. At that time only the burglars knew what had happened.

Margaret Craig, however, had a good idea. She lived at 17 Watt Street and early that same morning she had been awakened by a 'chap at the door'. Her shoemaker husband Hugh opened the door and two men walked in – Samuel Steel and Neil McPherson. It was disturbing enough for Mrs Craig to have two men enter her house in the wee small hours of the morning, but worse when she saw Steel carrying what she could only describe as a 'big green box'. Mrs Craig was not the most serene of women and when it was obvious that something illegal was happening she became so agitated that her husband thought she was having a fit. He ordered the two men and their mysterious box out of the house.

Perhaps Mrs Craig thought that was the end of the affair, and that evening she left to visit her sister. But when she returned home about nine o'clock her house was full of men. As well as her husband, Steel and McPherson, there were two other men, James McDonald and James McKenna of Pennycook Lane. As soon as she stepped indoors, her husband asked McKenna to stand outside and then ushered his wife out again, taking her back to her sister's where all three stayed the night.

The situation was ludicrous. Steel and McPherson had broken into McGavin's shop and had found the safe. As they were unable to crack it on the premises, they were carrying it through the streets of Dundee, searching for some method of opening it. There were two reasons for choosing Craig: firstly because he was known to own some chisels, and secondly because McKenna, who was involved in the theft, had once employed him.

In the meantime, McKenna kept watch outside the house as the others chiselled their way into the safe and extracted the contents. Replacing Craig's chisels where they had found them, they carried the broken safe outside. Bridget McMahon, a near neighbour, found it dumped in a back green behind 18 Watt Street and told the police. In the morning, James McDonald banged at the door of Mrs Craig's sister's house, woke up Hugh Craig and handed him four pounds, presumably in payment for use of his house and tools.

The police were already hard at work. Having been shown the discarded safe, they brought David McGavin to identify it and shortly afterwards an informer whispered an address to detective Hugh Patterson. It was fairly obvious that in a place as tight-knit as Dundee and as congested as the Hawkhill, somebody must have seen a group of men hefting a safe from door to door. When Patterson searched Craig's house he found three chisels and a sledgehammer – not normally tools used by a shoemaker – and what was more damning, one of the chisels was still flaked with green paint. Craig, however, was missing, as were most of the other suspects.

It was not long before the telegraph wires were humming and police forces the length and breadth of Scotland were aware of the break-in and the suspects. The Edinburgh police arrested McKenna and Craig together and McDonald separately, while the other suspects were found in various corners of Dundee. At the beginning of May 1888 Neil McPherson and Samuel Steel appeared before Lord McLaren at the Dundee Circuit Court, charged with the theft, and some other details came out during the trial.

At one time McGavin had employed and then sacked Craig. The jury must have wondered if Craig had some grudge against his ex-employer, and why he was not in the dock with McPherson and Steel. The jury also learned that McKenna was given two pounds and four shillings from the proceeds of the robbery, while McDonald got three pounds. McDonald agreed he had been in Craig's house but denied having seen the safe there.

The jury found the accused guilty and Lord MacLaren said it was a very daring act and 'equalled . . . anything of the kind he had heard before'. He also said that McPherson had not long been released from penal servitude and the sheriff also knew Steel well. He gave McPherson seven years' penal servitude and Steel five years'. Perhaps the judge and jury believed they had seen justice done, but McPherson did not agree. He left the court in anger, saying it was Craig who had broken into the shop. After this length of time, the final truth will never be known.

Paddy's Clock

Sometimes the crime was utterly petty, but the criminal still had to be tried, and the public wondered if the expense was worth the end result. Such was definitely the case with Paddy and his clock.

Sitting directly opposite the Tower Block of the University of Dundee, the Queen's Hotel is a splendidly Gothic creation. It was built in 1878, when the Victorians were at the height of their confidence and Dundee was riding the crest of a jute-financed wave. It is a beautiful building, with a three-storey French attic on top and an ornate oak staircase, while the arched windows gaze confidently down the Nethergate. There is possibly, however, an air of sadness, for the Queen's was intended to be the main hotel for the Caledonian Station. However, the station was not built in its original intended location at Seabraes, but deeper into Dundee, so the Queen's was a railway hotel without a railway. As a consequence there was financial ruin for one of its main developers, Andrew Meldrum, who instead of becoming rich became an assistant in a sports shop. Nevertheless, it remains a fine hotel and it was a fitting stop-over for the judges of the Circuit Court when they visited Dundee.

On the last day of March 1885 Lord Craighill presided over the Circuit Court. He arrived in Dundee on Monday 29th March, took up residence in the Queen's Hotel and held a levee. All the Dundee sheriffs, the Provost and the Magistrates attended, with the splendid display of the pomp and ceremony for which the Victorians were famous. The levee was followed by a fine procession from the hotel to the courthouse. His Lordship and his fellow dignitaries travelled in carriages, with Captain Primrose commanding the military escort, a brass band playing their hearts out and a solid block of blue-clad police.

Just before ten in the morning His Lordship reached the courthouse in West Bell Street, and with the dignified formality of high events, the court opened for business. All the usual suspects were in attendance: Mr Vary Campbell the Advocate-Depute, Mr Horace Skeete the Clerk of Court, and Mr Craigie the sole counsel amidst a bevy of bailies and sheriffs. Sixty-five men had been called up for the jury from all four quarters of Forfarshire and Dundee. Men either left their farms in the care of others, shut up shop or took an unpaid day off from their work. A large crowd waited for the free entertainment and some may have joined in as the Reverend Doctor Grant got the ball rolling with a prayer.

After all the preparations, the gathering, the expenditure and the expectation, there was only one case for the court. Patrick Martin was an old man, a petty thief with a poor track record and a history of failure. As he stood before the array of authority, flanked by immaculately uniformed policemen, he may have wondered what all the fuss was about; all this effort for Paddy and his cheap little clock.

The charge was put to him. On Friday 23rd January 1885 he stole a timepiece from the Nethergate house of Janet Bain. Martin pleaded not guilty, so the case went to trial. There was nothing complex for the jury to understand. The victim was an elderly woman and a millworker. She went to work in the morning, leaving her son in the house. When she returned about six in the evening her clock was gone. Her son had left the house about eleven, leaving the door unlocked.

The first witness was Elizabeth Glennan, an eleven-year-old millworker who lived in the same stair. She saw Patrick Martin leaving Mrs Scott's house with the clock under his arm. When he reached the street he began to run and within a few moments a gaggle of boys surrounded him, shouting, 'Come back, thief wi' the knock.'

Nine-year-old George Leslie also saw Martin running along Tay Street 'wi' a knock below his oxter' and all the local boys shouting after him. Presumably Martin outdistanced his followers, for he sold the clock to Patrick O'Rourke, a firewood merchant from the Hawkhill, claiming he had bought it for ten shillings.

It was not much later that Detective Edward Tooth arrested Martin, dragged him into the police office and charged him with stealing the clock. It was a petty, nearly pointless theft and would probably have been dealt with by the Police Court and a few weeks in jail if it had not been for Martin's previous record.

In 1869 Martin had four months in jail, in 1871 he got twelve months and in 1872 eighteen months for robbery, which is theft with violence. Finally, in 1880 he was given another twelve months for theft. His career stretched back fifteen years, peppered with the failures of arrest and nobody will ever know how many successful thefts. This last arrest may well have been for an article of trifling value, but its rightful owner would not agree and she probably had to work many finger-numbing hours to raise the extra cash to pay for it.

After all the fuss to open the court, Lord Craighill may have thought he had to justify his position by imposing a stiff sentence, or perhaps the accumulated crime of Martin spoke against him. His lordship sentenced Martin to five years' penal servitude.

'Thank you, My Lord,' Martin said in response. 'That will be a steady job for a while.'

With the sentence pronounced, the business of the court was finished. Lord Craighill congratulated Sheriff Comrie Thomson on the absence of crime in Forfarshire and finished his work. In all, the whole expensive day's business had taken just over an hour, and an elderly man had been sent to prison for five years for stealing a clock worth about two and sixpence. Paddy Martin had the last sardonic laugh, however, for he had hardly begun his five-year sentence before he ended it. He died in the General Prison in Perth in the middle of June that same year, a man remembered only for being the sole prisoner at the spring Circuit Court.

But not all cases of the 1880s were so petty; that decade also saw a crime that might tie Dundee in with one of the most notorious murderers of the nineteenth century.

Was Jack the Ripper Hanged in Dundee?

Carefully checked, labelled and packed away, the lengths of wood and bolts of iron sit quietly within a museum storage facility in Dundee. They are innocuous enough, obviously old, obviously historic, and to a casual observer they would mean nothing, but this collection of battered timber has as gruesome a history as any other artefact in the city. In March 1995 Dr Peter Davis, the curator of Her Majesty's Prison Service Museum, visited Dundee and inspected the carefully stored object. He declared that if assembled again it was 'in technical terms operable' and gave his expert opinion of its age. Dr Davis dated it from at least the 1840s, and perhaps as old as the 1820s, because of its relatively simple mechanism. This relic of old Dundee was the small, individual trap-door gallows that ended the lives of some of Dundee's most notorious criminals. There is a possibility that it was on this Dundee gallows that Jack the Ripper died.

There is certainly no certainty that the man who was hanged within Dundee Gaol on 25th April 1889 was Jack the Ripper, but there are indications that he might have been. The method of the murder for which he was committed was similar and after his execution, the Whitechapel murders stopped. His name was William Henry Bury, he was an Englishman and his short visit to Dundee was marked by his murder and dismemberment of his wife. The story of Bury reveals a degree of cold-blooded brutality that is still chilling, even when a hundred and a quarter years have passed.

Born in Stourbridge in Worcestershire, Bury hardly knew his father, who was run over by his own cart. Three weeks later, on 7th May 1860, Bury's mother was taken into the lunatic wing of Worcester Poorhouse. Bury was less than a year old. It was not an inspiring start to his life. His first job was as a factor's clerk, which shows he was reasonably educated, but he borrowed money, failed to pay his debt and left. He worked for a Wolverhampton lock manufacturer and was sacked for theft; by 1887 he was a petty street hawker in Birmingham, from where he moved to London.

By winter of that year Bury was working for James Martin, a sawdust seller and reputedly a brothel keeper, and here he met his wife, thirty-five-year-old Ellen Elliot, who may have been a prostitute. She was London born and bred, but had worked in a jute factory. The next year was significant, for Martin sacked him and he married Elliot. It is possible he married for money, for Elliot had inherited railway shares, some of which she sold to allow Bury to pay his debts, but if they married for love it was well disguised.

Less than a week after their marriage, Bury argued with his wife, knocked her to the ground and held a knife to her throat. Not surprisingly, the landlord evicted them. By now Bury was rumoured to have venereal disease, which was rife in London at the time, and when Ellen sold the last of her shares, they squandered the money in a drunken binge in Wolverhampton, with Ellen buying some jewellery with her share of her own money. It is possible that Bury's violence to Ellen continued, but the two stayed together.

Speaking openly about emigrating to Australia, Bury ordered two large wooden crates, presumably in which to store his effects. However, he also forged a letter from Dundee, purporting to be an offer from a jute factory offering Ellen a job. Prior to reading the letter, Ellen had no intention of moving to Scotland, but perhaps she thought regular employment would calm Bury's vicious temper so they could settle into a decent, ordinary life.

Disembarking from the Dundee, Perth and London steamer *Cambria* on 20th January 1889, the couple lived in Union Street for a week, and then moved to a basement at 113 Princes Street. When the jute mill job failed to materialise, Ellen worked for a day as a cleaner, while Bury met a painter and decorator named David Walker and returned to his old drinking habits. At this time Ellen was described by her neighbours as good-looking and tolerably well-dressed, while a newspaper picture of Bury shows a slender, sharp-nosed man, well-dressed and with a neatly-trimmed beard and moustache.

However, Bury did a little more than just drink. Over the next week he visited the courthouse, listened to the cases, and bought a length of rope from a local shop. He also borrowed a newspaper from his drinking buddy Walker, read an article about a woman committing suicide, but dropped it when asked to look up anything about Jack the Ripper. At about seven in the evening of Sunday 10th February 1889, he walked into the Central Police Office at West Bell Street and asked to see the lieutenant on duty.

It was now that the first connection between Bury and Jack the Ripper was made. Bury told Lieutenant James Parr that he had been drinking the previous night and when he woke in the morning he found his wife dead with a rope around her neck. So far there was nothing unusual: drunkards were ten a penny and Victorian Britain was used to suicides. What Bury said next was more disturbing, even to an experienced policeman. He claimed he had cut up Ellen's body and stuffed it in a box in their house in Princes Street. His mention of 'Jack the Ripper' appears to have been incoherent, but it seems Bury was afraid he might be arrested on suspicion of being the Whitechapel murderer. Bury was incomprehensible at first, but he eventually calmed down and made a statement, giving his background and some details of the death of his wife. Lieutenant Parr listened intently, arrested Bury and sent Lieutenant Lamb, who headed the detective department in Dundee, to find out exactly what had happened at 113 Princes Street.

Lamb and Detective Campbell found a scene of horror. Number 113 was a two-room basement flat, with the front room completely empty of furniture and the back having only one bed and a large whitewashed packing box, presumably one Bury had made in London. Naturally the detectives examined the box. Two boards in the top were loose, so Lamb removed both of them and a bed-sheet that concealed the contents: he possibly wished he had not.

A glance inside revealed the legs and feet of a dead woman, and Lieutenant Lamb immediately stopped operations. Only when the police surgeon arrived was the packing case fully emptied. As well as what was probably the household property of the Burys, the case held the body of Ellen. She lay on her back at the bottom of the case with her left leg twisted over her right shoulder, her right equally contorted and the shin broken. Ellen's stomach had been slashed with a sharp blade and her bowels had spilled out. More investigation found rope weals around Ellen's throat, and graffiti around the flat saying 'Jack Ripper is at the back of this door' and 'Jack Ripper is in this seller [sic]'. The police also found a knife soiled with human blood and the rope Bury had so recently bought, with twists of Ellen's hair among the fibres.

The next step was probably inevitable. Bury was taken to the Police Court, where he was reported as being agitated, charged with murdering his wife and dragged back to the cells. As he waited there, Mr Dewar, Chief Constable and Procurator Fiscal, telegraphed the Metropolitan Police with details of the crime, with its similarities to the Jack the Ripper murders in Whitechapel in London. The Metropolitan Police made a few local enquiries in London, and there is a legend that two London detectives travelled to Dundee, but if so, nothing further was done.

It was the 18th March 1889 before Bury appeared before the High Court. Rather than wear prison clothes, he appeared in ordinary dress, with a white collar, a spotted tie and a dark tweed suit beneath a brown coat with a velvet collar. He also looked calm and composed. Despite all the evidence against him, he pleaded not guilty, claiming that Ellen had strangled herself and he had only packed her body in the box. He did not give a reason. The doctors proved that Ellen had been strangled from behind, which was impossible for a suicide, and after a trial of thirteen hours, the jury took only twenty-five minutes to find Bury guilty. Strangely, they recommended mercy, which seemed to surprise the judge, Lord Young. He was not so kind, and sentenced Bury to death.

Hustled back to Dundee jail, Bury was placed in the condemned cell, some distance from the main block, and while he waited, various people petitioned for clemency. His solicitor, David Tweedie, wrote to Lord Lothian, Secretary of State for Scotland, arguing that the medical evidence was conflicting, and Bury might have inherited the insanity of his mother. The Reverend Gough of St Paul's Episcopal Church in Dundee also wanted clemency but on 22nd April the reprieve was rejected and the sentence confirmed. Bury was to be hanged on 24th of the month.

Even with the obviously planned and cold-blooded nature of the murder, many people in Dundee were against the execution, and the *Courier* opposed capital punishment in principle. Although they could not know it, Bury's hanging was to be Dundee's last. Perhaps in gratitude for his attempts to save his life, Bury confessed to the Reverend Gough that he had indeed murdered Ellen as they argued drunkenly over money, but even this virtual deathbed confession did not tally with the facts. He said he had tried to cut up Ellen's body the next morning, while the doctors said the slashes across her abdomen had been made within ten minutes of death.

While he waited for his execution, Bury was reported to be composed, spending his time writing a forty-four-page summary of his life. At no time did he say he was Jack the Ripper. On 24th April he was escorted the forty yards from his cell to the scaffold. It was only after the hanging that rumours began that Bury had been Jack the Ripper. Most are based on circumstantial evidence. For example, Bury had lived near Whitechapel when the murders had taken place; Bury's wife may have once been a prostitute and Bury had slashed open her abdomen in the same fashion as the Ripper. It was also said that Bury took off his wife's rings, which is something Jack the Ripper did, and the Whitechapel murders stopped when Bury left London. Lastly there are some remarks that Ellen allegedly made, saying, 'Jack the Ripper is quiet now' when speaking to her neighbours. Strangely, it was the *New York Times*, a newspaper which had no connection with either Dundee or London, that made a direct connection between Bury and the Ripper, and James Berry, the official hangman, supported the claims.

So what is the evidence?

1. Bury was near the area at the time of the five 'Jack the Ripper' murders.
2. The murders stopped at the time Bury left London.
3. Bury ripped open his wife's abdomen in a similar fashion to the Ripper.
4. There was chalk graffiti near Bury's flat implicating him.
5. Ellen Bury made some remarks about Jack the Ripper.

On the surface, these are not particularly damning pieces of evidence, but taken together they might be formulated into a case. Euan Macpherson in *The Trial of Jack the Ripper* has painted a full picture of the connection, and it remains an intriguing possibility that one of history's most elusive murderers met his end at the end of a rope in Dundee. The gallows remains in pieces, as a macabre reminder of Dundee's last hanging, and the storage facility of Dundee's museum also holds an inscribed sandstone slab with the initials J. H. B. and the date 1889, which is thought by some to commemorate Bury, but that too is merely conjecture. Of one thing there is no doubt: if anybody deserved hanging for murder, William Henry Bury did.

Epilogue

And that is a picture of Dundee crime in the nineteenth century. Of course it is only fragmentary. For every theft or robbery or drunken brawl mentioned, a hundred have been left out and for every recorded act of kindness or Christian charity, there are a thousand un-noted and long forgotten. But the text is intended to reveal something of the realities of life in Dundee when 200 chimneys pumped out smoke and the jute mills provided hard, hard work for many thousands. For the majority of the population, to live in old Dundee was to live with grinding labour or desperate poverty; drink competed with crime to blight the streets and a petty theft was all that was required to crash a family from marginal security to destitution and hunger.

As the century progressed, so the population increased. From the uncertain justice of the Charlies, Authority tightened its grip. The 1824 Police Act introduced new professionalism to the smoke-swirled streets of the city. Uniformed police paced their portentous beats, public houses faced tightened regulations and new concepts of justice replaced transportation with penal servitude and the lottery of freedom or death with the certainty of terrible silence behind enclosing walls. Some patterns of crime altered; grave robbing stopped; train robbing began. Some remained the same: husbands and wives abused each other behind the paper-thin partitions of tenement walls, men and women over-indulged in alcohol and exchanged insults and blows outside the gaudy glow of public houses, sneak thieves slithered through windows and predatory eyes watched for the unwary in the yawning mouths of closes.

According to figures released by the Scottish Government in 2011, Dundee still has problems with crime. Robbery and indecency are above the national average; drug crime, which the Victorians never knew, and crimes of dishonesty are well above. Petty assault and breach of the peace are as prevalent as ever, and Donald Mackay would not be surprised to learn that drunkenness in Dundee is well above the national average too. However, there is proportionally less crime concerning offensive weapons in Dundee than elsewhere, fewer miscellaneous offences and mercifully fewer serious assaults. The gang problems that so blight some communities are markedly fewer in Dundee and the two local football teams share an intense rivalry without the near hatred that afflicts sporting fixtures in other communities.

And yet in many ways Dundee remains as she was. She is one of Scotland's major cities, a bustling, very human place spreading along the coastal plain between the Sidlaw Hills and the Firth of Tay. The dynamism of the nineteenth century remains in her constant reinvention of self. Now the city is a centre of education, with two quality universities, Dundee and Abertay, a college of further education and the Islamic Al-Maktoum College of Higher Education. All share the same city and co-exist in harmony. There is talk of Abertay and Dundee Universities merging, talk of Dundee College linking with Angus College. Both may happen, but the underlying dynamism will continue. Dundee is like that.

In other ways Dundee has altered radically. Many of the tenements remain but more have gone, with the once crowded inhabitants moved to local authority housing schemes that encircle the city and provide far superior accommodation but possibly lack the community spirit that saw the Dundee people so often rise against what they perceived as injustice. The whaling ships also have gone, along with the jute mills, and the economic structure of the city has altered. New buildings and new roads have blossomed and two bridges now take the place of the once-busy ferries. Patrick Mackay the messenger is long dead, but his wife's grave still sits in the Howff graveyard, carefully tended by the hard working men and women of Dundee City Council. Some say the ghosts of the Wallace gang may be sensed on dark nights around Brook Street, and David Crockatt is no longer even a memory, but others of his type still linger. Baffin Street has forgotten its ghost, but the gallows where the Ripper may have bid his last farewell still lie in storage, possibly waiting for a new twist in the justice game.

Overall, Dundonians are proud of their city, and with good reason. It enjoys an enviable position between the Firth of Tay and the Sidlaw Hills, it is a notably accessible shopping centre and is constantly improving itself. And although crime still remains, Dundee can no longer be termed a 'Sink of Atrocity', if indeed that accolade was ever deserved. With few exceptions, most crimes in the nineteenth century were crimes of opportunity; murder was rare and organised criminality ever rarer. Dundee may have been a dangerous place, but probably no more so than any other industrial port town.

And through it all one sentiment remains: the warm-heartedness and genuine humanity of the Dundee people, and for that, residents should be proud and visitors thankful.

Select Bibliography

Adshead, Joseph, *On juvenile criminals, reformatories, and the means of rendering the perishing and dangerous classes serviceable to the state* (1856) Knowsley Pamphlet Collection, University Of Liverpool

Barrie, David, *Police in the Age of Improvement: Police development and the Civic tradition in Scotland, 1775–1865* (2008) Devon

Barrie, David, *The City of Dundee Illustrated* (1890) Dundee, Winter, Duncan and Co.

Baxter, Thomas Handyside, *Diary 1820–1830*

Beatts, J. M., *Reminiscences of an Old Dundonian* (1883) Dundee

Cameron, Joy, *Prisons and Punishment in Scotland* (1983) Edinburgh

Chesney, Kellow, *The Victorian Underworld* (1970) London, Maurice Temple Smith

City of Dundee Police 150th Anniversary

Colman, Henry, *European Life and Manners, in Familiar Letters to Friends* (1849) Boston

Dundee Council Minute Books, Dundee City Archives

Dundee Courier and Argus

The Dundee Directory and Register for 1829–30

The Dundee Directory for 1837–38

The Dundee Directory for 1840–41

The Dundee Directory for 1850

The Dundee Directory for 1853–4 (1853) Dundee

Dundee Perth and Cupar Advertiser

Dundee Police Board Minute Book, 1824–1832, Dundee City Archives TC/PBM Series

Engels, Frederick, *The Condition of the Working Class in England* (1846, 1969) London

The Factory Act of 1833: eight pamphlets 1833–1834 (1972) New York

Fraser, Derek, *Power and Authority in the Victorian City* (1979) Oxford

Groome, Francis H. (editor), *Dundee: A Historical Perspective, drawn from the Ordnance*

Hughes, Robert, *The Fatal Shore* (1987) London

Hunt, Tristram, *Building Jerusalem: the rise and fall of the Victorian city* (2004) London

Kidd, William, *The Dundee Market Crosses & Tollbooths* (1901) Dundee

Knight, Alanna, *Burke and Hare* (2007) Kew

Livingstone, Sheila, *Confess and be Hanged: Scottish Crime and Punishment Through the Ages* (2000) Edinburgh

Mackie, Charles, *Historical Description of the town of Dundee* (1836)

McCraw, Iain, *The Fairs of Dundee* (1994) Dundee

McKean, Charles and Walker, David, *Dundee: An Illustrated Introduction* (1984) Edinburgh

McKean, Charles and Whatley, Patricia, with Baxter, Kenneth, *Lost Dundee: Dundee's Lost Architectural Heritage* (2008) Edinburgh

McKean, Charles, Harris, Bob and Whatley, Christopher, *Dundee: Renaissance to Enlightenment* (2009) Dundee

Mackie, Charles, *Historical Description of the Town of Dundee* (1836) Glasgow

Macpherson, Euan, *The Trial of Jack the Ripper* (2006) London

Millar, A. H., *Glimpses of Old and New Dundee* (1925) Dundee

Miskell, Louise, Whatley, Christopher A. and Harris, Bob, *Victorian Dundee: Image and Realities* (2000) East Linton

Morris, R. J. & Rodger, Richard (editors), 'An Introduction to British Urban History, 1820–1914', in *The Victorian City: A Reader in British Urban History* (1993) London

Murray, Patrick Joseph, *Not so bad as they seem: The transportation, ticket-of-leave, and penal servitude questions* (1857) Knowsley Pamphlet Collection

Phillips, David, (editor) James Myles, *Chapters in the Life of a Dundee Factory Boy* (1850, 1980) Dundee

Rodger, Richard, 'Employment, Wages and Poverty in the Scottish Cities' in *The Victorian City: A Reader in British Urban History 1820–1914* (1993) London

Smout, T. C., *A Century of the Scottish People 1830–1950* (1987) London

Sword, Jessie, *They Did Wrong: Public Hangings in the Angus Area 1785 to 1868*, Dundee, Friends of Dundee City Archives

Tobias, J., *Nineteenth Century Crime, Prevention and Punishment* (1972) London

Whatley, Christopher A. *The Diary of John Sturrock Millwright Dundee 1864–65* (1996) East Linton

Whatley, Christopher A., Swinfen, David B. and Smith, Annette M., *The Life and Times of Dundee* (1993) Edinburgh